Halfway to Tax Reform

Halfway to Tax Reform

JOSEPH A. RUSKAY *and* Richard A. Osserman

FOREWORD BY CONGRESSMAN HENRY S. REUSS

INDIANA UNIVERSITY PRESS

BLOOMINGTON / LONDON

Published in Canada by Fitzhenry & Whiteside Limited, Don Mills, Ontario

Library of Congress catalog card number: 78-126216

ISBN: 253-13675-X

Manufactured in the United States of America

Contents

Foreword

CONGRESSMAN HENRY S. REUSS

The Taxpayers' Revolt has subsided, but we may be just in the eye of the storm. Congress responded to the Revolt by enacting the Tax Reform Act of 1969, tightening some of the more egregious tax loopholes and easing somewhat the tax burden on the average taxpayer. But the Act is a time bomb. The problem is that the extra revenue coming into the Treasury from the Act's modest loophole-closing does not begin to cover the losses from its tax reduction and relief provisions (such as increased exemption and standard deduction, and the low-income allowance). By 1975, the Treasury estimates, the Tax Reform Act is going to be costing the federal government nearly $8 billion a year in lost revenues.

At the same time, the demand for government spending on education, health, housing, transportation, welfare, crime control, and the environment continues to increase. What this means is that federal spending will soon outstrip federal revenues by a substantial margin, and when this happens the government will start looking around for more tax money. If the government decides that this money is going to have to come from the average, middle-income taxpayer, the Taxpayers' Revolt will be back again with a vengeance. Fortunately, there is a solution to the government's revenue problem which does not involve further burdening the average taxpayer—it is to complete the business of tax reform and loophole-closing so timidly begun in 1969. The additional revenue from this source—estimated at $10 to $50 billion a year—can avert the coming fiscal crisis.

Joseph Ruskay and Richard Osserman point the way toward such a thoroughgoing tax reform. Along the way, they demonstrate just how difficult real reform is. Time after time, the authors spell out the irrationality and unfairness of large portions of our tax code, and then conclude with a description of the Congressional response to these inequities. The response, all too often, is feeble tinkering and patching, leaving the real job of reform undone.

The problem, as the authors point out, is that tax reform is complicated—too complicated, seemingly, for the average taxpayer (or even the average Congressman) to grasp. But it is not too complicated for the beneficiaries of tax loopholes and their highly-paid lawyers and lobbyists. *Halfway to Tax Reform* goes a long way toward redressing that imbalance. Here, in understandable and readable form, is a tax reform handbook for citizens and legislators who want to know what is wrong with our tax system and what they can do about it. The authors show who wins and who looes under our current tax laws, who got what in the Tax Reform Act of 1969, and what has to be done to make sure that tax burdens and benefits are more fairly distributed in the future.

An immense literature has grown up around the subject of tax reform in the last two decades, much of it generated by economists, lawyers, and accountants writing for each other in arcane language that only they can understand. Ruskay and Osserman pull all the best of this together and make it understandable to the layman. If every citizen read this book, I doubt that the next Taxpayers' Revolt could be appeased as easily as the last one.

Preface

Stanley S. Surrey, Assistant Secretary of the Treasury during the Johnson administration, has repeatedly argued that if the goal of tax reform is to be realized the support of the average citizen must be enlisted. Awakening public interest in the reform of our income, gift, and estate tax structure involves educating and informing the general public. This in itself is a formidable task, requiring more writing for the interested layman. This book then is designed to give persons interested in tax reform, but who lack the specialist's or expert's knowledge of tax law, a basic understanding of the reforms that have been sought and from time to time achieved in recent years, and major areas where further revision and reforms are urgently needed.

We do not pretend to have explored or even to have mentioned every one of the innumerable tax preferences that permeate our income, gift, and estate tax laws. Instead we have concentrated on what are often characterized as the "major loopholes," those on which tax critics have chiefly focused their attention. It is these major areas of tax immunity and tax preference—the percentage depletion allowance for oil and other minerals, the special tax treatment of stock options, and the exemption from income tax of the interest on state and local bonds, to name but a few—the advantages of which are usually enjoyed by the upper-income groups of the population, that are dealt with seriatim in this volume. Many other preferences—the exemption from income tax of workmen's compensation and unemployment benefits, for example—have either been omitted entirely or mentioned briefly in passing. In general they represent tax concessions to those who have small or moderate incomes, although perhaps they should be included as income in an ideal tax structure.

It is the thesis of this book that many unjustified tax preferences still exist, and that despite passage of the Tax Reform Act of 1969 further reform is still imperative. But it does not follow that those who benefit from such preferences can be accused of evading their civic duty or even be criticized on moral grounds. On the contrary, they can hardly be blamed for taking advantage of opportunities that the tax law affords them. The legislators who have the responsibility for enacting and amending the law are at fault. It is the Internal Revenue Code, not those who profit from its loopholes, that must be reformed.

The income, gift, and estate tax rates used in the various examples cited in the text are those currently applicable without any adjustment for the income tax surcharge. The changes that the tax surcharge would have made would not have materially affected the figures in the examples.

We wish to acknowledge our indebtedness to our editor Mrs. Natalie Wrubel, to Professor Herbert J. Kiesling and Professor William D. Popkin of Indiana University for their valuable suggestions, to Robert Lewis, Esq., for reading parts of the manuscript and making helpful comments, and to Miss Carolyn Bremer for typing and correcting the manuscript. Portions of this book appeared previously in *New Republic* and are included here with the kind consent of the editors.

J. A. R.
R. A. O.

Halfway to Tax Reform

1

Some of Our Taxpayers Have Been Missing

The Tax Reform Act of 1969 has been hailed by many as a landmark of reform. While it did not succeed in closing all the loopholes in our tax structure, it did sweep away several long-standing preferences and reduce the advantages flowing from a number of others.

Pressure for tax reform started in 1967. The controversy that arose over President Johnson's request for a 10% income tax surcharge prompted a number of congressmen and senators to call attention to the tax loopholes favoring specially privileged groups.[1] Suddenly the ranks of the small corporal's guard on Capitol Hill that for years had been demanding the elimination of tax inequities started to attract a number of new recruits.

The late Senator Robert Kennedy made the headlines when he cited the number of millionaires and near millionaires who year after year had been paying no income taxes at all, and suggested that their income be subjected to a minimum tax "which would prevent the wealthy from continuing to get away completely."[2] The Democratic Study Group, about one hundred and forty House liberals, lined up in support of a bill introduced in October 1967 by Congressman Henry Reuss of Wisconsin that sought to wipe out many of the major tax shelters referred to in this book.[3]

President Johnson had promised to submit a tax reform program to Congress by the end of 1968, but in the fall of the year, following the election of a Republican administration, he changed his mind, and shortly before leaving office he instructed his Treasury officials to forward their *Tax Reform Studies and Proposals* [4] to Congress. The Nixon administration, sensing a change in the public mood, announced that it would make its own recommendations for reform. In the spring of 1969 it began submitting its reform package to Congress. [5]

The result of all this reform talk was that an increasing number of taxpayers, upset over their own escalating tax burdens, were for the first time alerted to the fact that many of their well-to-do fellow citizens were managing to escape paying their share of it. This public dissatisfaction gradually assumed the proportions of a "taxpayers revolt." It did not take long to reach the ears of Chairman Wilbur Mills and other members of the House Ways and Means Committee and was, more than anything else, responsible for the changes enacted in the Tax Reform Act of 1969.

Admittedly the Act made significant progress in the direction of greater tax equity, especially when viewed in the light of the dismal record of the 1950s and 60s. Some loopholes that had been successfully exploited for years by religious organizations, foundations, contributors to charity, real estate operators, and multi-corporate businesses were closed entirely, and the advantages of a number of others were reduced. In addition, a minimum tax designed to subject certain types of tax-free income to partial taxation was introduced into the Internal Revenue Code for the first time.

Nevertheless the tax reform forces were only partially successful, and most of the major avenues of tax avoidance are still with us. It will probably require something in the nature of a political upheaval, a resurgence of broad popular support for liberal and progressive legislation, before we will have a Congress that is determined to eliminate the remaining tax preferences. At the moment the emergence of this kind of widespread and insistent pressure by the electorate appears doubtful.

Statistics That Are Highly Disturbing

Our tax law is riddled by benefits that are given to the wealthy, and for the most part the benefits that are given to the average man are negligible.[6]

This candid appraisal was submitted to the House Ways and Means Committee by a tax expert about ten years ago. More recently sentiments hardly less critical were voiced by the head of the Treasury Department himself. At the 1963 Congressional Tax Hearings, Secretary Douglas Dillon, a graduate in good standing of the Wall Street investment banking fraternity, conceded that the country's tax code was honey-combed with loopholes and inequities favoring wealthier taxpayers.[7]

Data furnished by the Treasury during the 1963 hearings underscored these indictments. For example, during the sample year 1959, twenty people with adjusted gross incomes ranging from half a million to $5 million paid no income tax whatsoever: Five of the adjusted gross incomes were over $5 million, ten were between $1 and $5 million, and five were between $500,000 and $1 million.[8]

Other Treasury figures disclosed that thirty-seven individuals, each of whom had total incomes over $5 million, realized an average of $6,280,000 each in capital gains, which were taxed at the maximum rate of 25%. Each of them had been allowed an average of $3 million in other deductions as well.[9]

The fact is that people with incomes of $1 million or more who do not manage to avoid the payment of income taxes altogether, do not pay the high and so-called "confiscatory" rates complained of by advocates of tax reduction, but pay an effective rate of about 24%; while others with only a small fraction of such income pay much higher rates.[10] Treasury studies of two taxpayers, each with gross incomes of $300,000, showed that one paid 71% of his income in taxes while the other paid 4%. Two other individuals had gross incomes of approximately $1.3 million and $600,000, respectively; the former paid about .2% in taxes, while the latter paid almost 75%.[11] Another taxpayer, taking advantage of the privilege of the unlimited charitable deduction, received a credit of some $21 million against other income subject to tax by conveying to charity property which had a present value of $21 million, but which had originally cost him less than $500,000.[12]

The allowances for percentage depletion and other deductions permitted the oil and gas and other extractive industries, which cost the government billions each year in tax revenue, constitute one of the most important tax loopholes. It has not been unusual for a number of major United States oil companies, some with annual incomes as high as $62 million, to pay no income taxes at all,[13] while many others pay no more than minimal amounts.

One 1967 newspaper source revealed that:

Atlantic Oil Company, for example, has cleared a total of $410 million during the past five years but hasn't paid a penny of federal taxes. Marathon Oil, after getting by without paying taxes for four years, finally coughed up 1.8 percent of its earnings last year.[14]

The ability of many persons with very large incomes to pay so little of it in taxes, or to avoid tax liability altogether, has never been a mystery to critics of our tax system in and outside Congress. As Senator Russell B. Long of Louisiana put it, a person who has a large income would

go to a good tax lawyer or a good tax accounting firm . . . and they would advise him of a number of things he could do to keep his tax liabilities low.

For example, he could invest money in tax-exempt securities. He could invest it in state or municipal bonds or subdivisions and agencies.

He could set himself up as a private foundation and make contributions to that private foundation and deduct amounts that he put into that.

He could set up a number of corporations with a qualified pension and profit sharing plan on which he would pay no tax on the amount that was contributed for his benefit.

He could benefit from trust income accumulated for his advantage. He could benefit from interest paid on indebtedness for property that was owned for personal use.

He could engage in a number of transactions where he would have an interest expense and where the income would be taxed only for half, and that half at 50 percent, which works out to an overall tax of 25 percent for his profit, with a complete deduction for the interest expense that might finance that capital transaction.

He could go in the oil business and drill a bunch of wells and take the intangible drilling costs for a deduction, which ofttimes works out to as much as 80 percent.

He would have the advantage of percentage depletion in that industry as well as a lot of others.[15]

Persons with substantial incomes who manage to minimize or even escape tax liability entirely are in no way violating the law. On the contrary, they are following the law to the letter, and are merely taking full advantage of the myriad of special provisions, exceptions, and loopholes (ex-Senator Paul Douglas calls them "truckholes") which the law provides. It is the tax law itself, not the people who exploit the opportunities it offers for tax avoidance, that is the proper target for criticism.

At the 1963 Congressional Tax Hearings, Senator Douglas voiced the frustration of those whose repeated calls for tax reform had gone unheeded, in words that are as appropriate today as they were then:

Mr. Secretary, how can members of the Congress face the taxpayers, how can they face the workman or small farmer who . . . on an income of $5,200, pays $456 in taxes, how can we face them when these tremendous holes exist in the tax structure; people with incomes of over $5 million paying no taxes whatsoever; with $12 to $13 billion of capital gains completely evading taxation through transfer at death; with $3 billion of depletion allowances completely free from taxation; with $2 billion of intangible drilling and developmental costs written off virtually in the first year; with stock options, personal holding companies, and the whole range and gamut of special privileges?

. . . it seems to me that the administration is always taking a position that tax revision is important, but when you throw reform overboard to speed tax reduction it is permitting the pirates to take over the ship.[16]

Today the situation is no better. Indeed with the number of persons with million-dollar incomes and large fortunes increasing rapidly each year,[17] a comparable set of current statistics would probably be equally shocking. Testifying before the Congressional Joint Economic Committee, Joseph W. Barr, Secretary of the Treasury in the latter part of the Johnson administration, emphasized that middle-income taxpayers, with incomes from $7,000 to $20,000, were paying a larger share of their incomes to the federal government than high-income taxpayers; and that in 1967, 155 taxpayers with incomes over $200,000, including 21 with incomes of $1 million per year, showed no income tax liability whatsoever.[18]

Recent data assembled by the Treasury disclosed that the pattern of previous years was being repeated—that when tax-sheltered sources of income were taken into account a higher proportion of the extremely wealthy were paying taxes at an effective rate of 30%, which was lower than the rate paid by those with one-twentieth of their incomes; that the effective tax rate for most millionaires and multi-millionaires was in the same range (20%–30%) as those with adjusted gross incomes of $20,000–$50,000, while people whose substantial incomes were derived from ordinary non-tax-sheltered sources were obliged to pay taxes at rates as high as 70%.[19]

Impairment of the Principle of Tax Equity

These instances of disparity in the sharing of the tax burden offend commonly accepted notions of fairness, and underscore the extent to which various forms of income escape taxation and an incalculable amount of revenue is lost to the government every year because of a host of exemptions, preferences, and allowances. The essence of tax justice lies in the adherence to the principle of neutrality or uniformity, as opposed to preference and discrimination, and requires that income arising from different sources or economic activities be taxed alike.

Equity in taxation is both "horizontal" and "vertical." Horizontal equity requires that persons having equal incomes and otherwise similarly situated pay an equal amount in taxes. Thus two taxpayers, each enjoying an income of $25,000, one from a salary and the other from stocks and bonds or from an oil property, and each with a wife and two children to support, should be liable for the same amount of income tax.

Vertical equity, on the other hand, demands that those with

larger incomes should pay significantly more than those with smaller incomes.[20] Theoretically, vertical equity between taxpayers having unequal incomes has been achieved by the imposition of a progressively higher tax rate as income increases. The justification for this type of tax structure is that the higher the income the greater the ability to pay. Above a certain income level the payment of a larger percentage of income involves no greater hardship or sacrifice than the payment of a smaller percentage on an income at or below that level.

Accordingly, vertical equity presupposes that a third taxpayer, who also supports a wife and two children, but who is blessed with an income four times that of the other two, will pay an income tax not just four times as much as theirs, but perhaps six or seven times as much (according to a progressive rate schedule which increases from 14% for a married couple with a taxable income up to $1,000 to 70% for a couple with a taxable income of $200,000 or more).

Departures from equity and neutrality are justifiable under only two sets of circumstances: If some important public or social objective is to be achieved by singling out certain classes of taxpayers for exceptional or preferential treatment (such as persons over 65, or those devoting part of their income to soil conservation or flood control); or if imposing or collecting the tax presents insuperable problems of measurement or other administrative difficulties.[21] A proposal to tax parents for the benefits their children receive from a free public school education would be an example of the latter.

Unfortunately our tax laws are so honeycombed with provisions granting preferential treatment that persons with similar incomes and family responsibilities frequently bear widely disparate tax burdens, and the supposedly progressive tax structure becomes a mere fiction. Apart from the huge annual loss in tax revenues to the Treasury, this discrepancy between the taxes paid by specially privileged groups and others less favored creates a situation basically so unfair that, in the words of former Senator Paul Douglas, it threatens "to destroy people's faith in government and in the democratic system." [22]

In many respects the principle of progressivity—of imposing a substantially larger portion of the tax burden on those with larger incomes—has received a further setback by the Tax Reform Act of 1969. The overly generous cuts in the tax rates for higher-bracket taxpayers, including a 50% maximum rate on salaries and earned income no matter how large, was aptly characterized as a "major assault upon the principle of progression" by Senator Albert Gore. He confronted the Secretary of the Treasury with a comparison of the rates that would now be payable by one of his secretaries, who earned a salary of $26,000, and that payable by the president of U.S. Steel, on his salary of over half a million dollars:

> SENATOR GORE: . . . for instance, one of my secretaries told me this morning that his marginal rate would reach 40 percent. Yet by your recommendation and this bill Roger Blough's salary would be taxed at the marginal rate of 50 percent.
>
> Now when we get to the ridiculous extreme that there is only 10 percentage points' difference between the tax on the salary of one of my secretaries and the tax on the salary of Roger Blough, who earns perhaps $600,000 or $700,000, we have just about abandoned the principle of progressivism in our system of income taxation.[23]

The Effect of the New "Minimum Tax"

One of the major reform achievements of the new law was supposed to be the Minimum Tax on "items of tax preference." Under this provision well-to-do persons with large amounts of income from oil operations, accelerated real estate depreciation, stock options, capital gains, and other tax-sheltered sources are now required to pay some tax on these receipts.

The minimum tax is computed by adding up all the items of a taxpayer's tax-sheltered income (called "tax preferences") and subtracting from the total: 1. the amount of income tax payable on his normally taxable income (salary, dividends, interest, and the like), and 2. the sum of $30,000. The remainder is then taxed at the rate of 10%.

As an example, assume that taxpayer A, a retired investor, has an income of $80,000 from dividends and interest and a $300,000 long-term capital gain from securities sold at a profit during the year. He is subject to tax on the $80,000 of dividends and interest and on one-half of his long-term capital gain ($150,000). Assuming that he is allowed the usual deductions and exemptions for a married man in his station in life, he will pay approximately $110,- 000 in ordinary income tax. However, on the $150,000 of his long-term capital gain that he is not ordinarily required to report, but which is subject to the "minimum tax," he will pay a mere $1,000. The computation is as follows:

A's Ordinary Income Tax

Dividend and interest income		$ 80,000
One-half of $300,000 long-term capital gain		150,000
Total		$230,000
Less personal deductions and exemptions		30,000
Taxable Income		$200,000
Ordinary income tax	approx.	$110,000

A's Minimum Tax

Untaxed half of $300,000 long-term capital gain		$150,000
Exemption allowed on the minimum tax	$ 30,000	
Ordinary income tax	110,000	
Deductions allowed on computation of minimum tax		140,000
Difference		$ 10,000
Minimum tax at rate of 10%		$ 1,000

Actually, if A had a little more ordinary income subject to tax and only slightly less long-term capital gain, he would have paid no minimum tax at all on the untaxed portion of his long-term capital gain.

Obviously this minimum tax on income previously sheltered entirely from taxation by various preferential provisions is exactly that—a minimum tax. Despite this provision, many individuals who formerly resorted to tax preferences to avoid taxation will continue to enjoy incomes of over $200,000 a year without paying any tax, or will at most contribute a tiny fraction of their tax-sheltered income to the Treasury. The most glaring omission of the minimum tax provision is its failure to include interest on state and local bonds from the items now subject to the tax.

The impact of the new tax would have been more meaningful if Congress had adopted the Treasury's companion proposal requiring an allocation of deductions. Under present law, persons who have large amounts of tax-sheltered income in addition to incomes from normally taxable sources (such as salaries, dividends, and interest) can use their deductions for interest, taxes, charitable deductions, medical expenses, and so forth to reduce the tax due on their ordinary income, while their tax-sheltered income is in no way affected. Under the Treasury's proposal, such a taxpayer would have been obliged to pro-rate his personal deductions between his tax-sheltered and his taxable income, thereby substantially increasing the amount of his tax. This proposal was passed by the House of Representatives, but was stricken from the final bill by the Senate Finance Committee.

2

The Immunities of Religious Property—Little Rendered unto Caesar

With more and more people feeling the pinch of higher taxes, with federal, state, and local governments engaging in a constant scramble for new sources of revenue, and with the phenomenal growth in the property, wealth, and business activities of religious organizations in the past twenty-five years, there has been considerable pressure, even from the clergy themselves, for a reexamination of the traditional tax immunities of the churches.

A prominent leader in the Lutheran Church has suggested that religious groups should voluntarily consent to modifications of their tax exemptions "and thus render unto Caesar the things that are Caesar's, and to God the things that are God's." [1] Another leading churchman, a proponent of drastic religious tax reform, paraphrased the same proverb into the warning:

Let the churches render unto Caesar what is Caesar's before he comes to take it with a sword.[2]

The Tax Reform Act of 1969 eliminated one tax privilege of the churches that was so palpably inequitable that even legislators who were traditionally reluctant to consider any legislation that might conceivably offend the sensibilities of religious groups voiced little opposition. Churches and religious organizations are now required to pay a tax on their income from business operations that are unrelated to their regular religious and charitable activities. Other tax immunities of religious organizations remain unchanged.

Origin of the Tax Privilege

Tax exemption for religious institutions goes back to ancient times. The privilege was enjoyed by the priestly classes in Egypt and India, and in biblical times by the Levites and other functionaries of the Temple in Jerusalem. When Emperor Constantine the Great was converted to Christianity in the 4th century, immunity from taxation was conferred upon the Catholic Church.[3] Thereafter the practice became embedded in European tradition and was brought to America in Colonial times. Subsequently provisions for the exemption from taxes of church property found their way into most state constitutions, and where not conferred by state constitutions the exemption was accomplished by statute or judicial decision.[4]

The moral and judicial rationale by which tax exemption for religious property and activities has been traditionally justified is that churches serve a beneficial social purpose in fulfilling the spiritual needs of the community, and that church-operated educational, medical, and charitable facilities relieve state and local governments of a financial burden they would otherwise have to assume.[5] Indeed, tax exemption for religious property in this country has been virtually taken for granted. As one judge put it more than one hundred years ago:

It is presumed that in the nineteenth century, in a Christian land, no argument is necessary to show that church purposes are public purposes. . . . To deny that church purposes are public purposes is to argue that the maintenance, support, and propagation of the Christian religion is not a matter of public concern. Our laws, though they recognize no particular religious establishment, are not insensible to the advantages of Christianity, and extend their protection to all in that faith and mode of worship they may choose to adopt.[6]

Only a small minority of radicals and free-thinkers who insisted that such privileges were an indirect subsidy, in violation of the

First Amendment principle of the separation of Church and State, have in the past opposed this consensus. The most important public figure who ventured to suggest some modification of public policy in this regard was President Ulysses S. Grant, who stated in his seventh message to Congress:

I would suggest the taxation of all property equally, whether church or corporation, exempting only the last resting place of the dead, and possibly, with proper restrictions, church edifices.[7]

However, in recent years an increasing number of Protestant and some Catholic churchmen have expressed the view that the privilege of tax immunity for churches, and particularly the exemption of income of church and church-related organizations from business and commercial enterprises operated by them in competition with private taxpaying businessmen, was not only inequitable, but was also harmful to the long-term interests of the churches themselves.

Nature of Religious Tax Exemptions

The tax immunities of the property and income of churches and church-related organizations may be summarized as follows:

1. The real and personal property owned by religious organizations is generally exempt from real estate and personal property taxes in every state; the exemption extends not only to churches, sacristies, auxiliary church buildings, denominational schools, colleges, seminaries, monasteries, hospitals, orphanages, homes for the aged or poor, summer camps, and cemeteries, but to the land adjacent to church property and church-related facilities as well.[8]

2. The income of religious organizations is exempt from federal income taxes,[9] and usually from state income taxes.[10] Until the Tax Reform Act of 1969 was passed, income from business and commercial enterprises wholly unrelated to their religious purposes was also exempt.

3. Religious organizations are generally exempt from state and local sales, use, and similar taxes.[11]

4. The value of benefits received in lieu of salary by many min-

isters, priests, nuns, brothers, and other employees or functionaries of churches in the form of food, housing, clothing, use of servants, automobiles, and other maintenance generally escapes personal income taxes.[12]

5. Contributions by individuals and corporations to religious organizations are deductible for federal income tax purposes within certain limitations (50% of adjusted gross income in the case of individuals, and 5% in the case of corporations) [13] and are similarly deductible for state income tax purposes.[14]

6. The liability for federal and state gift, estate, and transfer taxes may be reduced without limitation by lifetime donations or bequests to religious institutions.[15]

Amount of Tax-Exempt Church Property

There is really no accurate statistical data on the amount or value of church-owned or operated property and income. Other private educational and charitable organizations must file reports of their financial operations on I.R.S. Form 990, but religious organizations are not required to file similar federal or state reports.

It has been estimated however that the value of church property in this country amounts to some $80 billion.[16] This estimate has been supported by studies made of the real property holdings of religious organizations; the best known studies are those prepared by Martin Larson.[17] He judges the value of real estate owned by churches to be a minimum of $79.5 billion,[18] basing his estimate on a detailed analysis of property records in four representative American cities, Buffalo, Washington, D.C., Baltimore, and Denver, and extrapolating the results for the rest of the country. Larson concludes that about $7 billion is owned by Jewish organizations, about $28 billion by Protestant and miscellaneous groups, and about $44.5 billion by Roman Catholic organizations. The $79.5 billion total is almost twice the combined 1965 value of the assets of the five largest United States industrial corporations—Standard Oil of New Jersey, General Motors, Ford Motors, General Electric, and Chrysler Corporation.[19] According to conservative calculations, real estate owned by religious organizations escapes taxation at the rate of approximately $4 billion annually; and the amount of federal income taxes avoided by them on their business and investment income is at least as much.[20]

Although the salaries received by religious functionaries are supposedly subject to federal and state income taxes, the value of benefits received in lieu of salary by members of sacred orders and other employees of the Catholic Church escapes such taxation, either because it is treated as maintenance or cost of operation of the religious institution, or because it is considered income of the church rather than that of the individual, and thus exempt. Rabbis and Protestant ministers pay no income taxes in respect to homes given to them by their congregations. When they themselves purchase a home, they may use the tax-free rental allowance provided by the congregation to defray virtually every expense of providing for it—interest and principal payments on the mortgage, taxes, utilities, and many other expenses. Moreover, although they have already used part of their tax-free rental allowance to pay for these items, under applicable revenue rulings they may in addition deduct the cost of interest and taxes from their other income.[21] The combined tax liabilities avoided by clerical personnel whose compensation escapes taxation in this manner has been estimated at $200 million per year.[22]

Furthermore, the amount of property and investments of religious organizations that is immune from tax is growing at an alarming rate.[23] When capital is allowed to accumulate at compound interest, any large amount of wealth invested conservatively in banks or mutual funds will double in one generation and multiply eight times in three generations. But the tax-free wealth of religious organizations has pyramided even more rapidly since it has frequently been invested in business enterprises that produce a much higher rate of return than savings bank deposits or investments in mutual funds yield.[24]

A leading executive of a religious foundation described how the investment funds of churches have multiplied:

Suppose a church buys a million-dollar business that in view of tax exemptions shows an annual profit of $120,000. It can borrow $800,-000 to purchase the business at the preferred loan rate of four percent, or $32,000. Hence, on an investment of $200,000, the church will net $88,000 or 44 percent.

Suppose, however, that the net were only 25 percent. An investment at 25 percent compounded doubles in less than three years, quadruples in six, in thirty years will multiply itself one thousand times. Starting with $1,000,000 and encouraged by the present tax exemptions for religious bodies engaging in unrelated business activities, any church by using this procedure could own America in 60 years.[25]

Mrs. Murray's War Against the Churches

By 1964 Madalyn Murray (now Mrs. O'Hair), a 45-year-old divorcee who lived with her two sons in Baltimore, Maryland, was already regarded by many people as "the most hated woman in America." [26] The Supreme Court of the United States had upheld her claim, as plaintiff in a suit against the Maryland school authorities, that the practice of reciting prayers in the Baltimore public schools violated the First Amendment's prohibition against laws respecting the establishment of religion. In May 1964 she took the lead in starting a new action in the Maryland courts attacking the exemption of church property and income from local real estate and federal income taxes. She claimed that the special tax immunity conferred upon churches forced her and other taxpayers to pay higher taxes, thereby in effect compelling her to support church activity in conflict with the constitutional prohibition against laws in aid of religion. Her suit was dismissed by Maryland's highest court, and ultimately the Supreme Court declined to pass on the question,[27] as it had declined in a number of previous similar suits.

Mrs. Murray, whose forebears came to America in 1650, was brought up in a rigidly conformist, Presbyterian atmosphere, but later became a militant atheist as a matter of personal conviction. As the result of her battles against compulsory school prayers and tax exemption for church property, she was subjected to a campaign of persecution by those whom she sarcastically referred to as her "Christian neighbors." A writer for a national magazine described this harassment with considerable understatement as "one of the less appetizing chapters in America's defense of civil liberties." [28] Although she had served as a WAC officer in World War II, later was graduated from law school, earned credits toward a Master's degree, and had seventeen years of training as a psychiatric social worker, she was unable to find employment. The local stores not only declined to give her credit, but refused to sell to her at all. Her sons, one of whom was suffering from a rare blood disease, a condition in which the slightest bruise caused bleeding under the skin, were beaten up over a hundred times by neighborhood gangs; and when she complained of these assaults in the local courts, the judges insisted that her sons had provoked them. Every window of her house was broken at least once, her car windows were smashed, the tires slashed, and the plants and flowers in her modest garden trampled and uprooted. She received thousands of letters full of the vilest, crudest abuse and vituperation, many containing threats of death. One such letter enclosed a newspaper photograph of Mrs. Murray smeared with excrement. Eventually for the safety of herself and her family she was obliged to move to Hawaii.

Whether Mrs. Murray's claim that tax exemptions for church property and income were unconstitutional violations of the principle of separation of Church and State was valid was a matter of some difference of opinion among legal authorities for several years.[29] On May 4, 1970, in the case of *Walz v. Tax Commission of the City of New York,* the U.S. Supreme Court settled the matter. With only Justice Douglas dissenting, it held that the Constitution's prohibition against state support of religion was not violated by state statutes providing for such exemptions. Further reform in this area will now come about only as the result of strong public pressure. Until now support for such reform has come chiefly from more liberal-minded church leaders—Protestant, Catholic, and Jewish—among whom a consensus has developed that a modification of the church's traditional immunities is urgent.[30]

A Significant Reform—The Tax Immunity of Church-Owned Business and Commercial Enterprises Comes to an End

The Tax Reform Act of 1969 at long last made church and religious organizations subject to tax on their unrelated business activities, and prohibited "boot-strap" transactions, which enabled churches to acquire businesses and other properties with borrowed funds, and to operate them without paying income taxes on the profits. In doing so, the Act brought to an end the one tax privilege that religious leaders in general and a large segment of public opinion had come to regard as particularly objectionable. While this reform is not likely to produce much additional tax revenue and will probably not seriously diminish the huge income of church organizations, it must be counted as an important step forward, and one that was long overdue. Its significance may be appreciated by an examination of the extent to which religious bodies have until recently been engaged in profitable business and commercial activities entirely free from any tax burden.

During the last twenty-five years religious institutions have been participating to an ever greater extent in practically every type of commercial and business activity, none of which are even remotely related to their religious or charitable functions. Some ventures have resulted from gifts or bequests, but in many cases the church organization itself has taken the initiative of investing its money in the enterprise. Churches or church-related organizations have owned radio and television stations, hotels, motel chains, shopping centers, office buildings, residential developments, chains of nursing homes, apartment houses, parking lots, laundries, a professional baseball stadium, warehouses, department stores, drug stores, retail stores, industrial plants, book stores, banks, farms, textile mills, cattle ranches, publishing companies, sugar refineries, insurance companies, and large tracts of land. They have marketed food and other consumer goods.[31] Until passage of the Tax Reform Act of 1969, no federal income tax was due in connection with these operations, and even today they are frequently exempt from state income taxes. In most cases the church or church-affiliated organization has not even been obliged to contribute to local property taxes.

Religious institutions have reaped enormous profits by the sale and lease-back of property and businesses, a device that has been used with increasing frequency. Churches and church-affiliated organizations, because of their tax-exempt privileges, were able to offer more attractive terms in the form of higher purchase prices or lower rents than taxpaying businessmen.

In a typical deal of this kind, the church organization purchased a hotel, an apartment house, or an office building from a private taxpaying individual or corporation. The church paid only a small percentage of the purchase price in cash, and in some cases no cash at all, but financed the purchase with a twenty-year mortgage. The purchasing church immediately leased the property back to the seller on a net lease whereby the lessee paid all taxes, insurance, and other operating expenses, plus a net rental. These payments, all tax-free, often amounted to a 20% or 25% return on the church's investment, and enabled the church, as owner-landlord, not only to pay the interest on the mortgage and to liquidate the mortgage principal over the twenty-year period, but to realize a tidy profit as well. The seller in turn had many tax advantages. The installments of the purchase price were taxable to him at the more favorable capital gain rates rather than as ordinary income. Further, as a tenant under the lease-back arrangement, he was able to deduct the rent, taxes, and other expenses from the profits of operation, thereby materially reducing his income taxes. Finally, the sizeable proceeds that he realized on the sale were immediately available to him as additional capital, which he could invest profitably in the same business or in some other enterprise.[32]

Such deals were often made for the purchase of property on which all permissible depreciation had been taken, so that the additional tax savings to the private seller made the sale–lease-back arrangement doubly attractive. Frequently before the twenty years had expired, the church organization would sell the property back to the former owner, or to a third party, at a large profit, on which no income or capital gains tax was due.

In an arrangement involving the purchase, lease-back, and resale of a hotel, a group of Baptist and Presbyterian churches recovered its original investment; received $25,000 a year for ten years, tax-free; and realized a tax-free capital gain of $450,000.[33] Purchase and lease-back deals involving supermarkets and service stations were reported to have accounted for 17% of the $2.8 million gross income of the Baptist Federation of Texas for the single year of 1962.[34]

Purchase and lease-back transactions involving tax-immune religious organizations became so common as to be regarded as almost routine. Most large owners of real estate and of commercial and industrial properties around the country were bombarded daily with sale–lease-back propositions from church groups offering lucrative tax avoidance arrangements for all concerned. Multi-million dollar sale and lease-back deals involved substantial properties and even whole businesses, and millions of dollars of taxes were saved by both parties. The only loser was the government, which was deprived of hundreds of thousands, and sometimes millions of dollars in tax revenue.

But perhaps the most objectionable feature of the manifold business and commercial activities pursued by religious organizations was the fact that in many cases they competed with taxpaying businessmen, often the owners of small concerns, over whom they obtained an unfair advantage because of their tax-exemption. Occasionally, as in certain operations of the Mormons, the church-owned commercial venture was operated by a subsidiary of the religious body, and paid federal income taxes on its profits. But usually these profits were tax-free, since churches and sacerdotal orders, unlike charitable and educational organizations, were not required to pay taxes on business income even though it was entirely unrelated to their religious functions.[35] Even where a religious organization operated through a business subsidiary that paid corporate income taxes, unlike the case of its private taxpaying competitors, the dividends paid over to the parent church body were tax-free. Furthermore since church-owned business corporations did not need to pay out as much in dividends as their taxpaying competitors in order to produce the same net return for their stockholders, they could retain more of their earnings for financing internal expansion and additional business, and were able to sell their products or services at a lower cost.[36] Because of such advantages, many small business firms suffered sharply reduced profits or operating losses, and were even threatened with being put out of business altogether.[37]

Church-operated enterprises competed in this manner with hundreds of local businessmen. In one city a church leased a lot to an oil company for a filling station; the church received one cent per gallon on all sales. No tax was paid on this business income, giving the church an advantage over every other filling station in town.[38] Sometimes churches even competed with their own members. In one Missouri town, a prominent church member whose business was selling real estate to prospective home owners found that his church owned similar property that was being sold for home sites. When his church sold acreage at a profit, he complained, the profit was tax-free, whereas when he sold his holdings he was obliged to pay a capital gains tax.[39] In New Orleans, Loyola University, a Jesuit institution, operated Television Station WWL-TV and paid no taxes on its income. The general manager of another New Orleans TV station, himself a Loyola alumnus, complained that the commercial rates for TV advertising charged by WWL were so low that he was unable to compete.[40]

Extensive as the property ownership and business operations of Protestant churches have been, they pale into insignificance when compared with the holdings of the Catholic Church. The assets of the Knights of Columbus, a Catholic fraternal order, are reported to have grown from $163 million in 1960 to over $200 million in 1965, and included department stores, warehouses, and a steel mill. Numero.s Catholic religious orders of monks and nuns are said to have marketed and advertised for sale to the general public products such as fruit cakes, hams, bacon, sausages, preserves and jellies, candy, beef, fishing equipment, bread, and religious articles—

all without the necessity of paying income, social security, and unemployment taxes, and often exempt from local real estate taxes as well.

A series of articles in a German magazine analyzing the business and financial interests of one Catholic order in the United States and other countries claimed that this group owned 51% of the stock of Bank of America, one of the world's largest banks, and a majority interest in Di Georgio Fruit Company, which in turn owns processing plants, citrus groves in California and Florida, banana plantations in Central and South America, and a fleet of more than one hundred steamships. In addition this order is said to control international banking systems, factories, and armament plants throughout Europe, and substantial interests in a number of America's largest oil, steel, and aircraft companies. Its United States stockholdings alone, apart from other American business interests, are stated to have a market value of $6 billion and yield an annual income of about $250 million a year.[41]

Father Richard Grider, a Catholic priest, was quoted as saying:

The Catholic Church must be the biggest corporation in the United States. . . . Our assets and real estate holdings must exceed those of Standard Oil, A. T. & T. and U. S. Steel combined.[42]

Growing Opposition to Tax Exemption for Religion

Although challenges to the tax immunities of religious organizations have been heard more and more frequently in recent years, most have come, strangely enough, not from outraged businessmen and representatives of taxpaying groups, but from members of the clergy whose churches have enjoyed these privileges for so long.[43] One of the leading critics is Eugene Carson Blake, a former president of the National Council of Churches of Christ, and Stated Clerk of the United Presbyterian Church. In a frequently quoted article that appeared in 1959, he wrote that in view of their favored tax position:

it is not unreasonable to prophesy that, with reasonably prudent management the churches ought to be able to control the whole economy of the nation within the predictable future.[44]

Blake and some of his colleagues coupled their agitation for a reappraisal of the churches' traditional tax-exempt status with an ominous warning: Unless the churches themselves took the lead in eliminating the abuses inherent in their tax immunity, they would ultimately become so rich and powerful that history would repeat itself; and forcible expropriation of church property and privileges similar to that which took place in England in the sixteenth century, France in the eighteenth, Italy in the nineteenth, and Mexico and Russia in the twentieth century would be carried out by an aroused public, and perhaps even by the government itself. "A government with mounting tax problems," Blake wrote, "cannot be expected to keep its hands off the wealth of a rich church forever." [45]

A number of influential clergymen, especially among the Roman Catholics, still resist any change in the status quo. But probably a majority of church leaders, including some liberal Catholics, now feel that while the churches are entitled to exemptions on church edifices and auxiliary property, and on other facilities essential to the pursuit of their religious, educational, and welfare programs, the elimination of their tax immunity on profit-making business and commercial activities was entirely justified.[46]

Many churchmen feel that although the loss of some of their privileges may cause churches financial hardship, the gain they will achieve in moral stature will more than compensate for it. Billy Graham, for example, has said that the abuse of religious tax exemptions has destroyed the spirit of voluntary giving and deadened the spiritual life of the churches; [47] and an officer of the National Council of Churches of Christ feels that tax exemptions are causing damage to the church's image, and that it is "high time that businessmen themselves should be getting up in arms." [48] Leaders of the United Presbyterian Church concluded that as a result of the church's tax-sheltered status clergymen have been less inclined to speak their minds on pressing and controversial social issues.[49] In some denominations a bitter struggle is going on between those who feel that churches must participate vocally in the vital issues of the day, and even attempt to influence legislation, and those who fear that by doing so they may jeopardize their tax-exempt status.[50]

Although not all Protestant church leaders agreed with him, Bishop Pike felt that in the long run the churches would benefit from the loss of some of their tax benefits. They would be compelled to stop spending money on over-elaborate and unnecessary church structures and to concentrate their plans on community usefulness and proper spiritual goals. Only when free of what he termed their "edifice complex" and dependence on wealthy contributors will the churches be free to speak out boldly on burning social and political issues.[51]

Most Roman Catholic leaders disagree sharply with all of these arguments. They claim that the power to tax is the power to destroy, and that tax exemption for religious organizations is essential to the separation of Church and State. They insist, furthermore, that their churches more than make up for the taxes they would otherwise pay by the social, educational, and charitable services they render through their parochial schools and welfare activities.[52]

Ineffective Half-Measures

There has recently been a trend on the part of some federal, state, and local taxing authorities seeking additional tax revenues to impose taxes on church properties and earnings from business. These efforts have not proved very successful however.[53] To improve their public relations or to avoid the threat of legislation that might modify or eliminate their tax exemptions, a growing number of church organizations are voluntarily paying local property taxes on church-owned real estate held for investment or operated for commercial purposes and sales taxes on items sold in church establishments open to the public. Others are making voluntary contributions in lieu of taxes to help defray the costs of water, sewers, police and fire protection, and other public services from which they benefit.[54]

But these situations are isolated. What is needed are standards and requirements that will produce uniform practices at least in the same state or locality. In fact, in a number of instances, religious organizations that had been making such voluntary payments or contributions abandoned the practice when they observed that other church groups were not doing the same.[55]

A Program for Reforms and the Limitations of the Tax Reform Act of 1969

Attitudes among church leaders toward tax exemption for religious organizations range from one end of the spectrum to the other—from that of traditionalists who say that now that the churches are being taxed on their unrelated business activities the status quo should not be further disturbed, to that of extremists like Madalyn Murray who would like to see all church property and income, whether devoted to religion, education, or charity, taxed across the board, exactly as if it belonged to secular persons.[56]

A program that would probably command strong support from most clerical advocates of reform would consist of the following modifications of present tax exemptions:

1. Sales, franchise, license, and excise taxes should be paid by church organizations just like other organizations.

2. The exemption from state and federal income taxes of the income of ministers, priests, nuns, and members of sacred orders, whether received in the form of salary or other forms of maintenance, should be eliminated.[57]

3. Church and church-related organizations should contribute to the local real estate tax burden to the extent that their property and auxiliary facilities receive the benefit of police and fire protection, water, sewers, and other public services.[58]

4. While church and church-related organizations should continue to enjoy exemption from federal and state taxes on their rents, dividends, interest, and other "passive" income, they should be required to disburse such income on a current basis. The same provisions prohibiting the accumulation of income by private foundations should be applicable to religious bodies,[59] including the requirement that if their funds are invested in non-income or low-income producing investments, the organization must meet any deficiency below some standard income formula from contributions

or even from their capital assets. As in the case of foundations, a certain amount of flexibility would be provided, permitting income to be accumulated to finance specific projects and programs upon application to the Treasury.

Some representatives of religious bodies have proposed that the "passive" or investment income, including realized capital gains, be subject to federal and state income taxes, either wholly or in part, because they believe that this area is the one in which the "wealth" of organized religion has grown most rapidly.[60] There are some who would go so far as to eliminate the exemption from local property taxes of church real property used exclusively for religious purposes.[61]

The latter, however, are decidely minority viewpoints. Since it is doubtful that even the relatively moderate measures suggested here will evoke much enthusiasm among lawmakers, and since proposals to tax religious organizations are invariably treated warily by Congress and the state legislatures,[62] it would be completely unrealistic to propose anything more drastic. The pyramiding of wealth in the past cannot be undone except by outright expropriation. However, the changes in tax exemptions suggested here, in combination with the new tax on unrelated business income, should go a long way toward discouraging such accumulation of wealth and assuring that future income and resources of churches are channeled exclusively into expenditures for religious, charitable, and educational activities.

Any meaningful tax reform in this area, however, especially at the federal level, must be preceded by a thorough investigation by the appropriate Congressional committees. One of the greatest problems at present is the fact that no one, not even the Internal Revenue Service, has any knowledge of the wealth, income, and financial operations of religious organizations, nor even of their numbers and identities. A necessary first step should be the requirement that all such organizations file complete reports with the Treasury Department of their property, income, and financial activities. Under the Tax Reform Act of 1969 churches and other religious organizations are exempt from income tax audits except under extraordinary circumstances.

Other Private Charitable, Educational, and Welfare Organizations

A number of those advocating modification of the special tax privileges of religious organizations contend that whatever reforms may be adopted with respect to religious bodies should be equally applicable to other private charitable, educational, and welfare institutions.[63] This action would seem only fair, especially now that the Supreme Court has ruled in effect that churches are not constitutionally prohibited from receiving the same statutory tax treatment as other charitable organizations.

Doubtless many college presidents and trustees will claim that the tax exemptions of their institutions are based on the traditional recognition of the services they render to society, and that any curtailment of their tax-exempt status would be an infringement by government on their independence. It is difficult, however, to see how the reforms envisaged here can have serious adverse effect on private institutions of higher learning. Many of them already pay local property taxes or contribute voluntarily to the cost of local government in return for public services from which they benefit; those who do not, should in all fairness be required to do so.

There remains only the requirement of current disbursement of the income from their endowments and the prohibition against accumulating income except for specific long-term projects and programs. Since this is precisely the practice that private colleges and universities are presently following, it is difficult to see how such an injunction would be burdensome. While in recent years their endowments and other capital funds have grown enormously in size,[64] this growth has utterly failed to keep pace with their expanding needs.[65] Private colleges and universities have not been hoarding their funds. On the contrary, due to ever increasing enrollment, higher faculty salaries, the need for new equipment, rising maintenance costs, increased scholarships and other student aid, all aggravated by inflationary pressures, their operating expenses far exceed their income, with the result that most of them are faced with enormous and ever-mounting deficits.[66] So much so, that it is generally agreed that a drastic increase in government aid to private colleges and universities will be needed in the next decade, and that unless such aid and increased contributions from other sources are received, many of them in the foreseeable future will become tax-supported public institutions or disappear from the scene altogether. In the Spring 1967 Report of the Ford Foundation, its head, McGeorge Bundy, said:

The present need of deans and presidents [of the private institutions of higher learning] strung end to end, would go three times around the endowment of the Ford Foundation without a pause for breath.

Under these circumstances it would hardly seem that requiring the private colleges and universities to disburse their income on a current basis, with adequate provision permitting exceptions for specific programs, would pose any problem

Proposed tax reform along the lines here suggested would place most tax-exempt institutions—charities, welfare organizations, hospitals, religious bodies, and private foundations—on an equal footing. While the proposed reforms will doubtless encounter bitter opposition in many quarters, at least it can be urged in their favor that, in addition to their inherent equity, they have the advantage of impartiality and uniformity.

3

Private Foundation Field Day Comes
to an End

At the end of 1966, Congressman Wright Patman, whose House
Subcommittee on Small Business [1] had been studying the operations of charitable foundations since 1961, summarized his conclusions as follows:

> The tax exempt private foundation—that strange creation of Ameri-
> can folkways, a holdover from the conscience-stricken moments of the
> robber barons at the turn of the century—is an indulgence which the
> taxpayer may soon have to decide he can no longer afford to support
> in the manner to which its founders have become accustomed. The
> present economy makes rising demands on the taxpayer for both ex-
> ternal defense and internal improvements, yet the privileged founda-
> tions do not share the pinch of citizenship. Their increased hoarding
> and building of untaxed wealth makes warnings such as expressed by
> Senator Albert Gore—that the proliferation of tax exempt foundations
> raises the threat of a dangerous "concentration of wealth and control
> over the economy"—sound indeed temperate. [2]

Congressman Patman, a veteran of some thirty-five years in
Congress, has been known for years as an ardent champion of the
small businessman and a critic of "big business" and Wall Street
bankers. While his indictment of the operations of charitable foundations was widely criticized as far too sweeping, even his critics
agreed that he had turned up enough evidence of abuses to warrant

Congress' taking a closer look at the tax privileges foundations enjoyed.

A private tax-exempt foundation or charitable trust is simply a legal entity, usually created by some well-to-do taxpayer, which has applied for and received a tax exemption from the Treasury Department. The contributions or donations that the foundation or trust receives from its founder or benefactors are supposed to be disbursed by the foundation or trust itself for charitable, educational, or religious purposes, or turned over to other institutions devoted to such purposes. For many years the granting of such exemptions by the Treasury was a mere formality, and once the exemption was granted, as the Patman Committee investigation disclosed, there was little check on the foundation's operations. Now for the first time, under the Tax Reform Act of 1969, the activities of foundations will be subject to a number of restrictions and to more rigid supervision by the Treasury. In order to defray the expense of such supervision, foundations will be required to pay a 4% tax on their annual investment income.

Tax-Exemption for Foundations and Its Abuse

As a matter of public policy our tax laws have always encouraged people to contribute to charities, hospitals, churches, and educational institutions, as well as private foundations. But for years wealthy taxpayers have resorted to the creation of private foundations as a tax device.[3] An individual could deduct 20% from his taxable income for contributions to a private foundation, and an additional 10% for gifts to publicly supported institutions; a corporation could deduct 5% of its taxable income for the same purposes.[4] In addition, donations to foundations and other tax-exempt organizations were fully deductible to reduce gift and estate tax liability.[5] Private foundations and other charitable, religious, and educational institutions paid no tax on the contributions received nor, generally, on the income earned on their assets.[6] While these deductions for gifts and bequests to foundations are still permitted, the new strictures on the activities and transactions of foundations eliminates their use as tax avoidance devices.

There is general agreement that on the whole the funds of private foundations have made impressive contributions to education, medicine, and scientific research, and have helped foster artistic achievement and an environment for the creation of new ideas and experimentation. However, until recently, there has been so little regulation and scrutiny of foundation operations that for many years some private foundations have been able to engage in activities constituting an abuse of their tax-exempt status.

As far back as 1916, the Walsh Committee of the United States Senate warned the country of abuses that might flow from the creation of privileged tax-exempt trusts and similar organizations. In 1948–49 the House Ways and Means Committee conducted hearings that revealed that certain tax-exempt institutions and private charities had moved into the commercial and industrial area; and that some, like the Ford Foundation, had acquired substantial interests in a number of the country's wealthiest industrial enterprises. In his tax message to Congress on January 23, 1950, President Truman was highly critical of tax exemptions granted to charitable foundations which were "used as a cloak for business ventures."

The Revenue Act of 1950 was intended to put a brake on some questionable foundation practices, but Congress was unwilling to adopt any really drastic reforms. A tax was imposed on foundation business income "unrelated" to charitable functions, and hitherto uncontrolled accumulation of income was limited by a requirement that accumulations be "reasonable." However, a recommendation of the Treasury Department that Congress enact an absolute prohibition of dealings between foundations and the donors controlling them was rejected.

The Patman Investigation

In 1961 Congressman Patman initiated the most comprehensive analysis of the activities of tax-exempt foundations ever attempted.

From time to time his subcommittee submitted a number of lengthy reports and conducted extensive public hearings.[7] By the end of 1962 Patman had become convinced that private foundations were being used as a device to evade taxes, and that the enactment of corrective legislation and stricter supervision of foundation activities was essential. In his interim report of December 31, 1962 the chairman stated:

Today funds are being put into foundations which yield no taxable income. Since the money lost to the public's Treasury must be found somewhere, the burden is shifted to people who are obliged to work for a living—to the widow with a cottage instead of a palace, to businessmen, and to the farmer.[8]

The time has come, I think, to take a close look at the types of operations in which tax-exempt foundations are engaged. Already our survey indicates a number of apparent abuses or irregularities which would seem to conflict with the intent of Congress when it relieved certain institutions from the burden of taxation. An "agonizing reappraisal" is overdue.[9]

The charge has been made, and with considerable justification, that Patman's condemnation of foundations was too indiscriminate and that many of his conclusions were unjustified.[10] He gave scant, almost grudging acknowledgment to the constructive philanthropic role played by most foundations, and by over-emphasizing the questionable role played by most foundations, conveyed the impression that the abuses were more common than they were.[11] Finally, he criticized the Treasury Department unmercifully for the fact that foundations disregarded reporting requirements and for the infrequency of Treasury audits of their operations, even though the Department's admitted failures in this regard (which have since been corrected) were due to insufficient manpower, rather than to inefficiency or neglect.

Yet when all this is said, it must be admitted that the committee revealed improper practices by many private foundations that called for a thorough review of their activities by Congress and serious consideration of remedial legislation. Indeed many of Patman's concerns were echoed by the Treasury Department itself, as witness the following colloquy between the committee chairman and Bertrand M. Harding, Acting Commissioner of Internal Revenue, during the 1964 hearings:

THE CHAIRMAN: Would you agree that foundations are established, at least in some cases, for the following purposes: (1) to reduce estate taxes and thereby lessen, or do away with entirely, the necessity for liquidating holdings in a family-owned or controlled business; (2) to retain active control of a business, although ownership is divested, by appointing family members or close associates as directors of the foundation?

MR. HARDING: I think there has been some evidence to that effect, Mr. Chairman.[12]

. . .

THE CHAIRMAN: Would you agree that there is ample evidence that some donors find it hard to forget that the foundation's assets once belonged to them?

MR. HARDING: I think that we have seen some of that, yes, Mr. Chairman.

THE CHAIRMAN: Would you agree that there is ample evidence that some donors seem to regard their foundations as reservoirs of capital to be tapped in time of personal need?

MR. HARDING: I think there has been some evidence along that line, too, sir.

THE CHAIRMAN: Would you agree that it is not at all unusual for a donor to call upon "his" foundation to lend him money, to purchase his property or to sell or to lease to him its property?

MR. HARDING: There have been indications; yes, sir.

THE CHAIRMAN: Would you agree that there is a lack of legally enforceable fiduciary standards to restrict self-dealing by those in control of foundations?

MR. HARDING: Yes, sir.[13]

. . .

THE CHAIRMAN: Since foundations are funded with tax deductible contributions and earn tax exempt income, would you agree that the problem of self-dealing may appropriately be considered at the Federal level?

MR. HARDING: Yes, sir.

THE CHAIRMAN: Would you agree that although loans to a donor must be at a "reasonable" rate of interest with "adequate security," and although his purchase and sale transactions with his foundation must be at "adequate" consideration, these are hardly fiduciary standards?

MR. HARDING: Yes, sir.

THE CHAIRMAN: Would you agree that, when directors of a foundation are selected because of their familial relationship or personal loyalty to the donor, it is too much to expect that they will rigidly adhere even to those guidelines in approving the donor's self-dealing?

MR. HARDING: I think it raises a very difficult problem, Mr. Chairman.[14]

. . .

THE CHAIRMAN: Would you agree that there is ample evidence that, in order to avoid possible loss of tax exemption, some foundations, which contemplate the operation of a business, find it expedient to incorporate their business ventures in the form of wholly-owned "feeder" subsidiaries?

MR. HARDING: Yes, there is that, Mr. Chairman.

THE CHAIRMAN: Do I understand correctly that the business profits of these corporate "feeders" are taxed at regular corporate rates and only the dividends which they pay to their "parent" foundation are exempt from income taxation?

MR. HARDING: That is correct.

THE CHAIRMAN: Would you agree that there is ample evidence that a substantial number of foundations are known to have tax-paying subsidiaries which compete for business with other commercial enterprises which have taxpayers for shareholders?

MR. HARDING: Yes, Mr. Chairman.

THE CHAIRMAN: Would you agree that the difference in tax liability at the shareholder level may afford a competitive advantage to the subsidiary of a foundation through forbearance of dividend payments?

MR. HARDING: It could have that result, Mr. Chairman.[15]

In fact tax-exempt foundations have frequently been recommended by lawyers and accountants as a tax avoidance gimmick. The committee summarized a law review article by a well-known firm of tax attorneys that pointed out the refinements of controlling property without ownership through creation of a foundation, as follows:

What can be accomplished by creating a foundation?
1. Keep control of wealth.

2. Can keep for the donor many attributes of wealth by many means:
   (a) Designating the administrative management of the foundation.
   (b) Control over its investments.
   (c) Appointing relatives as directors of foundation.
   (d) Foundation's assets can be used to borrow money to buy other property that does not jeopardize its purposes. Thus foundation funds can be enhanced from the capitalization of its tax exemption.
3. The foundation can keep income in the family.
4. Family foundations can aid employees of the donor's business.
5. Foundations may be the method of insuring that funds will be available for use in new ventures in business.
6. We can avoid income from property while it is slowly being given to a foundation by a combination of a trust and the charitable foundation.
7. We can get the 20 percent charity deduction in other ways:
   (a) By giving away appreciated property to the foundation, we escape a tax on the realization of a gain.
   (b) We can give funds to a foundation to get charitable deduction currently in our most advantageous tax year.
   (c) Very often local personal and real property taxes can be avoided.
   (d) We can avoid speculative profits.
   (e) We can give away valuable "frozen assets," white elephant estates, residences, valuable works of art, and collections of all arts.[16]

Growth of Foundations

Tax-exempt foundations and charitable trusts have grown by leaps and bounds, both in number and size. No one, including the Treasury Department, seems to have had any precise idea of how many tax-exempt foundations there were in the country. The Patman Committee estimated that there were as many as 100,000.[17] Until recently the reporting requirements of the Treasury Department were blithely ignored by most foundations, and audits by the Internal Revenue Service were few and far between.[18] Thus for many years the operations and dealings of foundations were, for all practical purposes, virtually unsupervised.

A key factor in the rapid growth of foundations has been the ability of a founder to contribute substantial wealth to a foundation, receive a tax deduction for his contributions, and still maintain control of his wealth through control of the foundation for an indefinite period. In this manner foundation assets have remained under family domination for generations. Earnings could accumulate since they were tax-free, and grow much more rapidly than those of businesses subject to taxation.[19]

The 534 foundations studied by the Patman Committee had assets of over $10 billion,[20] and during the period 1951–1965 their aggregate untaxed receipts amounted to about $11.5 billion. Between 1961 and 1964 their receipts of $4.6 billion were nearly 30% more than the combined net operating earnings after taxes of the fifty largest banks in the United States. As of the beginning of 1961, 111 foundations had stock ownership ranging from 10% to 100% in many of the largest corporations in the country. At the same time only about 48% of their "receipts" (a term that Patman applied to both income and capital gains) were being distributed to charity. The balance, much of it capital gains, remained unspent.[21]

In at least five respects Patman's criticism of the activities of private foundations was on solid ground—in regard to self-dealing, business operations in competition with private businessmen, excessive accumulation of income, the use of gifts of stock in family corporations for tax avoidance, and perpetual control of foundation management by founders or their families.

Self-Dealing Between Donors and Their Foundations

Clearly the founders and principal benefactors of some foundations exploited the organization's tax-exempt status for their own personal gain or for the benefit of members of their families, friends, and business associates through sales, purchases, loans, and other financial transactions. The Patman Committee reports are replete with instances of such self-dealing, which was facilitated by the fact that the donor or founder was permitted to, and generally did, select or control the selection of the foundation's directors, officers, or trustees, filling these positions with members of his family, employees, friends, or business associates.

The J. M. Kaplan Fund, Inc. whose operations were analyzed in considerable detail by the committee, is a good case in point. This fund was granted an exemption from income tax in 1946 as an organization operated exclusively for charitable purposes. At various times it held two promissory notes of J. M. Kaplan, its founder, in the amounts of $720,000,000 and $967,000, respectively. Neither note called for the payment of interest nor provided for collateral security, and both notes matured at his death. Another investment held by the foundation was a large loan to a corporation burdened with substantial obligations, in which relatives of Kaplan were interested as stockholders. The committee characterized the amount of interest payable on this loan as unreasonably low and its collateral security of questionable value.[22]

Some foundations used their funds to pay benefits to employees of corporations affiliated with the founder, to make low-interest loans to the founder or members of his family, or to help defray federal taxes on the founder's estate. Others held sizeable life insurance policies on the lives of officers, directors, or stockholders of corporations affiliated with the founder, or purchased the stock of such corporations and made loans to their executives so as to permit them to invest in the securities market. Purchases of securities from, and sales of securities to the creator of the foundation or his relatives, or affiliated corporations, were common practices.

The average taxpayer could not deduct a charitable contribution to reduce his income tax liability until it was actually paid. Not so in the case of some foundation "benefactors." A not uncommon device was the gift to a foundation of funds which were immediately "borrowed" by the donor in exchange for his promissory note. The donor was thus able to take an immediate deduction for income tax purposes for the amount of his contribution and still retain the use of the contributed fund.[23]

Frequently founders, large contributors, or their affiliated corporations even managed to reacquire securities that they had previously given away to a foundation, thereby reaping the double advantage of a deduction for income tax purposes equal to the value of their original gift, and the reacquisition of the same securities at a higher cost basis, without having to pay any capital gains tax.

In a number of instances foundation assets were employed to assist their founders or business associates of their founders in proxy fights for the control of other companies. Commenting on one such instance, the financial editor of the *Philadelphia Bulletin* wrote on January 17, 1961:

> Regardless of intent, the episode reveals in full nakedness how charitable foundations can be misused. A charitable trust, or foundation, is granted tax free status by Congress solely for a charitable purpose. Assets are not to be employed to enrich the donors, or founders or to aggrandize their economic power.
>
> A person can build up a foundation by contributing, every year, part of his income. If the investments are well chosen, the fund may grow rapidly through capital appreciation. Only income must be disbursed.
>
> The foundation's sponsor may be able to use the assets to buy control of companies. In so doing, he becomes an indirect beneficiary of the trust through the power it confers on him. He can install himself as president of a corporation so acquired. He can find jobs for friends, relatives and business associates. He can favor friends with business.[24]

Salaries and other expenses paid out to relatives of the donor were sometimes disproportionate to the amounts disbursed for charitable causes. One foundation established by a Southern newspaper owner accumulated over $5 million in unspent income between 1961 and 1964, during which time its assets grew from virtually zero to over $7 million. Its administration and operating expenses, which averaged well over $100,000 a year, included a $20,000 salary for the founder's widow and a $15,000 salary for a secretary. Another foundation, in the period 1961–64, disbursed between $244,000 and $283,000 a year for charitable purposes; but its three trustees collected "commissions" aggregating $40,000 to $43,000 per year—something over 15% of its charitable gifts. In another instance the "expenses" of the foundation exceeded its gross income, so that nothing at all was disbursed to charity.

Some foundations have afforded opportunities to members of the family of the creator or donor to travel about the world on trips ostensibly for foundation purposes, and to reap other personal benefits with tax-free foundation money. The directors of certain prestigious foundations have received exceedingly generous fees. One of the members of the Ford family was paid $5,000 per day for attending meetings of the Ford Foundation's Board of Directors.

In 1950 the Treasury Department recommended that the tax law be amended so as to provide an absolute prohibition of dealings between a foundation and the donor who controls it, but Congress declined to do so. The law merely provided that where there were transactions involving the transfer of assets, lending of money, or payment for personal services between a foundation and its donor, founder, members of their families, or controlled corporations, the terms had to be at arms-length. That is to say, there had to be a reasonable consideration for the transfer of assets; any compensation paid had to be reasonable in amount; and in the case of a loan, reasonable interest had to be paid and security furnished.[25] But deciding what was "reasonable" was a matter of interpretation,[26] and the courts all too frequently were overly lenient and formalistic in deciding whether the transaction had been fair and reasonable or had "inured to the benefit" of any individual.[27] Moreover, since it was often difficult to fix a reasonable value in the case of transfers of securities in closely-held corporations, interests in real estate, copyrights, moving picture rights, and other intangible property, there was infinite room for evasion; and the Treasury Department lacked the staff and personnel to police and scrutinize adequately the often intricate ramifications of such transactions. As a consequence, many instances of improper self-dealing escaped detection. Furthermore there was a number of loopholes in the statute. Transactions, for example, between foundations and corporations in which a donor owned or controlled less than 50% of the stock were not prohibited, although it was common knowledge that in many large corporations a far smaller percentage constituted effective control.[28]

In 1965 the Treasury Department submitted its own report.[29] At the request of Congress, it had for some time been conducting a separate analysis of private foundation operations. The Treasury proposed barring all donor-foundation dealings as well as all transactions between foundations and their officers, directors, and trustees, or their relatives, or relatives of the donor.[30] This proposal was adopted as part of the Tax Reform Act of 1969. It had been urged that such a flat prohibition might deprive a foundation of the personal services of a uniquely talented or productive trustee, or foreclose investment in a donor-affiliated business from which the foundation might secure a higher yield than from more conventional investments.[31] However, on balance, the Treasury proposal was sound and an amendment of the law along these lines was long overdue.[32]

Private Foundations Operating as Tax-Free Business Organizations

Many tax-exempt foundations directly or through subsidiary "feeder" corporations, have actively carried on extensive business activities. Their tax-exempt status gave them an unfair advantage over individuals and firms with whom they competed. It was one thing for a charitable foundation to have the privilege of receiving dividends, interest, rents, and royalties from its investments without having to pay a tax on such items of "passive" income. But it was another matter when foundations or their subsidiary corporations actively engaged in business and commercial enterprises in competition with private business and professional people. Foundations have acted as securities dealers, business brokers, and real estate operators; and they have operated manufacturing, banking, and research and testing organizations that offer their products or services to the public.

One tax-exempt foundation was found to have built up its assets from about half a million dollars to over $28 million by operating as a multi-million-dollar tax-free securities dealer. It granted millions of dollars of loans and credits to customers and business associates of the foundation's donor or managers, in return for commissions, interest, participations in stock investments, and finder's fees.[33] Another, whose founder was a leading real estate operator, was found to have been borrowing money from banks at one rate of interest and lending it out at a higher and often usurious rate to finance the purchase of New York City mortgages, real estate, and other assets.[34]

Foundations appear to have been particularly active in the research, scientific testing, and engineering fields. While they were supposed to be engaged in theoretical, basic scientific, or other technical research designed to produce significant new information or techniques having a broad application, a number of foundations, usually via a wholly-owned subsidiary, were busily involved in the preparation of technical studies, systems analyses, engineering work, and computer programming. They would furnish these services to private concerns or to federal, state, and local governmental authorities in return for substantial fees. In so doing they were competing directly with private taxpaying research and engineering concerns seeking the same type of clientele. Not only were they able to take business away from their taxpaying competitors, but they sometimes succeeded in putting them out of business entirely. The foundations' tax-exempt status enabled them to charge lower fees, and even to furnish such services below their competitors' costs. The Patman Committee rightly characterized all this as unfair competition.[35]

A trade association of private research and testing laboratories complained of having to compete with research institutes operated by tax-exempt foundations that did over $100 million in research and testing business in 1959. The president of one of the oldest nationwide school textbook and test publishers in the country informed the committee that a division of a tax-exempt private foundation was offering the same services to public schools and taking away $10 million worth of business a year from private companies in his field. A trade association of consulting engineers wrote Patman that one of its members had submitted a bid to the United States Department of Interior for a study of the possibilities of developing an adequate water supply at the Hopi Reservation in Arizona. The firm lost out when a Chicago-based tax-exempt private foundation offered to do the work for 10% less. The association estimated that its members in private practice were losing at least $10 million a year in fees to tax-exempt research institutes.

The influential Rand Corporation of Santa Monica, California, and the Institute for Defense Analyses of Cambridge, Massachusetts—two well-known tax-exempt scientific research organizations whose main activity was carrying on research projects for the United States Department of Defense and other governmental agencies in competition with private taxpaying companies—reported gross incomes in 1961 of more than $17 million and $8 million, respectively.[36]

In 1950 Congress enacted an amendment that was designed to deal with this competitive advantage over private taxpaying business; the amendment imposed a tax on the "unrelated business" income of foundations and their "feeder" subsidiaries.[37] But the Treasury Department was generally unsuccessful in convincing the courts that income from various commercial activities of foundations was "unrelated business" income, and should be taxed as such.[38] As often as not, such income was held not to be taxable, either because it was claimed to have been derived from an activity bearing a sufficiently close relationship to the functions of the foundation, or because it fell within one of the exceptions enumerated in the statute. Sophisticated tax specialists encountered little difficulty in circumventing the effect of the tax by converting the foundation's business income into a form specifically excluded from the "unrelated business" income tax.[39]

But even if all this income from business and commercial activity received by private tax-exempt foundations, usually via "feeder" subsidiaries, had been taxed as "unrelated business" income, the foundations would still have had formidable economic advantages over private businessmen with whom they competed. Even where the "feeder" subsidiary paid the regular corporate income tax on its business profits, the dividends it disbursed to its foundation parent were tax-free. The foundation could afford to forgo part or all of these dividends, or it could make available to its business subsidiary, from the foundation's tax-free funds, low-interest loans or other capital to permit the subsidiary to expand its business operations. The result was that, even assuming the same tax liability at the corporate level, the difference in taxpaying liability at the shareholder level gave the foundation-sponsored business an advantage over its competitors.[40]

One of the results of the growing business activity by foundations, or sponsored by them, was the funneling of substantial amounts of untaxed business profits into foundation coffers. Perhaps equally important was the tax revenue the government lost and which it would have otherwise derived from the operations of taxpaying business competitors whose profits were reduced or eliminated entirely as the result of foundation-sponsored competition.

To meet this problem the Tax Reform Act of 1969 prohibits foundations from engaging directly in business activity unrelated to their charitable or educational purposes, and limits the combined interest of a foundation and its donor in any unrelated business enterprise to 20% of the equity or voting power. A suitable grace period is provided for foundations to dispose of interests in excess of the 20% limitation. These measures were originally proposed by the Treasury Department in 1965.[41]

Some critics opposed the proposal on the ground that it would discourage future gifts to foundations of stock in family corporations, and force foundations to dispose of controlling stock interests in business corporations under unfavorable market conditions.[42] On the other hand, if Congress was to deal with the problem of foundation business activity at all, anything less than the Treasury's recommendation would have been ineffective.[43]

Unreasonable Accumulation of Funds

From 1951 through 1960 the aggregate gross "receipts" of the 534 foundations studied by the committee were almost $7 billion (Congressman Patman included in this figure almost $1.5 billion in capital gains). In this period the foundations dispersed about $3.5 billion, roughly 50%, for charitable and educational purposes.[44] Between 1961 and 1964 the aggregate of such receipts totaled about $4.6 billion (including some $1.3 billion of capital gains), of which some $2.2 billion, or about 48%, was disbursed for charitable and educational purposes.[45]

Although from an accounting and strictly legal point of view Patman was in error in lumping the capital gains of foundations with their "income," he was, in the view of many observers, including executives of many of the private foundations themselves, correct in insisting that their income should be distributed more quickly.[46] Referring to the $1.3 billion of foundation capital gains from 1961 through 1964, Patman commented:

Here is a huge amount of income, this capital gains mountain— growing and growing year after year, as if from some volcano of bullion—which should be distributed to charity on a reasonably current basis. The country's antipoverty needs, the war in Vietnam, the Nation's health needs, the Nation's education, research and scientific needs, and all other worthwhile causes demand that Congress force these funds into charity by law.[47]

The funds of some private foundations have accumulated to a fantastic degree. The Rockefeller Foundation has a well-deserved world-wide reputation as the generous supporter of a host of important and worthy causes. Nevertheless its assets grew from $35.9 million in 1913 to over $860 million in 1966. The funds of other foundations have similarly swollen in size—the Richard K. Mellon Foundation from $1,000 in 1947 to $121 million in 1964, the Bollingen Foundation from some $101,000 in 1945 to $5.1 million in 1964, the Ford Motor Company Foundation from nothing in 1949 to $38 million in 1964, and the Standard Oil Foundation from nothing in 1952 to almost $49 million in 1964.[48]

All that the law required was that exempt foundations refrain from accumulating income "unreasonably." [49] But under Treasury Department regulations, contributions received by foundations did not have to be counted in determining whether there had been an accumulation of income, and their capital gains not only escaped all tax, but were likewise not required to be dispersed to charity if they were reinvested within a reasonable period of time. The law's generosity went even further If they incurred a capital loss in disposing of their funds, foundations were permitted to deduct that amount from income, thereby further reducing the amount of income subject to scrutiny as having been "unreasonably" accumulated.

In fact the prohibition against "unreasonable" accumulations of income by tax-exempt foundations were so vague and flexible that it was not surprising that many foundations accumulated more income than they dispersed to charity. When the Treasury Department went to court to compel foundations to disburse greater shares of their income, it was usually unsuccessful, according to former Secretary of the Treasury Douglas Dillon. The courts were generally extremely lenient with foundations in this regard.[50]

Patman had a drastic solution [51] for what he considered a jealous hoarding of their resources by tax-exempt foundations, in some cases contrary to the desires of the great financiers who founded them.[52] Instead of being permitted to carry on their functions in perpetuity, he suggested that the life of private foundations be limited to twenty-five years. At the end of that period they would be required to distribute their funds to active charities and other beneficiaries and wind up their existence. Meanwhile, to minimize the accumulation of funds, he recommended that contributions and capital gains should be added to foundation income for the purpose of determining whether there has been an "unreasonable accumulation" of income, and that contributors should not be allowed tax deductions for gifts to foundations until the contributed asset has been donated by the foundation to active charities or devoted to charitable purposes.[53]

While agreeing with Patman that amendments to the law were needed to force foundations to distribute their income more rapidly, the Treasury Department considered his proposals arbitrary and unnecessary. Instead the Treasury proposed in 1965 (and Congress passed in 1969) a requirement that foundations invest their assets so as to generate current income to be spent on a current basis.[54]

Under the 1969 Act a private, non-operating foundation (that is, a foundation that does not spend substantially all of its income directly for active charitable and educational activities, and does not have more than half of its assets devoted directly to such activities) has to spend all of its net income on a current basis by contributing it or devoting it directly or indirectly to active charitable organizations or activities. At the same time a certain amount of reasonable flexibility is permitted; for example, a foundation may, with the approval of the Treasury Department, accumulate income over a period of years for a specific charitable project.

In order to deal with the situation in which a foundation's assets are invested for the most part in "growth stocks" or unimproved real estate that may appreciate greatly over a period of time, but yield little or no current income, the Treasury suggested, and the new act provides, an "Income Equilavent Rule." A foundation whose assets are invested in low-income-producing assets is required to spend for charitable, educational, and other exempt purposes the equivalent of what it would have received in current income if its funds had been invested in more conventional types of investment. If the foundation's investment assets yield less than 6% it is obliged to turn over cash gifts from contributors or part of its growth stocks to other active charitable organizations.

In addition, the Treasury proposed that boot-strap operations and other borrowing for investment purposes by foundations should be prohibited, that they should be prohibited from making loans not within their charitable functions, and that the use of their funds in connection with short-selling, margin trading, and other speculative stock market operations be forbidden.[55] While the 1969 Act did not adopt this suggestion, it accomplishes the same result by imposing taxes on the foundation and those involved in such transactions.

The rationale for the tax-favored treatment of contributions to foundations is that the tax revenue that the government loses is offset by the benefit the public receives from the contributed funds in the form of expenditures for charitable and educational activities. The new tax law, which includes in essence the Treasury's 1965 proposals, will go far toward forcing foundations to distribute their investment income more rapidly.[56]

Gifts of Stock in Family-Owned Corporations

A favorite tax avoidance device employed by innumerable founders and other benefactors of private foundations involved the gift to the family foundation of part of the stock in the family-owned corporation. The donor got an immediate income tax deduction for the value of the stock, but continued to keep control of the corporation and its assets within the family. (Typically, the officers of the foundation consisted of the donor and close relatives.[57]) Since the donor was in control of both the foundation and the business, he could siphon off most of the corporation's income by way of salaries for himself and members of his family; and since he generally found it more advantageous to retain the rest of the earnings in the corporation than to pay them out as dividends, the foundation received little if any benefit from its ownership of the stock. The foundation was not permitted to sell the stock and use the proceeds to finance a current charitable program. Instead it continued to hold it in its portfolio as a dead asset. In this way, the Patman Committee pointed out, many wealthy taxpayers achieved sizeable tax benefits from a transaction that left them no poorer after the transaction than before, and that usually resulted in no benefit to charity.

The Treasury's solution to this problem was to deny the tax benefits of the charitable deduction to donors of stock in family-owned corporations until the receiving foundation disposed of the stock, or until the donor and members of his family terminated their control over the corporation. As long as the donor, certain related parties, and the foundation continued to have 20% or more of the corporation's combined voting power, control of the corporation would be presumed to exist.[58] The Tax Reform Act of 1969 accomplishes much the same result by imposing a penalty tax on holdings of more than 20% in corporations or other businesses controlled by the foundation, its donor, and other related persons.

While it is true that these new provisions will sharply reduce gifts of family corporation stock to private foundations, since the tax benefit from such contributions will be eliminated,[59] unless foundations are pressured into disposing of family corporation stock, and reinvesting the proceeds in publicly traded securities, they will continue to retain these unproductive investments indefinitely. On the whole it would appear that the public's loss in gifts to foundations of stock in family corporations will be less than the cost to the Treasury in terms of tax deductions allowed to the donors under former tax laws.

Perpetual Control by the Founder and His Family

One of Patman's chief complaints was that in most cases private foundations continued indefinitely under the management and control of their founder and members of his family. Long after the death of the founder, the foundation was managed by his relatives or descendants, who frequently lacked any particular imagination, judgment, or concern for charity. They continued to make contributions to the same public organizations favored by the founder, were incapable of channeling its funds into more useful or productive activities, and at the same time were unwilling to liquidate the foundation. To correct this stagnation Patman suggested that after twenty-five years foundations be required to terminate their existence and distribute their assets and accumulated income to publicly-supported charitable and educational organizations.

However, the Treasury Department, and most commentators, considered that arbitrarily limiting the life of private foundations to twenty-five years, or any other fixed period of time, would be unwise. It would eliminate one of the great advantages that society derives from many well-operated private foundations, namely, the flexibility and imagination of their long-range and far-sighted charitable and educational programs, and their years of expertise.[60] In 1965 the Treasury suggested that after twenty-five years private foundations should be required to have 75% of their directors or trustees consist of outsiders, persons other than the donor and his relatives. Foundations already in existence for twenty-five years would be accorded a grace period in which to comply.[61] This proposal, however, was never adopted. Not only would it have eliminated the evils of perpetual family control,[62] but by requiring the introduction of independent outside management, it would have decreased the opportunities for abuse by insiders dealing with the foundation for their own advantage.

Foundation Tax Reform Adopted in 1969

Congress was well-advised in incorporating in the Tax Reform Act of 1969 most of the proposals contained in the 1965 Treasury Report on Private Foundations. Under the new law private tax-exempt foundations and charitable trusts are obliged to devote their income and assets exclusively to charitable ends, and speed up distribution of their funds to hospitals, medical research projects, universities, and other worthy causes. More federal resources can now be made available for poverty programs, urban renewal and development, mental health, air and water pollution, and other pressing needs that are largely dependent on government funds, and that are not presently being met.

The prohibitions against self-dealing and other abuses will reduce the amount of tax-sheltered income and increase tax revenues. The exclusion of private foundations from business and commercial activities that compete with taxpaying businessmen should have the effect of substituting for the profits earned by foundations from unrelated business operations on which no taxes were paid, the profits of small and intermediate size business enterprises whose tax payments to the federal and state governments will be correspondingly increased.[63]

The new provisions curtailing self-dealing, business operations, excessive accumulations of income, and gifts of stock in family corporations [64] have encountered little effective opposition in foundation circles. In fact, spokesmen for a number of the larger foundations went on record as agreeing with the Treasury's original recommendations in whole or in part.[65]

4

Special Tax Privileges for Corporate Executives—Stock Options Old and New

When Congress amended the tax law in 1964 in order to put a stop to some of the more flagrant practices connected with stock options, it was widely predicted that this legislation would sound the death knell for this tax loophole. But a cursory glance at recent corporate proxy statements indicates that these prophecies of doom were somewhat premature.

In the last few years Bristol-Myers Company, International Telephone and Telegraph Corporation, City Investing Company, and W. R. Grace and Company have granted stock options to a handful of their top executives. These options have yielded aggregate benefits of well over $12 million.[1] These companies are merely a sample picked at random from the thousands of concerns whose securities are traded on the New York and American Stock Exchanges. Obviously the tax avoidance device of executive stock options, with its "heads I win, tails you lose" philosophy and specially favored tax treatment, was still very much alive. It is still thriving, even after passage of the Tax Reform Act of 1969.

Stock Options before 1964

Back in 1945 the Supreme Court decided that when a corporation had given one of its officers an option to buy its stock below the market price, the spread between the option price and the value at the time the option was exercised was to be treated as additional compensation, taxable to the executive at ordinary income rates.[2] This ruling threatened to deprive top corporate management of a valuable tax loophole. In 1950, under pressure from the business community, Congress obligingly came to the rescue and changed the law to permit the lower capital gains treatment of benefits arising from stock options.

Thereafter it was common practice for most leading U.S. corporations to grant their highly paid executives lucrative long-term options to purchase the company's stock. If the market price rose, as has generally been the case, the executive had a tidy profit, which cost him nothing. Furthermore, the gain was either not taxed at all, or taxed at favorable capital gains rates, with a maximum of 25%, rather than at the much higher ordinary income tax rates.

Before the Revenue Act of 1964, a corporation could grant its key executives options over a ten-year period to purchase its stock for a price as low as 85% of the market. The options were in effect gifts, granted purportedly on the theory that they would provide an incentive to better managerial performance, and give the executive "a stake" in the enterprise. The option cost the executive nothing, nor was he bound to purchase the stock. But if the price of the stock rose, he could purchase it at the original option price, and hold the securities indefinitely until death, or he could give them away to members of his family or to charity without paying any tax on the profit. If he chose to sell the stock, the profit was taxable to him, not at the high ordinary tax rate applicable to persons with large incomes, but at the advantageous capital gains rate, a maximum of 25%, provided he had waited two years after receiving the option and six months after exercising it.

What is more, if the market declined below the option price, so that exercising the option would no longer prove profitable, the corporation was permitted to lower the price so as to assure the executive a profit on his purchase. Sometimes when the market dropped, the corporation simply granted a new option at a lower price, and the prior option was abandoned or allowed to lapse.[3]

The degree to which the stock option device was abused by corporate executives was illustrated by the following account of a Washington, D.C. newspaper reporter:

Stockholders of the Aluminum Company of America, who suffered the humiliations of watching their stock drop from more than $120 a share to less than $70 in the last two years, may have read with mixed emotions the decision of the corporation's top executives to spare themselves and some 300 other officers and employees a similar indignity.

A fairy godmother stock option committee consisting of the six highest paid directors and officers, voted to cancel options on 193,000 shares of Alcoa stock at $117.25 and to re-issue options share for share at $68.50. This put all optionees (a) even with the current price of Aluminum stock and (b) 48¾ points up over the patient stockholders who held their shares without benefit of a fairy godmother Committee to bail them out of their investment venture.[4]

Kennedy Reform Proposal

The Kennedy administration included a proposal in the tax bill it submitted to Congress in 1963 for the outright repeal of the provisions that had made this loophole possible. The presidential tax message of that year called on Congress to eliminate the special capital gains treatment for profits arising from stock options, recommending that the spread between the option price and the market price at the time of exercise be treated as ordinary income and taxed like other forms of compensation. The administration stated that

Stock options represent compensation for services. . . . To the extent that the stock option provisions allow highly paid executives to pay tax at capital gains rates or to escape all tax on part of their compensation, they are not consonant with accepted principles of tax fairness.[5]

The administration marshalled an impressive array of evidence in support of its position. A series of Treasury Department studies covering the 1950–60 period revealed the huge profits that had been amassed through stock options.[6] They showed that a number of corporate executives, all drawing salaries in six figures, received extra benefits from the exercise of stock options ranging from $1 million to over $3 million. One executive with a yearly salary of about $1 million received additional benefits of almost $4 million over the ten-year period through the exercise of stock options. Three hundred and fifty large U.S. corporations granted their top-level executives benefits in the form of stock options totaling some $200 million in 1959 and $164 million in 1960.[7]

The Harvard Business Review studied 166 top executives from thirty-one of the fifty largest U.S. industrial corporations for the 1950–60 period. Option benefits for the group, resulting from the favorable spread between the prices they paid for their stock and market prices, averaged $83,000 per year, about 65% of their average annual salary of $128,000. After paying the capital gains tax on their stock option profits, the group enjoyed an average benefit of $72,000 per year, or 122% of their average annual after-tax salary of $59,000. Two-thirds of these executives had option gains averaging $25,000 or more per year after reduction for capital gains tax, while 7% enjoyed benefits of over $200,000 per year after taxes. Almost two-thirds received after-tax option gains which were more than 50% of their after-tax salaries, while 38% had after-tax gains that exceeded their after-tax salaries and bonuses.[8]

The traditional rationale advanced by those opposing reforms in the stock option area—that stock options provided an inducement which would attract and retain talent and an incentive for better managerial performance—was largely demolished by the statistics furnished to Congress by the Treasury. The market price of corporate stock, it was shown, generally rose during periods of business boom, irrespective of the special talents of management, and during recessions stock prices fell, often in spite of excellent management policies. In actuality, the large benefits reaped by highly paid corporate executives through stock options appeared to result, not so much from their superior management, as from changes in investor outlook and a rapid rise in the price-earnings ratios of most stocks between 1950 and 1960. The market price of many stocks rose more rapidly than corporate earnings, and sometimes rose in spite of a decline in earnings, because of the willingness of stock market investors to pay higher and higher prices in relation to current earnings.

Most significant of all, the Treasury demonstrated that despite the claim that stock options were an indispensable means of giving key executives "a stake" in the business, most of them did not hold it for investment. On the contrary, approximately two-thirds of those acquiring stock through stock options sold all or part of it within three years.[9]

Moreover it was shown that the real beneficiaries of the stock-option device were the upper classes in the corporate hierarchy— those in the highest income tax brackets. The inclusion of middle and lower salary bracket executives in company stock option plans was often mere window dressing to give the plan the appearance of impartiality.

Finally, the practice was and continues to be detrimental to public stockholders, since it dilutes their financial interest in two ways: It results in the issuance of thousands of additional shares for a fraction of their value; and, in contrast to the payment of other forms of employee compensation, the corporation can take no deduction for income tax purposes for what is essentially a gift to the recipient, i.e., the difference between the option price and the market price when the option is exercised.

A Gesture toward Reform

During the 1963 tax hearings the House Ways and Means Committee and the Senate Finance Committee were literally inundated with testimony and formal statements by representatives of the business and financial community who opposed the proposal to do away entirely with favored tax treatment of stock options. Under this kind of pressure, as is so often the case, the reform that emerged was a compromise. A few of the most flagrant abuses were rectified, but the loophole according capital gains treatment to certain executive stock options remained intact.

In substance the new code provisions reduced the period for which options could be granted from ten to five years, and increased the option price from 85% to 100% of the market value. The optioned stock had to be held for at least three years (instead of six months) before being sold for the profit to be considered capital gains and not ordinary income. The new code prohibited lowering the option price if the market price decreased after the original grant; and the favored tax treatment was denied to executives who owned a significant percentage of a corporation's outstanding stock [10] (under the prior law executives owning up to 10% of a corporation's outstanding stock were eligible). Finally, qualified stock option plans had to be submitted to and approved by the corporation's stockholders.[11]

Stock Options since 1964

The effect of these amendments at best was to make the device a little less of a one-way street for the benefit of the recipients. Under present stock option plans top executives still receive gratis options good for five years to purchase their company's stock at the present market price. For example, on June 30, 1965 Corporation A grants X, one of its vice presidents, an option to purchase 2500 shares of its stock at $100 a share, the current price on the New York Stock Exchange. Thereafter the price of the stock rises steadily, and by June 30, 1967 it is selling for $150 a share, at which time X exercises his option and purchases the 2500 shares. The purchase at $100 a share gives him an unrealized profit of $50 a share, or $125,000.

Three years later the stock is selling for $200 per share. If X decides to sell the stock, having waited three years after purchasing it, he pays only a capital gains tax on the $250,000 profit. X may continue to hold the 2500 shares until his death, may give the shares to his wife and children over a period of years, or may donate the 2500 shares to charity or to his private foundation, without any tax being due from anyone on the $250,000 profit. On X's death his heirs are deemed to hold the stock at the "stepped up" basis, i.e., the value at death, thereby reducing or perhaps eliminating entirely future capital gains taxes on a future sale.

This granting of capital gains tax treatment to the stock option profits of a favored minority, while the vast majority of taxpayers —wage and salary earners, professional men, and owners of individual businesses—pay taxes on their compensation at regular rates, is offensive to every principle of equity. Yet qualified stock options, in spite of the 1964 amendments, are still available as a convenient tax loophole.[12]

They are still the only method sanctioned by the Code for rewarding personal services on a capital gain's basis in a completely discriminatory manner.[13]

By October 1, 1964, among companies whose securities were traded on the New York Stock Exchange, the number of stock option plans adopted or expanded since the enactment of the 1964 amendments was greater than the number of such plans adopted or expanded during the preceding two years.[14] Current annual reports and proxy statements indicate the sizeable monetary profits and special tax advantages still being enjoyed by recipients of stock options.

The Bristol-Myers Company granted options on 84,000 shares of its stock in 1965 and 1966 to five executives. On the basis of stock market quotations early in 1968, the combined benefits were over $2 million; one officer alone made a profit of $940,000.[15] Under a 1966 stock option plan, City Investing Company granted options on some 65,000 shares of its stock to seven of its executives. Again based on the market price of the stock early in 1968 the group had already achieved aggregate benefits of over $4 million; the president alone made a profit of some $3½ million on 50,000 shares on option to him.[16] International Telephone and Telegraph Corporation disclosed the granting of options to five of its top executives at prices which, by January 1968, yielded combined benefits, realized or unrealized, of more than $4 million; one executive had a profit by that time of over $2¼ million.[17] Options granted by W. R. Grace and Company on some 83,000 shares had by early 1968 yielded benefits to three of Grace's top executives of more than $2⅓ million; one of them had already made a profit of $1,400,000 on 45,000 shares.[18]

These are only samples. The list of companies whose stock option plans continue to yield comparable benefits to top management is endless.

Restricted Stock—A New Loophole

The Tax Reform Act of 1969 effectively curbed the corporate community's most recent device for providing executives with special tax benefits—the sale of restricted stock under an executive incentive compensation plan. The key to the tax advantage lay in certain Treasury regulations dealing with stock options. One such regulation [19] provided that if the transfer of stock was subject to a restriction, such as requiring resale to the corporation at a reduced price, the restriction had a significant effect on the stock's value, and that therefore no income was realized on the grant of stock subject to such a restriction. The regulation went on to provide, however, that when the restrictions were removed, the taxpayer had income amounting to the spread between the price paid, if any, and the value of the stock at the time he acquired it or at the time the restriction lapsed or was removed, whichever value was the lower.

For example, if an executive received stock subject to restrictions at $100 per share at a time when the stock was selling on the market for $150 per share, when the restrictions expired he would have realized $50 of ordinary income per share. But if at that time the stock was selling for less, say, $130, he would be deemed to have realized only $30 of ordinary income per share.

If the executive bought restricted stock at $100 per share when the market price was $150, and the market price rose to $300 a share when the restrictions lapsed, the fortunate executive found himself in the following circumstance: On his tax return he had to report ordinary income of $50 per share. He could immediately sell his stock for $300 per share and realize a capital gain of $150 a share, the difference between the market price at the time he purchased and his selling price. He would then have received $300 a share for stock that had cost him $100 a share; of the $200 per share spread $50 was taxable at ordinary income rates, and $150 at the more favorable capital gains rate.

Many leading public corporations, including American Cyanamid, Armco Steel, Borg Warner, General Tire and Rubber Company, and Upjohn, had incentive compensation plans under which grants of restricted stock were made along the above lines. The plan generally provided that a fund of money, depending on the corporation's earnings, was set aside. An executive committee of the corporation allocated the fund among executives and other employees. It could pay out the benefits in the form of cash or in restricted stock that, for a period of years, could be sold only to the corporation for $1 per share or some other nominal value. An executive receiving restricted stock under such a plan had nothing to lose and considerable to gain. He made no investment, but received stock of the corporation at no cost to himself. If the market price rose, he received a handsome profit, taxable for the most part at capital gains rates.

The device of conferring capital gains tax treatment on the sale of stock subject to transfer restrictions and given to corporate executives under arrangements of this kind, was simply another species of tax favoritism granted to a special group of taxpayers. Instead of the major part of the profits in the above example being taxed at capital gains rates, the entire spread between the original cost and the eventual selling price of restricted stock should have been treated as ordinary income, and taxed at ordinary income rates.

The Loophole Is Partly Closed

Under the Tax Reform Act of 1969 restricted stock options are no longer an effective tax avoidance device. The capital gains treatment has been eliminated, and the gains are taxed at ordinary income rates.[20]

However the special tax treatment accorded the more widespread device of qualified stock options for corporate executives remains practically untouched. During the 1963 tax hearings, the executive editor of the *Commercial and Financial Chronicle* told the House Ways and Means Committee that the executive stock option is nothing more or less than "a free stock market ride" without risk of loss, "that has nothing to do with managerial effort." [21] Unfortunately the Committee members were not listening. But that candid appraisal is applicable to the stock option and all of its progeny.

5

Waning Days of a Tax Windfall for
Multi-Corporate Operations

Until the passage of the Tax Reform Act of 1969 groups of related corporations could enjoy a tax advantage in the form of multiple corporate surtax exemptions and other benefits that were entirely unwarranted. While the new law has not swept away these privileges abruptly, it at least provides for their gradual elimination over a period of years.

Misuse of Multiple Corporate Surtax Exemptions

In keeping with the theoretically progressive nature of our tax system, the federal income tax on business corporations has for years contained a feature that was designed to aid small new business ventures, which generally require incentives not needed by their larger and financially more powerful competitors. Built into the corporate tax structure is a provision for a relatively low normal tax of 22% on the first $25,000 of corporate net income with the excess subject to the much higher tax rate of 48%.[1] Infant business enterprises, it was thought, should be encouraged to grow by allowing them to pay a relatively low tax on a modest amount of net profit, while subjecting them to the same higher rates as their more affluent competitors as soon as their profits exceeded $25,-

000.[2] Unfortunately it has not worked out that way. Many multi-million dollar businesses with units all over the country, including large food, clothing, shoe, drug, and gasoline chains, have taken advantage of the provision by splitting up what is essentially a single business into numerous corporate entities. By forming separate corporations for each local operation, they obtained a $25,000 surtax exemption for each of their corporate units. As a result, instead of paying 48% of its overall net profit in excess of the first $25,000, a large business controlled by the same interests was able to shelter hundreds of thousands of dollars of combined profits from taxes at the higher rate.

What has resulted is a perversion of what Congress originally intended as a benefit for small business. It gives business giants operating what are essentially single enterprises in multi-corporate form unfair economic advantages over even their large competitors who have been unable to take advantage of the multi-corporate device. The advantage over their small business rivals is, of course, even more pronounced. The administration, as part of its 1963 tax proposal, suggested that a group of corporations under common ownership should be limited to a single surtax exemption.[3] In this way only the first $25,000 of their combined net profits would escape taxation at the higher surtax rate, and the advantage of the lower rate would be confined primarily to the small business corporations for whose benefit it had originally been designed.

However Congress rejected this eminently fair and sensible proposal, with the result that many large business enterprises continued to enjoy the tax advantages of the multi-corporate form much as they did before. Indeed, under the 1964 tax legislation reducing corporate tax rates,[4] the advantage of doing business in multi-corporate form was more attractive than ever.[5]

If a group of corporations under common control elected to obtain the benefits of multiple surtax exemptions, it paid a small 6% penalty tax,[6] but the penalty amounted to a maximum of only $1,500 per year for each corporation (6% of $25,000). When the family consisted of three or more corporations, each additional surtax exemption saved up to $6,500 in taxes (the difference between 48% and 22% of $25,000). Even when the 6% penalty reduced this saving to $5,000 per corporate unit, it was still advantageous for such a business to operate in multi-corporate form.[7]

Circumventions Yielding Even Greater Tax Advantages

If a multi-corporate enterprise was organized in such a manner as not to constitute a "controlled group" of corporations,[8] it not only obtained all the tax advantages of its single corporate competitor, including multiple accumulated earnings credits and multiple exemptions from estimated tax filing and payment, but it could also utilize multiple surtax exemptions without even having to pay the 6% penalty tax. An enterprise with a $500,000-a-year net income could have saved more than $123,000 a year in corporate income taxes if it were organized as twenty corporations instead of one.

In most cases the "controlled group" designation was not difficult to circumvent. Generally speaking there were three types of corporate families that fell into the classification of a "controlled group": the parent-subsidiary relationship, the so-called brother-sister relationship, and combinations of the two.

A parent-subsidiary group of corporations was considered a "controlled group" if the parent owned, directly or indirectly, 80% or more of the voting power, or 80% or more of the value of all classes of stock of one or more members of the group. A brother-sister group was considered a "controlled group" if a single individual, estate, or trust owned 80% or more of the total combined voting power, or 80% or more of the value of all classes of stock of each of the corporations in the group.[9] There were innumerable possibilities, by careful family planning, often involving only minor adjustments in family ownership, for circumventing the "controlled group" classification.[10]

It was relatively easy to avoid the "controlled group" designation in family businesses by shifting the ownership of the stock so that no one member of the family owned more than 80% of two corporations. However, this method of avoiding the "controlled group" classification was ended by the Tax Reform Act of 1969, which provides that if five or fewer persons join together and own 80% of two or more corporations, each of the corporations is treated as a member of a "controlled group."

Correcting the Abuses

The Internal Revenue Service was aware that many large chain store operators, real estate companies, and other businesses using the multi-corporate form in brother-sister or parent-subsidiary corporations were able to shelter large segments of their earnings from high tax rates, and to obtain other tax advantages. It was estimated that the loss in tax revenues from the unjustifiable use of multiple surtax exemptions alone amounted to $235 million each year.[11]

True, there was always the possibility that the tax authorities could challenge these arrangements as tax avoidance schemes and "sham" devices,[12] and seek to have income and deductions reallocated realistically among members of the corporate family, or to have multiple surtax exemptions, multiple accumulated earnings credits, and other benefits and allowances denied. But generally speaking, where it was shown that the multi-corporate set-up, however large, served some reasonable business purpose, the government was unsuccessful. If, for example, their respective activities—wholesaling, retailing, transporting—were functionally distinguishable from one another, or the limitation of each member's financial liability was shown to have been an important consideration, the group enterprise was safe from attack. Furthermore the burden on the Treasury in proving that tax avoidance was a primary motive frequently presented insuperable obstacles.[13] In one case contested by the Treasury, the court allowed separate surtax exemptions to be taken by sixty-seven separate corporations, all engaged in the same business, that of manufacturing hobby kits. All of the corporations used the same business office; none had any employees other than their officers and directors, who were the same for each corporation.[14]

At long last in the Tax Reform Act of 1969, Congress heeded

what the Treasury had been urging for years, and allowed a family of corporations only one $25,000 surtax exemption and only one $100,000 accumulated earnings credit. Unfortunately, as a sop to large business organizations that have been enjoying these special privileges for so long, the reform does not become fully operative until 1975.

6

The Submerged Iceberg—Capital Gains That Escape Taxation

Capital gains are defined as the gains from the sale at a profit of securities, real estate, or other investments. If the property has been owned for six months or more, only one-half of the gain has to be included in income subject to tax. In effect, then, capital gains are taxed at one-half the rate of ordinary income. Until the Tax Reform Act of 1969, the maximum rate applicable to the taxable half of capital gains was 50% (so that the maximum *effective* rate on the entire capital gain was 25%) no matter what the taxpayer's bracket was.

Under the new law the maximum effective rate for corporations was raised to 30%, but the 25% rate is still in effect for individuals for capital gains up to $50,000 a year. For larger gains the rate will rise from 29½% in 1970, to 32½% in 1971, and finally to 35% in 1972. The very low maximum effective rate may have been abolished, but capital gains in general will continue to be taxed at only one-half of the ordinary rate.[1] Many commentators regard this preferential treatment as highly discriminatory compared to the taxation of ordinary income from salaries, business, dividends, interest, and other sources at rates up to 70%.[2] How much more inequitable is a system that allows an enormous amount of capital gains to escape taxation altogether!

One writer has compared capital gains to a huge iceberg floating in the water.[3] The portion above the surface represents the capital gains resulting from sales and transfers of property on which a capital gains tax is paid. But the much larger portion of the iceberg, submerged and hidden from view, represents the enormous appreciation in value of the stocks, real estate, and other property on which no capital gains tax is ever paid because their owners retain the assets until death, and pass them on to their heirs.

Similarly, a gift of property that has appreciated in value escapes capital gains tax at the time of the gift, although when the recipient sells it, a capital gains tax must be paid on the ultimate gain, measured against the original owner's cost. However, since property given away in this manner may be held by the donee until his death and then passed on to his heirs, there is the possibility of an almost indefinite postponement of capital gains tax on such gifts. It has been estimated that every year $22 billion worth of appreciation in stocks, real estate, and other property passed on to heirs at death, or given away in the form of lifetime gifts, escapes the capital gains tax, and that as a result the Treasury loses about $3½ billion a year in tax revenues.[4]

Avoidance of Capital Gains Taxes at Death

Under present law, if a taxpayer owning stocks, real estate, an interest in a business, or other assets that have appreciated greatly in value since their original acquisition continues to own them until his death, both he and his heirs completely escape the payment of any income or capital gains tax on this appreciation.[5] On the other hand, another taxpayer who sells such assets before his death will have to pay a capital gains tax on the difference between his original cost and the proceeds at the time of sale.[6]

As an illustration, take the case of two taxpayers, otherwise similarly situated: Taxpayer A has stocks, real estate, or an interest in a business acquired ten years ago with an investment of $50,000. Today his holdings are worth $500,000. If A now sells them for

$500,000, he realizes a capital gain of $450,000 on which he must pay a capital gains tax.

Taxpayer B also possesses assets currently worth $500,000, consisting of securities, real estate, or an interest in a business acquired ten years ago with an investment of $50,000. B, however, retains the assets until his death, by which time their value has increased to an aggregate of $750,000. Neither Taxpayer B, his estate, nor his heirs will ever have to pay any income or capital gains tax on the $700,000 appreciation. B's heirs, under present law, are deemed to receive the assets at their value at the time of death, namely, $750,000. They may hold them indefinitely; but even if they decide to dispose of them for $750,000 they will not be liable for any tax on the gain. Only if the property continues to appreciate in value, and the heirs receive more than $750,000 on an eventual sale, will they have to pay a capital gains tax on the excess over $750,000.

Under present law, property that has appreciated in value passes at death, *not at the decedent's original cost, but at the appreciated value* (often many times the original cost) *at the time the decedent dies.* This rule is frequently referred to as the "stepped-up" basis.[7] A former Secretary of the Treasury described it as an "escape hatch by which our wealthier taxpayers can avoid all taxation on substantial amounts of capital gains." [8] In addition, it has a number of undesirable economic side-effects, and results in enormous loss of tax revenue to the Treasury.[9]

Inequities of the Present Law

The present system discriminates sharply between the investor who sells appreciated assets and pays a capital gains tax, and the one who retains them until death and completely avoids the tax. The taxpayer who during his lifetime disposes of property that has increased in value since he acquired it, pays a tax on the gain when he sells; and his estate is subject to the estate tax on his remaining assets (which may include the proceeds of the sale).[10] On the other hand the taxpayer who holds such property until death escapes paying the capital gains tax on the appreciation and so do his heirs. True, the size of his estate, and consequently his estate tax, may be increased as a result of not disposing of the property before death; but the financial impact of the estate tax on the retained assets is rarely as large as the savings gained by avoidance of the capital gains tax. Indeed, it is most unlikely that any estate tax will be due at all; because of the generous exemptions and deductions, including the marital deduction, permitted under the estate tax law, only about 3% of all estates pay any federal estate tax.[11]

The present system is likewise unfair to those persons who do not have the good fortune or financial resources to invest in stocks, real estate, or other assets which appreciate in value. People whose income consists principally of wages or salaries, or who invest their extra money in savings banks, pay an income tax at graduated rates every year on their earned income and savings bank interest. When such a taxpayer dies his children or other estate beneficiaries receive an inheritance that consists of the remainder of funds received by the decedent during his lifetime, every penny of which has been reduced by the payment of the graduated income tax. On the other hand, those who inherit assets that have grown in value over the years derive the enormous benefit of the "stepped-up" basis; the estate that they receive has been undiminished by the imposition of a capital gains tax.

Put another way, the present law accentuates the already large disparity between the taxation of ordinary income and of capital gains, and encourages a preferred class of taxpayers to convert ordinary income, which is of much less benefit to them, into the more advantageous form of capital gains.

Because of the high rate at which ordinary income would be taxable to them, wealthy taxpayers derive little net advantage from increasing their current income from dividends, interest, and salaries. They are primarily concerned with capital appreciation, which is taxable at the lower capital gains rate or which may indeed escape taxation altogether. Such persons can avoid being taxed on accrued earnings by investing in so-called "growth stocks"

—the securities of rapidly expanding companies that pay out little to their shareholders in dividends, but retain the major part of their earnings to be plowed back into the business. As these earnings grow, because of such factors as internal expansion and the development of new products, the market price of the stock will rise.[12] The owners of such securities are able to avoid for years payment of income taxes at very high individual tax rates on these earnings, which have been retained instead of being paid out in the form of dividends. Should they sell their growth stocks during their lifetime, they are subject only to the preferential capital gains tax rate; and if the shares are held until death, they can be passed on to the heirs free of capital gains tax. In many cases the capital appreciation amounts to hundreds of thousands, and even millions of dollars.

The process may be carried even further by the heirs who may pass the securities on, together with additional tax-free appreciation, to their own estate beneficiaries. The failure to tax the gains of assets held by investors until death sharply conflicts with the whole theory of the progressive income tax, which assumes that an increased rate of tax will be paid as the ability to pay increases. Not only are the gains of persons who hold on to appreciated assets until death not subject to the graduated tax scale, but under the present system they escape income taxation altogether.

Undesirable Economic Side-Effects

Most authorities agree that the knowledge on the part of investors, especially older investors, that they and their heirs will escape all tax on the accrued gain, deters them from disposing of such investments during their lifetime,[13] and in effect, "locks" them into their investments. This in turn tends to immobilize financial investment, discourages the flow of funds into new ventures, and leads to an artificial and inefficient allocation of capital resources. If the expectation of escaping tax on appreciated assets at death were removed and replaced by the knowledge that these gains would be subject to a capital gains tax, there can be little doubt that more investors would be inclined to dispose of their investments, pay the tax on their gains, and invest the profits in other business ventures.

Finally, the loss of tax revenue under the present system is staggering. In 1963, the Secretary of the Treasury, Douglas Dillon, told Congress that every year $12-$13 billion in gains were transferred from one generation to another free of capital gains tax. He estimated that the imposition of a capital gains tax on the transfer of appreciated property at death or by gift would add about $750 million a year to the Treasury's revenues.[14] More up-to-date figures compiled by the New York Stock Exchange indicate that probably $22 billion of appreciation per year escapes tax in this manner, and that the annual revenue loss estimated by the Treasury in 1963 was far too conservative. While admittedly any precise computation is impossible, it is likely that the tax revenue lost by the Treasury under the present system is about $3½ billion annually, and perhaps more.[15]

Avoiding Capital Gains by Gifts

If a taxpayer gives away property that has appreciated in value since he acquired it, he may be liable for a gift tax, but he avoids the payment of a capital gains tax on the accrued appreciation, and the recipient of the gift is not liable for any capital gains tax as long as he continues to hold the property. Only when the recipient sells the property does he become liable for the payment of a capital gains tax on the difference between the donor's original cost and the sales price.[16]

For example, Taxpayer C acquired stock ten years ago for $15,000; the stock is now worth $150,000. He decides to make equal gifts worth $30,000 to each of his five children. No capital gains tax on the tenfold appreciation in value of the stock has to be paid at the time of the gift; and although C may have to pay a gift tax on each gift, it will be about one-half of the applicable capital gains tax rate. Should the children eventually dispose of their stock they will be liable for a capital gains tax based on their father's original cost. If at a later date a child sells his shares for $40,000, he will be liable to pay a capital gains tax on the difference between the $40,000 sales proceeds and the $3,000 original cost. Of course the children may not sell the stock, but hold it until their own respective deaths.

Thus the present tax treatment of gifts of appreciated property, though not as inequitable as the treatment of transfers at death, also involves widespread opportunities for tax postponement and avoidance. Although ultimately a capital gains tax will be paid when the property is sold (if the proceeds exceed the donor's cost), payment may be postponed indefinitely if the donee holds the gift until death. This tax treatment encourages wealthy taxpayers in the higher tax brackets who own assets that have greatly appreciated in value to give such assets to other family members in the lower tax brackets; when the recipients dispose of them they will probably pay taxes at lower rates than the original owners.

Plugging the Loopholes

Most authorities seem to agree that the most effective way to eliminate the inequities and tax avoidance inherent in the present system is to amend the Internal Revenue Code so as to provide that capital appreciation in the value of assets transferred by death or by gift shall be subject to the imposition of a capital gains tax at death and at the time of the gift.[17]

Under the Treasury's 1963 proposal, which Congress rejected, all appreciation in value of assets held until death, or transferred by gift, would be subject to a capital gains tax.[18] To avoid the criticism of double taxation, the amount of the capital gains tax paid would be deducted in calculating both estate and gift taxes, and generous exemptions and exclusions were provided for. Property bequeathed or donated to charity would be exempt, personal residences and household effects excluded, and the usual marital deduction allowed on gifts or bequests to a wife or husband. If necessary, estates with liquidity problems would be given up to ten years to pay. Moreover there would be a three-year transition period after the law was enacted, during which only a partial tax would be imposed, with the full tax not becoming effective until the end of the third year.[19]

There is no doubt that the tax would create severe liquidity problems for some estates, especially those consisting primarily of stock in a closely held family business where the appreciation in value may be very substantial. Many owners of such businesses, in addition to being confronted with the troublesome prospect of paying an estate tax, would face the additional problem of having to pay a capital gains tax at death; in some cases this would require the sale of the business at a sacrifice. To escape this eventuality, it is argued, many such owners would sell out their businesses during their lifetimes to larger corporations, which would in turn accentuate an already undesirable trend toward the concentration of economic power and the disappearance of the small businessman.[20]

The difficulty in obtaining the cash needed to meet possibly enlarged tax liabilities at death would be greatest during the first few years after the new tax goes into effect; but the provisions allowing hardship cases up to ten years to pay the tax and the three-year transition period should meet this problem. During the transition period investors would have time to avail themselves of a variety of estate planning techniques so as to enable their executors to deal adequately with the liquidity problem.[21]

It is also true that the new tax would create additional administrative problems. In many cases executors of estates would find it difficult to locate records of decedents for the purpose of establishing the original cost of securities and other property that had been held for long periods of time.[22] But similar problems have arisen in other situations and have not proved insuperable. In a short while investors and businessmen would take greater care to maintain and preserve adequate records for use after their deaths.[23]

It is argued that the proposed reform calls for a change in the law which may in any case be unconstitutional. While the matter is by no means free from doubt, the majority of tax law authorities believe that the imposition of a capital gains tax on accrued appreciation of assets held until death would not be an unconstitutional exercise of the taxing power of Congress.[24]

Proposals in one form or another to impose a capital gains tax on appreciated property held until death have been urged by the Treasury and other supporters of tax reform for over twenty-five years. All such suggestions have met with a barrage of criticism from members of the banking and investment community and others who have attacked them as being double taxation and confiscatory.

One critic at the 1963 hearings before the Senate Finance Committee insisted that the event of death does not constitute a "realization" of a gain, and that the proposal to tax accumulated appreciation would be taxing what was merely a "paper profit." But only the day before, the committee had heard a witness describe in great detail how the "paper losses" from depreciation and depletion allowed him in connection with his oil operations had eliminated his taxes by offsetting profits of several millions of dollars in dividends on marketable securities. Several Senators were quick to point up the inconsistency of tax conservatives who are perfectly willing to take advantage of "paper losses" to reduce their tax liabilities, but who strenuously object to being taxed on their "paper profits":

SENATOR GORE: So a paper profit—the phrase "paper profit" has come to be a cliché. If in our economic currency of today, a person has realized $100,000 in paper profits in a marketable security, he has in fact very real profits which he has realized. . . .

SENATOR DOUGLAS: Well, now, since we have launched into this discussion of economic tax etymology, may I say my good friend from Tennessee [Senator Gore] is, I think, the best authority on the dictionary that we have in the Senate. I would like to say that the definition of paper profits is only exceeded in casuistry by the term "paper loss." We had an explanation yesterday of the term "paper loss," a loss which does not occur in reality but which, because of the tax law . . . , can be used as an offset against profits to diminish the taxes paid to the Federal government. When my good friend from Tennessee creates a "Gore Dictionary of Financial Terms" I suggest he define paper losses in satirical language just as he does paper profits.

SENATOR GORE: I shall accommodate you.[25]

Admittedly the imposition of a capital gains tax on transfers of property by death or by gift may involve hardship for some taxpayers and administrative problems for others, especially during the first years after its enactment; nevertheless a tax loophole as inequitable as this one should not be tolerated for such considerations alone.

7

Oil and Gas—A Major Leak in the Tax Structure

Probably no provision of the tax law is so associated in the public mind with special privilege as the depletion allowance for the oil and gas industry. In his 1950 tax message President Truman said: "I know of no loophole in the tax laws so inequitable as the excessive depletion exemption now enjoyed by oil and gas mining interests." It has been the target of tax reformers intermittently for more than forty years. Yet, supported by powerful majorities in both houses of Congress, it has survived every proposal for significant change, and has escaped virtually unscathed under the Tax Reform Act of 1969.

It Is All Perfectly Legal

A few years ago at a hearing before the Senate Finance Committee an oil operator gave a vivid explanation of how the special tax treatment of the oil and gas industry had helped him amass his fortune. Over a five-year period, by the judicious use of the percentage depletion allowance, drilling and development expenses, and other deductions permitted oil and gas producers, his company had managed to avoid paying any income taxes whatsoever, not only on its large oil and gas income, but on millions of dollars of dividends on marketable securities as well.

Some senators were astonished that a company with such extensive financial operations could escape paying income taxes for so many years. When the witness insisted that he had done nothing wrong, that his attorneys had assured him that everything his company had done was perfectly legal, Senator Douglas observed:

What you are saying is: "It has been legal in the past, it is not our fault." Of course it is not your fault, but poor Uncle Sam has made so many errors that sharp people can take advantage of, that one really feels tempted to come to the aid of the old gentleman.[1]

Tax-Sheltered Oil and Gas Incomes

The enormous fortunes amassed by certain individuals from oil and gas operations is fairly well known. Names like John Paul Getty, the billionaire head of Getty Oil Company, and H. L. Hunt, the Dallas-based oil executive, whose incomes are reputed to be at least $500 million a year,[2] are almost household words. Less well known to the general public is the fact that many of these wealthy oil operators and investors, and most of the major oil companies themselves, frequently pay only a small portion of their incomes in federal income taxes; that indeed in many cases they manage to avoid income tax liability altogether.

In 1964, with the general corporate tax rate at 48%, the five largest United States oil companies paid the following percentages of their incomes in federal income taxes: Standard Oil of New Jersey, 1.7%; Texaco, 0.8%; Gulf Oil, 8.6%; Socony Mobil, 5.9%; Standard Oil of California, 2.1%.[3] The top twenty-two oil companies, with a combined gross profit of more than $5.1 billion, paid only 4% of that profit in federal income taxes in 1964. The following year they paid only 6.9% of their gross profits in income taxes, and in 1966 only 8.5%.[4] From 1962 to 1967 Atlantic Oil Company had a profit of approximately $410 million, but managed to avoid paying a penny of it toward federal income taxes; while Marathon Oil Company, after incurring no income tax liability for four years, paid 1.8% of its earnings in 1966.[5] Another oil company earned $65 million in net income over a five-year period, did not pay a cent in income taxes, and in fact received a $235,000 tax refund.[6]

Wealthy individual investors in oil properties have fared equally well. In 1960 the Treasury Department made a study of six individuals with incomes of $1 million or more, part of which was derived from oil and gas properties.[7] Five of the six had an aggregate income of $8.3 million; [8] $3.8 million, or 46%, of this total was offset by the allowance of percentage depletion on oil and gas income, and $2.6 million was offset by deductions for intangible drilling expense. In two of the six cases the sum of these special tax allowances exceeded net income from oil and gas production, and this excess served to reduce tax liabilities on other sources of income. Three of the six millionaires, one of whom had an income of over $28 million, paid no federal income tax at all; and the taxes paid by the other three averaged a little over 7% of their incomes.

Special tax deductions have played a major role in achieving these tax savings. According to a report of the Treasury Department in February 1963, out of some $3.3 billion of depletion deductions allowed annually to all extractive industries, about $2.2 billion was granted each year to oil and gas. In addition oil and gas producers were being permitted current deductions of over $1 billion annually for drilling and development costs.[9]

The Treasury estimates that it is losing $1.6 billion in taxes every year as the result of tax preferences allowed the oil and gas and other mineral industries (with 80% of the benefits going to oil and gas).[10] Others believe the revenue loss is even greater.[11]

Unique Tax Position of Oil and Gas

The search for and production of oil and gas involves expenditures for exploration; drilling of wells, including test and unproductive wells; and the development of the wells when oil is found. Once oil starts to flow it continues until the well is exhausted or until what remains is deemed uneconomical to extract. Since a mineral body, as production continues, is eventually exhausted, oil and gas are considered wasting assets that are depleted in the course of exploitation. This is the theoretical basis for the depletion allowance.[12]

The tax advantages of oil and gas production arise from the combination or interaction of the following:

1. More than three-fourths of the cost of drilling, the so-called intangible drilling and development expenses,[13] are deductible immediately from other income.[14] In other industries such expenditures, which are really capital in nature, are not permitted to be deducted immediately for tax purposes. Instead they must be capitalized, and recovered gradually over a period of years in the form of depreciation.

2. The cost incurred for necessary physical structures or equipment used in drilling and development are, as they would be in any other industry, recovered in the form of deductions from income, called depreciation, over the life of the structures or equipment.[15]

3. Persons with oil or gas income are allowed a so-called depletion allowance. Every year they are permitted to deduct 22% (the allowance was formerly 27½%, but was reduced by the Tax Reform Act of 1969) of the gross income from the property, up to a limit of 50% of the property's net income.[16] There is no time limit to this allowance. It continues as long as oil or gas continues to flow. Nor does it in any way depend on the cost or the amount invested in the well. On the contrary, the allowance for percentage depletion permits the recovery of tax-free income far in excess of the actual investment.

4. While the cost and risk of unsuccessful drilling is considerable, oil and gas producers are permitted to deduct in full, against any other income, the cost of dry holes.[17] For a wealthy oil and gas investor in the 70% income tax bracket, this means that the government is in effect underwriting 70% of the cost of any unsuccessful operations.

Recovery of Investment Cost—Recoupment Unlimited

In any other industry, an investor is permitted to recover the cost of his original investment in plant and equipment only once, through tax deductions in the form of depreciation. But if he is in the business of extracting minerals or other natural resources, such as oil and gas, he may recoup his investment or any other cost, tax-free, a number of times.

Take, for example, a typical manufacturer who spends $1 million to erect a plant; the building costs $850,000, and the machinery and equipment, $150,000. Assuming that the factory building has a useful life of twenty-five years, and the equipment a life of ten years, the owner may deduct from income $34,000 (1/25 of $850,000) as depreciation on the factory building and $15,000 (1/10 of $150,000) as depreciation on the equipment and machinery each year.

If the manufacturer has a gross income of $175,000 per year, and operating expenses and overhead of $75,000, disregarding other possible deductions, his taxable income will be:

Gross income from operations		$175,000
Less operating expenses		75,000
Net income from operations		$100,000
Less depreciation:		
On factory building	$34,000	
On equipment and machinery	15,000	49,000
Net taxable Income		$ 51,000

After ten years in the case of the machinery and equipment, and after twenty-five years in the case of the plant itself, the manufacturer will have recovered the amount of his original investment in the form of deductions from taxable income. At the end of these periods the assets presumably have no value and no further deduction is permitted.

But the situation of an oil and gas producer is infinitely more advantageous. Take the case of C, a wealthy investor with over $100,000 of other income from dividends, who invests $135,000 in drilling and developing an oil well. Typically, $100,000 or more of this cost spent during the first year is treated as "intangible drilling and development expense," and may be deducted immediately against other income.[18] C can use the $100,000 of drilling expenses to eliminate the tax that he would otherwise have had to pay on his $100,000 income from dividends.

The remaining $35,000 spent for the cost of materials installed in structures, and tools, pipes, casing, and other machinery and equipment must be capitalized and recovered by depreciation deductions. Assuming a useful life of ten years, $3500 a year will be allowed for depreciation.

Even though he has recovered no oil so far, C has already been able to recoup his entire drilling and development expenditures of $135,000 by offsetting $100,000 against other taxable income, and by taking depreciation deductions of $3500 a year to reduce taxable income from the property over the next ten years.

Assume that during the following year C's investment has paid off and results in a well producing $100,000 of oil and gas income annually. After deducting annual operating expenses of $25,000 and the year's depreciation on equipment of $3500, C will have an economic profit from the property for the year of $71,500. However, he will not be obliged to pay taxes on anything like that amount. He now becomes the beneficiary of an additional allowance unique to the oil, gas, and other extractive industries—the allowance for percentage depletion. Under the Tax Reform Act of 1969, he is permitted to deduct 22% of the gross income from the oil property each year, or 50% of its net income, whichever is less.

In the second year C will figure the taxable income on his oil property as follows:

Gross oil income		$100,000
Less:		
Operating expenses	$25,000	
Depreciation on oil property equipment (1/10 of $35,000)	3,500	28,500
Net income from oil property		$ 71,500

Less percentage depletion allowance:
the lesser of:

22% of $100,000 (gross oil income)	$22,000	
or		22,000
50% of $71,500 (net oil income)	35,750	
Net taxable income		$ 49,500

Thus, during the second year, C has recovered an additional $22,000 tax-free, thanks to the depletion allowance. If we assume that oil production from the property continues in future years at the same rate or better, each year C will have an additional $22,-000 deduction for depletion, and in another four to five years he will have recovered his $135,000 original investment tax-free a second time. Depending on the flow of oil and his operating expenses, C may recoup his original investment many times more. According to Treasury Department figures, as the result of the depletion allowance, the cost of an oil well is recovered by its owners approximately nineteen times.[19] Even the new Minimum Tax will not offset C's benefit because of its generous exclusions.

If C is a wealthy taxpayer whose income puts him in the 70% tax bracket, he can continue to spend money on exploring for additional oil and gas wells, knowing that even if only dry holes result the government will be paying 70% of the expense, whereas for each producing well he finds, the lion's share of the benefits will be his. Each time he acquires another producing well, he will again enjoy the special tax deductions for drilling and development and percentage depletion, which will offset or reduce the taxes otherwise payable on the new oil and gas income.

Loopholes within Loopholes—Avoiding the Ceiling on Percentage Depletion

Some oil operators are able to reap additional tax advantages, even beyond those intended by an overly generous Congress, by circumventing the ceiling on the depletion allowance. The 22% of each year's gross oil income allowed as a tax-free depletion allowance is supposed to be subject to a limitation—that it shall in no case exceed 50% of the net income from the property (gross oil income less deductions, including those for drilling and development). But some operators are able to get around this limitation by careful timing of their expenditures for drilling.

For example, even before an oil property becomes productive, an oil operator can use the drilling and development expenditures incurred to offset, and thereby reduce or eliminate entirely, his liability for income taxes on other sources of income. But the following year, when the oil well is producing, one would expect that the drilling and development expenses incurred the year before would have to be taken into account so as to reduce the net income from the well, and bring into play the ceiling on depletion of 50% of net income. Not so.[20] He is able to get the full benefit of the percentage depletion allowance without being embarrassed by having it reduced by the 50% of net income standard.

As an illustration, assume that S, a high bracket taxpayer with a very substantial income from other sources, spends $160,000 to drill and develop an oil property. He succeeds in bringing in a well that produces $310,000 of oil income that same year, less $30,000 for operating expenses. S's depletion allowance would be figured as follows:

Gross oil income		$310,000
Less:		
Drilling and development expenses	$160,000	
Operating expenses	30,000	190,000
Net income from oil property		$120,000
Less percentage depletion allowance:		
the lesser of:		
22% of $310,000 (gross oil income)	$ 68,200	
or		
50% of $120,000 (net income)	60,000	
Allowance for percentage depletion		$ 60,000

Thus S's depletion allowance is limited by the 50% of net income ceiling.

But suppose S had the foresight to start his drilling operations later in the year, in July for example, and completes them late in December of the same year. Although S has no oil income from the property for the year, he can use the $160,000 of drilling expenses to wipe out the tax he would otherwise pay on that amount of income from other sources. Meanwhile, he arranges that the actual flow of oil does not start until the beginning of the following year, during which he achieves the same oil revenue with identical expenditures. Now S's depletion allowance is figured as follows:

Gross oil income		$310,000
Less operating expenses		30,000
Net income from oil property		$280,000
Less percentage depletion allowance:		
the lesser of:		
22% of $310,000		
(gross oil income)	$ 68,200	
or		
50% of $280,000		
(net income)	140,000	
Allowance for percentage depletion		$ 68,200

What S has managed to accomplish by simply concentrating his drilling costs in the first year of operations and postponing the oil flow until after the second year starts, is to obtain a tax-free depletion allowance that is $8,200 greater than 50% of the *total* net income ($120,000) actually earned over the life of the property. At the same time he has had the full tax benefit of the deduction of drilling costs to shelter his other income from taxation. If S were required to take into account, in figuring the property's net income, the drilling deductions taken the year before, his depletion allowance would have been only $60,000, and he would not realize the additional $8,200 of tax-free income.

Thus, under present law, an adroit oil and gas producer can maximize the benefits of his allowance for percentage depletion by judicious spacing or timing of his drilling operations. He can even accomplish this shifting of expenses by making a contract under which payment for the drilling is not required until the work is completed; or conversely, if he desires to concentrate the drilling expense at the beginning he can arrange to pay the drilling contractor in advance, even though the work may not be completed until the following year.[21]

Tax Advantages on the Sale of Oil Property

The owner of an oil or gas property often receives an additional tax break when he sells the property. Not only is the profit he realizes on the sale taxed at the lower capital gains rate, but part of the proceeds he receives consists of the recovery of expenditures previously made and which have already been used to eliminate taxes at the highest rate on other income.

Assume, for example, that J, whose large income puts him in the highest income tax bracket, acquires an operating interest in an oil property at a cost of $50,000. In the same year he spends $250,000 for intangible drilling and development costs in drilling a well on the property. Although obtaining no production from the property in that year, J is permitted to deduct the $250,000 of expenses, and use it to offset $250,000 of his income from a large portfolio of marketable securities, income that would otherwise have been taxable to him at the 70% rate. In the following year J sells his interest in the oil property for $1 million, realizing a capital gain of $950,000.

The $1 million sales price includes the value of the $250,000 that J spent the previous year in drilling and developing the property, expenses that are really capital in nature. He has already been permitted to use this $250,000 to eliminate tax liability at a 70% rate on $250,000 worth of other income, thereby saving him $175,-000 in taxes for the previous year. He now pays a tax on the $950,-000 gain (which includes the $250,000 previously spent and deducted), at a rate of about 35%. Even under the new Minimum Tax provisions, his rate will probably not be appreciably higher.

In other words, the $250,000 of expenses that J now recoups on the sale of the property is taxed to him at a rate of about 35% and costs him about $87,500 in taxes. These same expenses, used as a deduction against other income the year before, have already saved him $175,000 in taxes. He thereby achieves a net saving of about $87,500 in taxes, and has, in effect, succeeded in converting $250,-000 of ordinary income into $250,000 of capital gains.

Efforts to Correct Abuses

When the Kennedy administration submitted its proposed tax bill to Congress in 1963, it suggested a number of tax reforms, but it eschewed an outright attack on the depletion allowance for the oil and gas industry on the ground that to do so might delay the administration's tax bill "forever." [22] However, it did seek to eliminate certain abuses—loopholes within loopholes so to speak—of what the secretary of the treasury characterized as a "very generous" tax privilege.

Among other things, the Treasury proposed that the law be amended so as to prevent oil and gas producers, such as S in the example a few pages back, from obtaining an even higher depletion allowance than Congress originally intended, by the adroit timing or spacing of drilling operations. The effect of the proposal would have been to prevent an operator from recovering more than 50% of the overall net income of an oil property through percentage depletion deductions.[23]

For another, the administration sought to prevent an operator, on the sale of an oil property, from paying taxes at the lower capital gains rate on costs that he had previously used as deductions against ordinary income.[24] Under the Treasury proposal, taxpayer J, in the previous example, who sold his oil property for $1 million, which included the recovery of $250,000 previously deducted drilling costs, would have to pay a tax at his ordinary income tax rate of 70% on this part of his profit, with only the balance ($700,000) taxed at the more favorable capital gains rate.[25]

However, even these modest efforts by the Treasury to correct glaring abuses of the oil and gas tax loophole were rejected by Congress. In 1969, under a Republican administration, the Treasury did not even submit to Congress any meaningful reform proposals in this area.

Tax Breaks for All Parties in Oil and Gas Transactions

No deal involving the sale or lease of interests in an oil property is complete until arrangements have been worked out to assure maximum income tax advantages to all concerned—lessees with royalty interest, owners of working or operating interests, and holders of overriding royalties and net profit interests.[26]

Usually the transaction is arranged so that the lessee of the property receives a royalty, which is subject to a tax-free depletion allowance. Since the privilege of deducting drilling expenses from other sources of income is sometimes even more advantageous than the depletion allowance, especially for wealthy investors in high tax brackets, those who supply the capital for drilling are allocated the maximum share of drilling and development costs.

Unfortunately the typical small independent searcher for oil, the so-called wildcatter, does not derive much benefit from these manifold tax privileges since he generally does not have the large sources of outside income against which he can offset drilling expenses and losses from dry holes. The affluent investor, who acquires an undeveloped or partly developed oil property and proceeds to "drill it up," recovers most of the drilling costs by deducting them from his ordinary income. If the well proves successful he has a valuable capital asset that he can dispose of, and pay taxes on the profit from the sale at capital gains rates. In effect, he can use dollars costing him only 30¢ after taxes to do the drilling, and in return obtain an asset that can be sold for dollars worth 65¢ to him. Moreover, the cost of dry holes or unsuccessful drillings are likewise fully deductible.[27] If he is in the 70% tax bracket Uncle Sam pays 70% of any losses.[28]

Oil and gas investments are ideal vehicles for cutting down taxes among wealthy family groups if the transaction is carefully planned.[29] Arrangements are usually made to allow those in the higher income tax brackets to take the maximum number of tax deductions incident to operating the property, while shifting as much income as possible to low-income bracket family members. The revenue from an oil or gas property can often be split among a large number of children or grandchildren in the lower brackets so as to minimize or even eliminate income tax liabilities.

Assume, for example, that A, a taxpayer in the 70% income tax bracket, wishes to reduce the eventual tax on his estate and in the meantime minimize his tax on current income. He acquires a lease on a piece of property on which no oil has so far been discovered. Before commencing any drilling or development work, A assigns a non-operating interest in the property [30] to each of the trusts that he has set up for his various children. The gift tax, if any, will be very small because the transfer to the trust is made when the property has little value. (If the gifts had been made after the discovery of oil had shown the property to be exceedingly valuable, substantial gift taxes would have been due.)

A then proceeds to "drill up" the property, deducting the drilling and development expenses from his other income, so that the drilling really costs him only 30¢ for each dollar spent. After production commences the trusts receive the income from the oil at little or no cost, since their respective income tax brackets are relatively low; furthermore, each will have the advantage of taking generous percentage depletion deductions before computing income tax liability.[31]

Until the Tax Reform Act of 1969, an interest in an oil and gas property could often be acquired with largely tax-free funds, that is, with money on which the buyer never had to pay any taxes. It was accomplished by use of the so-called A B C deal, as follows: A, who owned a lease on a producing oil property, sold it for $1 million to an oil operator, C. C had only $200,000 to invest, so A assigned his lease to C for $200,000 in cash, and retained an oil payment of $800,000 payable out of 70% of future production, with 6% interest payable on the unpaid balance.[32] A, who wished to obtain his $1 million sales price immediately assigned the retained oil payment to an investor, B, for $800,000 in cash which B raised through a bank loan carrying 5½% interest.

The payments from the oil income and interest received by the investor B were paid over to the bank, and were offset by cost depletion deductions B was permitted to take. In effect B's only taxable income was part of the interest he received, namely, the difference between the 6% interest on the unpaid oil payment and the 5½% interest on his loan at the bank. But it was a virtually risk-free investment for both B and the bank, since the debt was amply secured by future oil income.

A obtained his entire sales price in cash, and the profit on the sale was taxable to him at the capital gains rate. As for C, he acquired the entire interest in the property with a minimum of cash. He paid no income tax on the $800,000 oil payment paid over a period of years to B, so that four-fifths of the $1 million purchase price was in effect paid from the production of the acquired property on which C paid no income tax. The balance of the oil income payable to C had to be included in C's income, but he could partially offset it by the deduction of certain operating expenses of the property.

The device of the oil or mineral production payment, including ABC deals like this one, was eliminated by the Tax Reform Act of 1969. Hereafter the Treasury will treat production payments as the repayment of loans, which is what they really are. The Treasury told Congress that this tax avoidance gimmick alone had been costing the government $200-350 million *yearly* in tax revenue.[33]

Oil Companies Operating Abroad

As far as the oil and gas industry is concerned, the Treasury Department has told Congress that it collects "almost no taxes from any of their operations abroad because of the way that foreign tax system works." [34]

American oil companies with foreign operations get the benefit of the same deductions for drilling and development and depletion allowances as domestic companies, even though it is generally believed that the risk of unsuccessful drillings in foreign countries is much less. In addition, the payments made by them to foreign governments, which are in reality royalties, are not merely treated as deductions against income, but are permitted to be taken as credits to offset their U.S. income tax liabilities dollar for dollar.[35]

These royalties (denominated "taxes") usually equal or exceed the amount of the U.S. tax on the American companies' foreign oil production, and usually wipe out all U.S. income tax liability on their foreign operations.

A former member of the Senate Finance Committee, Paul Douglas, has proposed that U.S. oil companies operating abroad should not be permitted to deduct these payments from their U.S. tax liability. Such payments should be treated, he insists, just like the royalty paid by any oil and gas developer to the owner of the property. That is, they should be permitted to be deducted merely as an operating cost to reduce profits, with the net profit after the deduction subject to U.S. income tax.[36]

Such a proposal would make quite a difference. Take for example an American oil company operating in a Middle East country, such as Kuwait. Assuming that it makes a profit from oil production of $10 million for the year, and pays $5 million in royalties to its host government, it will have a tentative U.S. tax liability of $4,800,000 (48% of $10 million). However, at present it can use the $5 million paid to Kuwait to offset and eliminate its U.S. tax. But if ex-Senator Douglas' suggestion were adopted, the U.S. Treasury would receive income taxes of $2,400,000 on these operations as follows:

Net profits from oil operations in Kuwait	$10,000,000
Less amount paid to the Kuwait government as royalties	5,000,000
Net profit from Kuwait operations	$ 5,000,000
U.S. income tax liability (48% of $5,000,000)	$ 2,400,000

Another privilege enjoyed by U.S. oil companies with foreign operations is the prerogative of using the cost of drilling and development abroad that results in operating losses to reduce the taxes they owe on income earned from their U.S. operations. The Kennedy administration's 1963 tax bill sought to eliminate this privilege among others.[37] However its modest proposals fell on deaf ears and were stricken out of the bill that was ultimately enacted.

Percentage Depletion—Pros and Cons

The arguments of those defending and opposing the special tax privileges of the oil and gas and other extractive industries, too numerous and involved to be enumerated here in full, raise a variety of economic, legal, social, and even political issues.[38]

In no other industry, say the critics, can an investor recover tax-free more than his original investment cost. Defenders of the special tax treatment argue that in other industries the value of the original investment can normally be recovered through depreciation, but normal depreciation of the original cost of an oil property, i.e., the cost of discovering the oil, bears no relation to the market value of the oil in the ground, and that the depletion allowance is intended to permit recovery of this discovery value.

But, reply the critics, how can one justify the fact than an oil investor recovers that value not once, but many times over, through a combination of deductions for intangible drilling and development expense and percentage depletion without time limit? The defenders insist that in the oil industry, unlike other industries, the capital asset acquired, the oil in the ground, is exhausted in the course of production. Special deductions and allowances, they say, are needed to encourage the search for new oil reserves, and to compensate for the cost of finding a new oil body to replace the one that has been depleted. Investment in other industries does not involve the high risk of loss through dry holes inherent in oil production, and if people are to be encouraged to invest their capital in oil exploration they must be given the opportunity to "make a killing" on successful ventures.

But, say their opponents, what about the fact that these tax bounties are enjoyed not only by the risk-takers, but by the owners of royalties, overriding royalties, net profit interests, and others, none of whom are exposed to the personal liability or cash commitments that the actual operators of oil properties face? While that may be true, say the defenders, the allowance of percentage depletion embodies a long-standing Congressional policy to encourage capital investment in the extractive industries, in order to build up oil reserves necessary to an expanding national economy and for national defense and security in the event of war. The same tax treatment must be extended to production abroad, because foreign oil reserves may also be needed in an emergency.

Opponents, however, ask: Why should the extractive industries be singled out for special treatment? With the increased use of atomic, nuclear, and other sophisticated weapons, oil may not prove to be so vital in future wars. Why not allow the steel, chemical, and other industries to receive similar tax favors on national security grounds? Moreover, it can hardly be contended that the building up of reserves of clay, sand, gravel, and oyster shells, the producers of which also benefit from this special tax shelter, is also vital to national defense.

One of the most effective arguments made by critics is that these tax incentives artificially stimulate a hasty, inefficient, and wasteful exploration of scarce natural resources, leading to a misapplication of capital that could be more effectively employed elsewhere in the private or public sector of the economy. The other side, however, vigorously denies that this is true. If the allowance for percentage depletion is eliminated or reduced, it is claimed, those who discover and develop oil properties, and especially the small independent producers, will sell their properties to the larger companies; this will have adverse effects on competition and accelerate the trend toward concentration of economic power and monopoly. Since the purchasers of such properties would be entitled to take depletion on a cost basis, which would result in larger depletion allowances than at present, it is questionable whether in the end the government would gain much additional tax revenue. Critics reply that the anti-trust laws can be relied on to prevent abuses of competition and monopoly, and that there can be little doubt that the overall tax effect of eliminating percentage depletion will mean billions in additional revenue for the Treasury.

Supporters of the present system claim that the reduction of the industry's special tax advantages will lead to increased prices for oil and oil products, including higher gasoline costs for millions of automobile users. Critics deny that such price increases are inevitable; and in any case, they say, it is fairer for gasoline users to pay more for gasoline than for the entire taxpaying public to pay higher taxes to make up for the tax revenue lost through percentage depletion.

Another argument of industry spokesmen and others is that if the oil industry's present tax privileges are reduced, costly government subsidization of oil and gas production, with attendant increased bureaucratic interference and control, will inevitably follow. Better a government subsidy than the present preferences, is the reply. At least subsidies are clearly defined, have a known quantity, and are easier to control than special tax privileges.

Above all, what offends most critics of the depletion allowance is that it is inherently discriminatory, conferring a special tax advantage on a privileged group of taxpayers on the theory that their assets are wasted and depleted in the course of being used.

A few years ago Pete Ratzloff, a former professional football player and president of the National Football League Players Association, appeared before the Senate Finance Committee to urge adoption of some sort of tax relief for the professional athlete "who depletes his natural resources of physical ability and muscular strength while earning a high income on which he is heavily taxed." He suggested that a professional athlete ought to be granted an annual tax deduction based on the average number of years that he had participated in a sport, thereby reducing the very high income taxes which he was required to pay in his few productive years. Senator Douglas sympathized with him, pointing out logically:

> Professional athletes should have a depletion allowance as well as oil, gas, sulphur, coal, iron ore, clam shells, oyster shells, sand and gravel

and adding, that what the athletes are asking by way of tax relief is modest compared to the percentage depletion allowance allowed without end to oil and gas producers as long as oil and gas keeps flowing. The trouble, however, Senator Douglas observed, was that if tax relief because of depletion of the natural abilities of athletes were permitted, the same privileges would have to be extended to movie stars, TV actors, poets, and others. He added that

Poets are in much the same position. Poetic impulse develops early in life, and then there are very few poets who write good poetry after the age of 40. It is part of the ebullience of youth, so to speak. Shouldn't they receive a depreciation allowance for the wasting away of their poetic inspiration?

Senator Carlson, joining in the fun, suggested that United States Senators should perhaps be included. Senator Douglas replied

This might be a good idea, but we will be suspected of enacting class legislation and conflicts of interest. As a matter of fact, frequently the earning power of a United States Senator increases after he is defeated because then he can become a lobbyist [laughter].[39]

Proposals for Reform

Some critics of the present tax treatment of oil and gas concede that the industry should be permitted to continue the privilege of immediately deducting intangible drilling and development costs, and some would include all costs of exploration and development.[40] Most reform proposals are directed at the allowance of percentage depletion over and above cost depletion. Such proposals run the gamut, starting at one extreme with the suggestion that all preferential tax treatment for the extractive industries should be eliminated, and that reliance for encouraging the development of natural resources should be placed on such non-tax incentives as subsidies, stockpiling, price supports, and development loans. Other critics would reduce the size of the percentage depletion allowance, the 50% of net income percentage, or limit the tax advantage of the depletion allowance in other ways.[41]

Recent data prepared for the Office of Tax Analysis of the U.S. Treasury Department supports the conclusion that percentage depletion is an inefficient method of encouraging exploration and discovery of new domestic oil reserves. In view of this study a major revision in the present tax treatment of the industry is called for.[42]

Token Reform in 1969

The reduction of the percentage depletion allowance for oil and gas producers from 27½% to 22% under the Tax Reform Act of 1969 was a somewhat one-sided compromise between the 20% rate voted by the House and the 23% figure approved by the Senate. It can hardly be described as a significant step toward closing this loophole.[43] Even the reduction of the percentage depletion from 27½% to 22% is deceptive. As Senator Harris of Oklahoma pointed out, even under the old law most of the larger oil companies had an effective depletion rate of about 23% [44] and would be almost totally unaffected by the so-called reform.

The Nixon administration justified its position in favor of a modest rather than a drastic cut in the oil depletion allowance on the ground that the tax preference was necessary as an incentive for oil producers to invest in further exploration. However, as one critic, Senator Jack Miller, reminded the assistant secretary of the treasury during the tax hearings, both corporate and individual oil producers would, under the terms of the bill, be rewarded whether they "plowed back" their savings from the depletion allowance into further exploration or not.

SENATOR MILLER: Let's say corporation A has percentage depletion from oil and gas which amounts to $25 million. Corporation B also has $25 million percentage depletion. Corporation A, pursuant to the intention and purpose of Congress, plows back that $25 million in exploration and development. But Corporation B, contrary to the intention of Congress, abuses the provision which Congress has enacted, and uses that $25 million to pay dividends to stockholders, and yet you are advocating precisely the same treatment for both corporations.

Is that correct?

MR. COHEN: Yes, Senator; that is correct under our present proposal, under our recommendations made to you yesterday.[45]

Needless to say, major reform of the tax privileges of the oil and gas industry still remains to be accomplished.

8

Another Tax Shelter for the Wealthy— State and Local Bond Interest

The Nature of the Exemption

Tax exempt securities are issued by state and municipal governments, school districts, and other local authorities to finance a variety of local improvements, from new highways and school buildings to bridges and tunnels. They pay interest that has ranged from 2½% to more than 8%. More than $100 billion worth of such bonds are outstanding, paying more than $3 billion in tax-free interest annually; a conservative estimate is that the Treasury is losing well over $1 billion dollars a year in tax revenue as a result of the exemption.[1]

Wall Street brokerage firms dealing in "tax-exempts" distribute attractive brochures that give the impression that almost anyone can profit from this type of investment. But in reality people in lower to medium tax brackets need not apply. They are meant for people of substantial means, and the higher the tax bracket, the greater the tax saving.

Holders of this virtually risk-free type of investment [2] are chiefly wealthy individuals, commercial banks, and insurance companies. A man who can afford to invest $2 million in "tax-exempts" may receive $60,000 to $80,000 in tax-free income. His neighbor, on the other hand, who receives the same amount from salary, dividends, or his business pays a very substantial part of it in income taxes.

A taxpayer in the lower income brackets does not generally have available the large sums needed to produce a substantial income from this type of investment, nor does he derive an advantage from investing in state and municipal bonds even though the interest on them is tax-exempt. If he is in a 20% tax bracket, for example, he is better off investing in good common stocks paying an average of 5½% in dividends. Even after paying a 20% tax on his dividend income, he is left with almost 4½% after taxes, more than he normally would receive if he had put his money into tax-exempt securities. A wealthy man in a 50% tax bracket, is better off investing in tax-exempt securities yielding 3¾% than in stocks paying an average of 5½% in dividends; in the 50% income tax bracket, the net return on his 5½% dividend would be only about 2½%.

At one time the special treatment accorded interest from tax-exempt bonds was frequently under attack, and the constitutional arguments raised in its defense were often criticized as having a very tenuous basis. Then for a number of years, until comparatively recently, the exemption had been virtually immune from criticism: indeed it had become so sacrosanct a tax loophole that the Treasury did not even mention it in presenting the administration's tax reform program to Congress in 1963.

When the Income Tax Act of 1913 was adopted, it was decided to exclude from Congress' broad authority to tax income, "from whatever source derived," the salaries of state and local officials and income from state and local bonds. But there was considerable debate on the matter. Those who favored the exemption relied on the dictum of Chief Justice Marshall that "the power to tax involves the power to destroy," [3] and argued that to tax such payments would amount to an unconstitutional encroachment on the powers of the state governments, in violation of the doctrine of the separation of powers. In the end the question was resolved in favor of the supporters of the exemption, in order to "avoid further acrimonious debate," [4] and because it was then thought that the amount of income that would be involved would be insignificant.[5]

Ever since, the defenders of the exemption have successfully resisted attacks on it, although some of the criticism has emanated from very high quarters. In 1922, echoing a similar request made by two of his predecessors a few years before, Secretary of the Treasury Andrew Mellon stated:

The most important consideration is that the existence of the growing mass of tax-exempt securities, coupled with the extremely high surtax rates still imposed by law, tends to drive persons of large income more and more to invest in wholly tax-exempt securities. . . . The result is to impair the revenues of the federal government and to pervert the surtaxes, so that instead of raising revenue they frequently operate rather to encourage investment in wholly tax-exempt securities, and even to encourage the issue of such securities by States and municipalities. This process tends to divert investment funds from the development of productive enterprises, transportation, housing, and the like, into non-productive or wasteful State or municipal expenditures, and forces both the federal government and those engaged in business and industry to compete with wholly tax-exempt issues and on that account to pay higher rates of interest.[6]

A succession of presidents, secretaries of the treasury, economists, and spokesmen for various business groups—including Presidents Coolidge and Roosevelt, Treasury Secretaries Morgenthau and Snyder, The Investment Bankers Association, and The National Association of Real Estate Boards—have called for the elimination of the exemption either by Act of Congress or by constitutional amendment. But well organized pressure by taxpayers in the high-income brackets and by representatives of various state governments, to which the majority of congressmen and senators have always deferred, invariably resulted in the defeat of such proposals in one or both houses of Congress.[7] In 1969 an effort to reduce slightly the advantages of this tax shelter was passed by the House but defeated in the Senate.

However, the doctrine of intergovernmental tax immunity, on which the defenders of tax exemption of state and local bonds rely, was pronounced one hundred and fifty years ago, long before the adoption of the federal income tax amendment. More recent decisions of the Supreme Court, holding that the federal government may properly impose an income tax on the salaries of state and local officials, have cast considerable doubt on the assumption that the doctrine is still applicable to protect the exemption. As a result, although some well-known tax experts disagree,[8] many authorities are convinced that if the question of the taxability of interest on state and local bonds were to come before it today, the Supreme Court would in all likelihood decide that such income is no longer immune from federal taxation on constitutional grounds.[9]

The Exemption Is Highly Discriminatory

Not only does the preferential tax treatment of state and local bond interest give advantages to the wealthy that, by the very nature of things, cannot be enjoyed by those with moderate or low incomes, but it also discriminates between different groups of taxpayers with large incomes. Enormous tax advantages are available to those who have the financial resources to purchase these bonds without borrowing, but they are unavailable to those who have to borrow the funds to do so.

Section 265 (2) of the Internal Revenue Code provides in substance that when a person borrows funds for the purpose of investing in tax-exempt securities, he may not take a deduction on his income tax return for the interest he pays on the debt incurred. As a result many high-income taxpayers who might substantially reduce their taxes by investing in tax-exempts with borrowed funds are effectively prevented from doing so.[10]

Take the case of taxpayers A and B. A receives a salary of $100,000 a year, but has no other financial resources. B draws $100,000 a year from a business in which all his financial resources are invested and which would be jeopardized if any of the investment was withdrawn. Neither A nor B have the funds available to invest in tax-exempt bonds unless they can borrow the money to do so, but borrowing would not be profitable unless they are permitted to deduct their interest payments from their taxable income. If they borrow $500,000 at 5% and invest it in tax-exempts yielding 3½%, they will have to pay the bank $25,000 interest on which they must pay income taxes. The yield from their investment, although tax-free, is only $17,500 (3½% of $500,-000).

Taxpayer C with a large fortune invested in conventional stocks and bonds has no such disability. C is not obliged to borrow in order to invest part of his resources in tax-exempts. All he has to do is sell part of his investments and reinvest the proceeds. If C sells $500,000 worth of stocks from which he derives $25,000 in dividends that are fully taxable, and invests the money instead in tax-exempts paying 3½% interest, he reduces his taxable income by $25,000 in return for $17,500 a year tax-free.[11] (The reduction of his income by $7,500 is actually a gain if his tax bracket is higher than 30%). Thus C accomplishes the same result without borrowing as he would have achieved if he had borrowed $500,000 at 5% interest and were permitted to deduct the $25,000 interest on the loan from his taxable income.

While we fully agree with the propriety of Section 265(2), the fact is that under its provisions some high-income taxpayers with cash or other financial resources available to invest in and carry tax-exempt bonds without borrowing have a distinct advantage over those who do not have similar financial resources.[12] The real remedy is to eliminate the exemption for interest on state and local bonds entirely.

The Overall Economic Effects Are Disadvantageous

The economic justification advanced by defenders of the exemption is that it enables state and local governments, school district authorities, and the like to borrow vast sums at lower interest rates than they would have to pay if the interest on their bonds were not tax-exempt. But for years critics have pointed out that the value of this bounty enjoyed by state and local authorities is outweighed by the revenue lost to the federal government. Put another way, the savings to state and local governments in interest paid is substantially less than the cost to ordinary taxpayers, who are obliged to make up the difference with their tax payments.

In recent years the Treasury has adopted an increasingly critical attitude toward the tax-free status of interest on state and local bonds. As more and more tax-exempt bonds are issued the interest rate is being forced upward, not only increasing the cost to the state and local governments, but also resulting in greater tax benefits to holders of these securities.

Some Treasury officials, it is believed, now favor eliminating the tax exemption entirely, as a costly and inefficient method of helping state and local governments finance local projects. If the tax-exempt status of these bonds were abolished, the interest rate would of course have to be raised. But state and local governments would receive federal assistance to meet the increased costs of their borrowings. All taxpayers, including those who hold portfolios of state and municipal bond issues, would be contributing to these federal funds. In this way the subsidy to state and local authorities would be under governmental control, since it would take the form of an increase in federal expenditures rather than a loss of tax revenue. The extent of the subsidies to local governments for schools, hospitals, highways, and other projects would be visible and open to scrutiny; Congress and the public would be in a better position to see to it that the amounts of these federal grants approximated more closely the benefits they were designed to achieve.[13] The suggestion that the federal government share part of its tax revenues with state and local governments, a proposal that has really gained increasing support from congressmen, governors, and others, would facilitate such subsidies.

Those who oppose replacing the tax exemption for state and local bond interest with a federal subsidy emphasize that whatever form such direct federal assistance takes, it will inevitably lead to increased federal involvement in and federal control of the affairs of state and local governments, a trend generally considered to be undesirable.

Recent Reform Proposals

In 1969 an attempt by the House of Representatives to close this loophole was frustrated in the Senate. The House's version of the Tax Reform Act of 1969 contained a provision under which owners of tax-exempt securities would have had to pay a so-called Minimum Tax under certain circumstances. If their tax-free or tax-sheltered incomes from such sources as interest on tax-exempt bonds, capital gains, charitable contributions of appreciated property, and accelerated depreciation on certain types of real estate exceeded their taxable income they would have had to pay a tax on 50% of the aggregate of the two. Also under the House bill, deductions previously taken by individuals against their taxable sources of income would have had to be allocated pro rata between their ordinary taxable income and their tax-free or tax-sheltered income. The result of these proposals would have been to require many wealthy taxpayers who previously paid no tax at all to pay some tax.

The House bill offered state and local governments the option of issuing taxable instead of tax-exempt bonds in the future. If they issued taxable bonds a federal subsidy would make up the difference in the interest rate they would have had to pay.

These worthwhile reforms were proposed by the House under the aegis of Chairman Wilbur Mills of the Ways and Means Committee, but were stricken by the Senate Finance Committee. Even an attempt by the Treasury to salvage the requirement that taxpayers with tax-exempt bonds at least pro rate their deductions between their taxable and tax-free income was unsuccessful.

Exemption of Interest on Industrial Revenue Bonds

From the point of view of the loss of federal tax revenue and discrimination between taxpayers, it is bad enough when tax-exempt bonds are issued by state and local authorities to finance new schools, highways, hospitals, and other public facilities and improvements. But when such bonds are used to underwrite what are essentially private rather than public enterprises, an already inequitable situation is aggravated by further and even more unjustifiable abuse. In effect the benefit of tax exemption belonging to local governments is being diverted to private business interests.

In recent years there has been a phenomenal growth in the use of tax-exempt industrial revenue bonds issued by municipal governments and non-profit "development corporations" for the purpose of attracting industry to local communities. The device enables private enterprises to expand by acquiring plants in new locations without investing their own capital, and at the same time reaping enormous tax advantages.

The device typically involves a community that is eager to attract new industry. The municipality issues bonds in order to construct a factory or other industrial facility that is then leased for twenty or thirty years to a private industrial concern. The rental payments are set at a figure far below what would normally be fair rental terms, but just high enough to permit the municipality to take care of the interest and amortization payments on its bond issue. At the end of the lease term, the industrial tenant may renew the lease for an additional term at a nominal rental, or perhaps purchase the land and building for a nominal amount. The rental payments made to the city are not only deductible by the industrial tenant for income tax purposes, but at the end of the lease the tenant usually winds up as the owner of the land and buildings that have cost it nothing or next to nothing. Meanwhile it has enjoyed the occupancy of a valuable facility at a cost far below the true rental value as an inducement to locate its operations in the community; the low rental and other advantages are possible because both the city's income from the rent and the interest received by the bondholders are tax-free.

Sometimes the construction and the issuance of the bonds are undertaken by a non-profit "industrial development corporation" organized by representatives of the city and the private industrial concern. In other cases the new plant is constructed by the manufacturer itself, "sold" to the city in return for the proceeds of the bond issue, and immediately leased back to the manufacturer.

Frequently the bonds are secured, not by the general credit and revenues of the municipality issuing them, but merely by the income anticipated from the rent payments. But whatever the variations, the advantages derived through the use of the tax exemption for private interests are the same.[14]

In 1963 there were about $500 million worth of industrial revenue bonds outstanding. In the year 1967 about $1½ billion of these bonds were marketed, and the figure for 1968 was expected to be even higher.[15] Their use is not confined to the financing of factories and other industrial facilities. It is not uncommon for them to be used to supply funds for the construction of department stores, motels, and even bowling alleys.[16]

Of course industrial revenue bond financing has its defenders in government and business circles. With some justification it has been pointed out that the practice has stimulated the expansion of industry to new locations, provided jobs in depressed areas, and increased real estate values and local tax rolls.[17] But in addition to the loss of federal tax revenues and the damage to the progressive tax concept the device has many adverse side-effects. It has been criticized by the Investment Bankers Association,[18] the Municipal Law section of the American Bar Association, trade union representatives, and the Treasury itself.

For example, the industrial concern favored by such financing receives an unfair advantage over local competing businesses who may not have the same recourse to tax-free funds to finance their expansion.[19] Labor unions have complained that the practice has enabled anti-union employers to close organized plants and re-open new ones in non-union areas. Local governments may be subject to "blackmail" by a manufacturer who threatens to relocate his operations in a different area unless the local authorities float a bond issue to provide him with a new plant or to modernize the old one.

Then, too, the municipality does not always gain by the transaction. Frequently the local community would have fared better in the long run if it had financed the new facility by the issuance of a conventional bond issue, and leased it at a fair rental to a new business enterprise.[20] The real beneficiary in these transactions is usually the private corporation; it receives tax advantages that sometimes include immunity from local property taxes and a long-term lease at bargain rates. After twenty or thirty years the city may be the owner of the project, but by that time the facility's useful life may be over, and the city obtains little of value.[21] Finally, since many industrial revenue bond issues are secured, not by the general revenues and credit of the municipality, but by the rental payments expected from the private business concern and the mortgage on the property, there is always the danger that the business will run into difficulties and that the bonds will be defaulted, with consequent loss to the bondholders, many of them members of the local community.

When bonds of this type are issued by regular local governmental bodies or agencies, the issues are at least open to public debate and the proposal is frequently submitted to a vote by the community. But, increasingly, when a private non-profit "development corporation" is created to promote a project, the decisions are basically made by private interests, the underlying facts are not made known to the public, and the element of public scrutiny and approval is lacking.

Criticism of the expanding use of industrial revenue bonds has been mounting in the last few years. Stanley S. Surrey, former assistant secretary of the treasury, takes the position that when private corporations resort to this type of financing, it

makes them accomplices with the local issuing agencies in an arrangement that distorts the tax-exemption privilege and forces the Federal tax system improperly to support their financing.

Indeed, the position of accomplice is often forced upon the local agency under the threat of locating the plant elsewhere. This is a far cry from the original use of those bonds for corporations willing to enter areas of high unemployment but lacking capital of their own.[22]

Early in 1968 the Treasury issued regulations calling for the complete termination of the tax-exempt status of these bonds. However the House and Senate, where the ultimate decision lay, were unwilling to go that far. In the summer of 1968 Congress enacted legislation which, as subsequently amended, set a limit to the tax-free treatment of interest on such bonds to issues under $5 million, the idea being to limit this form of tax-free financing to relatively small companies.[23]

While the 1968 legislation will undoubtedly curtail the use of industrial revenue bonds by some of the country's industrial giants for financing their large expansion projects and will somewhat slow down and reduce the aggregate amount of this type of financing, this tax avoidance device will continue to be available to many business enterprises. The only proper solution lies in eliminating all present exemptions from tax of the interest on state and local bonds, whether they are industrial revenue or development bonds or the more traditional variety. Not only are tax-exempt securities a source of gross tax inequity that permit wealthier taxpayers to avoid the progressive nature of the income tax, but they also tend to distort the allocation by investors of their capital funds, and thereby divert investment from more productive to less productive enterprises.

9

The Incorporated Pocketbook Is Not Dead

Most people with large incomes quite understandably try to keep from being taxed at the high individual tax rates normally applicable to them, and, if possible, from being taxed altogether. For years a popular device for accomplishing this has been the use of the closely held private corporation. By diverting investments and income from themselves to such corporations, sometimes referred to as "incorporated pocketbooks," income is sheltered from taxation at high individual income tax rates.

The individual income tax rate at present is 70% on an income over $100,000 (or 70% on the joint income of a husband and wife over $200,000). The corporate tax rate on the other hand, is only 22% of the first $25,000 and 48% on the excess. Moreover corporations are allowed an 85% dividend credit. At the 48% corporate tax rate their dividend income is really taxed at only 7.2% (.48 × 15%).[1]

The advantages of having investment and other passive income diverted to a corporation rather than having it taxed to the individuals to whom it really belongs are obvious, provided of course that the so-called Personal Holding Company Tax [2] and the tax on unreasonable accumulation of corporate earnings can be avoided.[3]

As an illustration, consider M, who is in the top marginal individual income tax bracket of 70%. He places $4 million worth of common stocks, which produce annual dividends of $160,000, into corporation X, which he has created. The advantage to M is as follows:

Tax With Incorporation (the stocks are owned by Corporation X instead of by M as an individual)

Dividend income to X Corporation on $4 million worth of securities	$160,000
Less inter-corporate dividend credit: 85%	136,000
Dividend income taxable to X Corporation	$ 24,000
Tax to X Corporation at 22%	$5,280

Tax Without Incorporation (the stocks are owned by M individually)

Dividend income on $4 million worth of securities	$160,000
M's individual tax rate	70%
M's income tax on the dividend income	$112,000

M has saved over $106,000 by channeling this income into his corporation. He will not dissipate this tidy saving by having the corporation pay the money out to him in the form of dividends, since he might then have to pay as much as 70% of it to the government in taxes. Instead he will retain the money in the corporation. Eventually, when it suits M's convenience, the "corporate pocketbook" will be liquidated and its assets paid over to him; and although he will be taxed on the profit, it will be at capital gains rates with a maximum of 35%. Even assuming that at some future time M will have to pay about $37,000 additional in taxes when the corporation is liquidated, he has still achieved a very large net saving. Indeed M may never have to pay the additional tax on liquidation of the corporation. He may escape this tax entirely by keeping the corporation in existence and leaving the stock to his heirs.[4]

If, in addition to these dividends, M's corporation has other types of income that are taxable at the top corporate rate of 48%, or if the corporation's securities portfolio consists of bonds rather than stock, so that it does not get the benefit of the 85% dividend received credit, the economic advantages of using the corporate tax shelter, while not so spectacular, will still be considerable.[5]

Prior to 1964 the use of private corporate tax shelters as tax avoidance devices was so widespread that some reform in this area was inevitable. Taxpayers in high-income tax brackets were able to form corporations owned by themselves and their relatives to shelter passive income from stocks, bonds, real estate, patents, and other assets, and were still in no danger of having the corporations subjected to the penalties of the Personal Holding Company Tax.[6] The income would be accumulated in the corporation,[7] where it would usually be subject to comparatively low tax rates. When the corporation was eventually liquidated, the amounts paid over to the stockholders were taxable to them at the preferential capital gains rates, and even this tax could be avoided by bequests of the corporation's stock to heirs. All that was necessary was that ownership of the corporation's stock was not concentrated too heavily among a few people,[8] or that a modicum of active business operations be conducted which yielded a little more than 20% of the corporation's gross income.[9] In other words, if one-fifth of the corporation's gross income was from some active business (no matter how little *net* income was realized from such activity), the remaining 80% could be of the passive variety, and was shielded from individual income taxation. In this way one dollar of active income could shelter about four dollars of dividends, interest, rents, and the like from high individual tax rates.

The 1964 Reforms

The tax provisions enacted in 1964 applicable to Personal Holding Companies [10] are too complex to be set forth here in any detail. However, in essence the law was tightened up in two important respects, making it much more difficult to use these corporate tax shelters:

1. The amount of a corporation's so-called "active income" required to shield its "passive" income was raised from 20% to 40%.

2. If this minimum of "active income" came from such previously popular activities as real estate or gas and oil operations, it had to be in a sense *net* income [11] rather than merely *gross* income.

Previously $50,000 a year of gross income from real estate or oil and gas operations could shield four times as much passive income from dividends or interest (i.e., $200,000) even though the actual (net) income from the real estate or oil and gas operations was minimal. But under the 1964 law it takes 40% of active business income to shield 60% of passive income, and the active income from rents or from oil and gas has to be reduced by offsetting expenses before application of the percentage.

Moreover, if real estate, mineral, oil, or gas operations are sought to be used as the active business ingredient, this activity must be the corporation's preponderant activity; adjusted gross income from the active business must equal at least 50% of the corporation's total adjusted gross income; [12] and the corporation's other passive income, such as income from dividends and interest, may not exceed 10% of its overall gross income. [13] It is this 10% limitation that now makes the personal holding company classification particularly difficult to circumvent.

"Escape Routes" for the Ingenious Taxpayer

In spite of the 1964 reforms of the Personal Holding Company Tax provisions, some avenues of escape remain that still make it possible for closely held corporations to be used as shelters to avoid high individual tax rates.

A taxpayer in a high-income tax bracket can set up a closely owned corporation controlled by him to operate a manufacturing business, a telephone answering service, an employment agency, or a television station with a gross income of $100,000. This business may not require more than a minimal investment because its net income is small. He can use the corporation to shelter a portfolio of stocks and bonds yielding $150,000 a year in dividends and interest which will be insulated from taxation at his high individual income tax rate. [14] Even if the manufacturing business has a bad year so that its gross income (gross sales less cost of goods sold) declines, the Personal Holding Company Tax can be avoided by having the corporation distribute a large dividend. [15] This measure may be painful for the stockholders when they fill out their tax returns, but they may be able to offset the added income by reducing their taxable income in that year by other measures.

Another type of tax shelter still available is the incorporated talent device. For years, actors, directors, writers, cartoonists, and authors whose talents commanded large compensation formed corporations to which they contributed their services. The payments for these services received from moving picture companies, book publishers, producers of television programs, and the like were channeled into the corporation where they were subject only to relatively low corporate income taxes and shielded from much higher tax rates that would have applied if these payments had been received by these individuals directly. Eventually the talent corporation would be liquidated and its accumulated earnings would be paid to the actor, director, or author stockholder as a capital gain, taxable to him at the lower capital gains rate.

The 1964 Revenue Act sought to prevent these arrangements by providing that if the corporation's contract with the moving picture company, publisher, or television network specifies that the services are to be performed by a stockholder owning 25% or more of its stock, the payment will be considered Personal Holding Company income and the penalty tax is applicable. But this obstacle is not difficult to circumvent. Contracts of this type are worded so that they do not specifically require that the services have to be performed by any particular person, but it is tacitly understood that it will be the well-known actor, writer, or producer who will actually do the work.[16]

Adjusting Investment to Avoid the Tax

It is much more difficult, because of the additional 50% and 10% tests that must be satisfied, to use income from real estate to shield large amounts of dividend or interest income from individual taxation. Still a wide variety of expedients are available.

For example, to meet the 50% rental test, which requires that adjusted rental income must amount to at least 50% of the corporation's total adjusted ordinary income, a closely held real estate corporation can: 1. change the nature of its investments by acquiring, by purchase or exchange, properties that yield more rental income; [17] 2. switch to properties on which the real estate taxes or interest on mortgages are lower; 3. arrange to refinance or pay off some of the mortgages on its properties so as to postpone or reduce interest payments; 4. change its methods of taking depreciation from an accelerated method to a less rapid write-off; or 5. adopt other operational changes to increase the net real estate income.[18]

If it appears that passive income from dividends or interest may exceed the limit of 10% of total gross income, such income can be reduced by substituting "growth stocks" that pay lower dividends for high dividend paying securities, or by switching from common stocks to corporate bonds at a time when interest rates are low; [19] although often some of these expedients will have the effect of diluting some of the advantage of the Personal Holding Company device.

If there is any likelihood that the corporation is retaining too much dividend, interest, and other passive income to pass the 10% overall percentage test, and consequently is in danger of being classified as a personal holding company, the best escape hatch of all is to pay out just enough in dividends to meet the percentage requirement.[20]

In spite of the 1964 reforms, the Personal Holding Company Tax leaves room for maneuver and tax avoidance. The present 40%-60% ratio still enables wealthy taxpayers to use closely held corporations to shield substantial amounts of passive income from taxation at high individual tax rates. One dollar of active income can shelter one dollar and a half of dividends and interest from personal income taxation.

It has been suggested that the penalty of the Personal Holding Company Tax should be imposed on closely held corporations unless at least 60% of their income is active rather than passive in nature.[21] Congress might do well to adopt such a provision as a first step toward more thoroughgoing tax reform in the Personal Holding Company area.

10

One Good Loophole Deserves Another— The Proliferation of Special Tax Treatment

The Mania for Capital Gains

Capital gains transactions receive such advantageous tax treatment [1] compared to ordinary income that it is no wonder that the pursuit of capital gains has been a veritable mania with many taxpayers.[2] Even for persons with moderate incomes the capital gains treatment has had distinct advantages. But for those whose incomes from ordinary sources are subject to the higher rates, the temptation to manipulate transactions and cast them in some capital gains formula has been well-nigh irresistible. Instead of paying ordinary income rates (up to 70%), only 35% of the profit need be surrendered to the government; and the higher the tax bracket the greater the benefit from transforming ordinary income into capital gain.[3]

Capital gains were not always preferentially taxed. From 1913 to 1926 gains from the sale of capital assets were taxed like any other income. Since then, however, they have been granted favored treatment of one kind or another. Some critics regard such preference as the biggest loophole in the tax law favoring the wealthy,[4] and advocate drastic increases in the capital gains rate, lengthening the holding period required for preferential treatment to several years, or both. Some even insist that capital gains should be treated and taxed in the same manner as any other income. On the other hand, there are those who claim that the tax rate on capital gains is too high; some even believe that such gains should not be taxed at all.[5] But whatever the conflicting view of tax authorities may be as to how "true" capital gains should be taxed, there seems to be general agreement that the capital gains label has proliferated beyond all reasonable bounds.

The Capital Gains Jungle

To begin with, the statutory standards designed to determine which transactions result in capital gains treatment and which in ordinary income and the court decisions that seek to apply them are so indefinite, confusing, complex, and inconsistent that it is often difficult or impossible to predict what will be taxed as capital gain and what as ordinary income. The result is that the boundaries between what is and what is not capital gain are often arbitrary, illogical, or capricious, and the entire capital gains area is a sort of "jungle" in which most taxpayers and even many tax experts wander about aimlessly and confused.[6]

One taxpayer may trade in stocks and bonds to his heart's content knowing that his profits will be treated as capital gains. Another taxpayer, who never before owned or traded a piece of real estate, may buy a parcel of property, subdivide it, make a few improvements, and advertise it in a newspaper before offering it for sale, only to discover later that he is in the real estate business, and that his gain will be taxed at the higher rates applicable to ordinary income.

An estate that acquires a large inventory of jewelry, antiques, or other property from a decedent who collected them over a long period of time may offer them for sale to the general public. Or a taxpayer in the auto rental business, after deciding to discontinue the enterprise, may choose to advertise his remaining automobiles and trucks for sale. One may have the good fortune to be taxed on his profit at the capital gains rate, while the other's gain may be determined to be ordinary income. There are any number of inconsistent tax treatments of such transactions as sales of movie rights or TV programs, assignments of exclusive agency contracts, and cancellations of favorable business leases or of profitable distribution agreements, to name a few.

The fuzzy distinction between capital transactions and those giving rise to ordinary income, in combination with other factors, sometimes permits shareholders in closely held corporations with accumulated earnings to find ways to siphon off these earnings to themselves without being taxed at ordinary income rates, and at the same time leave them in control of the corporation and its future operations. These maneuvers, which often successfully translate ordinary income into more advantageous capital gains, take a variety of forms,[7] but they usually result in the shareholders receiving cash which was part of the corporation's surplus, while their stock interest remains intact.

Proliferation of Capital Gains by Congressional Action

Most troublesome of all is the extent to which Congress, under pressure from one special interest or another, has time and again extended the favored capital gains treatment to transactions no more deserving of the preference than others "for no other reason than that the particular claimants involved were able to persuade Congress that a tax break was called for in their own case." [8]

In 1942 lump sum payments from pension, profit sharing, and stock bonus plans received by employees on death or retirement was made an exception to the rule that compensation for personal services was taxable at ordinary income tax rates, and was granted capital gains treatment.[9]

In 1943, under pressure from the timber industry, Congress decided that royalties or other income from the cutting of standing timber, although hardly differing from other types of income,[10] would be taxed as capital gain.[11]

In 1950, similar preferred treatment was extended to inventors who sold or licensed their patents,[12] even though the income of artists, writers, and composers from the sale or license of their copyrights was, and still is, taxed at ordinary income rates. Inventors, it was said, deserved to be rewarded by special tax treatment as an incentive to conceiving new inventions. But why writers or composers should not be similarly encouraged is difficult to understand.

In the same year the special dispensation was granted to the profits made by corporate executives on the exercise and sale of stock options,[13] although this preferential treatment of what is essentially additional compensation is a clear discrimination against other taxpayers not fortunate enough to receive such corporate favors.

In 1951, although the profits from such sales did not differ materially from those of other businessmen selling property to their customers, the sale of livestock used for breeding, draft, or dairy purposes and unharvested crops sold at the same time as the land on which they were located were singled out for capital gains treatment.[14] In the same year an exception was made in the case of royalties received by coal property owners in return for mining rights,[15] the argument being that since royalties received for timber cutting had been given this preference, why not give coal royalties similar treatment.

Each successive exemption granting capital gains treatment to some new business interest or group has encouraged other groups to seek similar tax privileges for themselves. During the 1951 debate in the Senate on whether coal royalties should be granted the capital gains bounty, Senator Hubert Humphrey opposed it on the ground that it would eventually lead to demands by owners of other mineral properties for the same preference:

MR. HUMPHREY: In recommending this provision, the Ways and Means Committee offered the explanation that timber owners now have capital gain treatment on their cutting contracts, and have had since 1943. How could one justify denying to coal what is accepted in the case of timber?

In other words, since 1943 the timber owners have had that benefit. Now we say, "That is bad, of course, but why deny the same privilege to coal-mine owners?"

. . .

This, of course, is always the argument made on behalf of one special interest from a privilege granted another.[16]

In 1963 the Kennedy administration made an effort to eliminate most of these preferences; the secretary of the treasury proposed to Congress that the special capital gains treatment for income from patents, lump sum withdrawals from pension plans, coal and timber royalties, sales of livestock, and a number of other transactions be removed.[17] Congress not only rejected the proposed reforms, but decided that iron ore royalties should be added to the list of preferred items.[18]

Not only are these privileges of capital gains treatment discriminatory, but often they have not accomplished the purpose for which they were originally enacted. Indeed, frequently the result was the very opposite. The granting of capital gains treatment in connection with the sale of livestock and unharvested crops and the similar exception made for standing timber were designed to aid small farmers, ranchers, and owners of timber. Instead, the chief beneficiaries proved to be wealthy investors in cattle raising, citrus groves, and other properties and the giant lumber, pulp, and paper companies who have utilized the privilege for large-scale tax avoidance.

Stock option profits were excepted on the theory that they provided an incentive to better business management and made it easier to recruit and retain competent employees. But experience has shown that the beneficiaries were for the most part high-salaried executives who, more often than not, instead of retaining the stock, sold it at handsome profits, which were taxable to them at the lower capital gains rate.[19]

Livestock and Farming

Although most of them had never before set foot on a cattle ranch or farm, many highly paid corporate executives, lawyers, doctors, and other investors with large incomes from non-farming sources have for many years been attracted to investments in cattle raising and other agricultural activities because of their special capital gains treatment. These "gentlemen farmers" and cattle breeders have secured unwarranted tax benefits by utilizing a provision of the tax law intended, not for them, but for true farmers.

While most taxpayers are required to deduct their inventory from the cost of goods sold, farmers, who traditionally operate on a simplified cash accounting basis, have been permitted to deduct from income all expenses of their operations, including the cost of raising their cattle and other crops; and when they sell part of this inventory, such as breeding cattle or unharvested crops, they have been allowed to treat the profit as capital gain, thereby transforming ordinary income into capital gains.

Taking advantage of this exception, which was meant for working farmers, investors and investing syndicates would, in a typical transaction, purchase cattle for breeding purposes, using a bank loan for most, if not all, of the purchase price. While the herd was being built up they could deduct all the expenses of the care, raising, and maintenance of the cattle and take large depreciation deductions as well, all of which was currently deductible against their large executive, professional, or other income. The cattle operations may have actually been conducted at a loss, but this did not worry them since such losses were offset by tax savings on their other sources of income. After the herd had been developed and cattle owned for a year or more were sold, the profits were taxed at a maximum rate of 25%, since they were considered long-term capital gain. Although the cattle business as such may have proved unprofitable, it enabled them to reap a substantial after-tax profit.[20]

Some organizations specialized in managing the livestock investments of wealthy absentee owners. The brochure of one such organization assured prospective clients that with a cash outlay of $94,750 over a five-year period they would reap substantial after-tax benefits. Although during the five years there would be a loss of $209,750 on the cattle raising operation, largely due to maintenance, interest, and depreciation costs, the investor would be able to use these losses each year to reduce taxes on his high-bracket income from other sources. At the end of the period he would enjoy long-term capital gains of over $150,000 on the sale of the cattle, subject to a maximum tax of 25%. And all these benefits could be enjoyed without the investor even having to visit the cattle ranch! [21] Similar tax shelters were available to wealthy investors in citrus groves, orchards, and farm crops. In each case the property, though operated at a loss during the period of development, was later sold or liquidated, and the profits taxed at capital gains rates.

The Treasury Department warned Congress that these investments by high-bracket taxpayers were enabling them to obtain unfair and unwarranted tax advantages. Moreover they created unfair competition for true farmers and ranchers who were not in the enviable position of being able to pay their operating costs and other expenses out of tax dollars, but had to operate at an economic profit in order to remain in business.[22]

Prodded by the unfavorable publicity given to the fact that thousands of wealthy persons had been achieving huge tax savings through farming and livestock breeding operations, Congress finally took steps in the Tax Reform Act of 1969 to reduce this tax shelter. While these provisions do not close the loophole, they make it slightly less attractive and more difficult to use.

The new law narrows the capital gains loophole somewhat for "gentleman farmers" (who are defined as those with incomes of more than $50,000 a year from other sources, in contrast to working farmers) by providing that their capital gains from farming will be treated as ordinary income to the extent that they had operating losses in excess of $25,000 per year. If their farming losses are less than $25,000 a year or their income from non-farming sources is less than $50,000, the new limitation will not affect them. Accordingly, "gentleman farmer" Jones can still have cattle-raising losses of $24,000 a year for three years, sell the livestock produced in those years for $100,000, and have the profit taxed at the favorable long-term capital gains rate.

To make the loophole a little less attractive, the depreciation previously taken by Jones on his original purchase of livestock will be taxed at full ordinary income rates when those animals are later sold. But he will still be able to benefit by taking ordinary deductions for the cost of raising the cattle and get capital gains treatment when he sells the offspring of the original livestock when they are two or more years old.

Another provision of the new act is aimed at discouraging wealthy people from engaging in cattle breeding and other activities as a "hobby" while using their losses from these operations to provide a tax shelter for their incomes from other sources. If they sustain losses from such pursuits for a number of years in succession their operations may be challenged as an activity not engaged in for profit, and the use of further losses to reduce taxable income will be disallowed.

In its attempts to deal with the use of farming operations as a tax shelter the new law is of course an improvement over the old, but on the whole it represents only a half-step toward reform in this area. What is needed is a complete overhaul of the old law, including a substantial tightening up of the exemptions still available.

Timber

The story in the timber industry is much the same, except that the tax shelter remains as inviting as ever. During World War II Congress was persuaded that high corporate income and excess profits taxes were a serious deterrent to fulfilling the nation's wartime needs for timber. It was said that farmers who sold their mature trees for cutting on a royalty basis (in accordance with good conservation and reforestation practices) had to pay taxes on the proceeds at high ordinary income tax rates. But they could obtain the advantage of the lower capital gains rate by selling their entire timber stand to a lumber company or sawmill operator for a flat sum, or by disposing of the timber together with their land. The result was a rash of outright sales leading to widespread and indiscriminate timber cutting. In order to encourage regular sales of mature trees on an annual basis rather than outright sales of whole tracts, the sale or cutting of standing timber held for six months or longer was accorded capital gains treatment.[23]

However experience has proved that the change in tax treatment has not aided those for whose benefit the law was amended. According to Treasury Department surveys, it is not the average farmer or other small timber owner [24] who has profited from the tax preference, but rather the big lumber, pulp, plywood, and paper companies with vast holdings of timber and large regular incomes from lumber processing and other operations who have reaped the rewards.[25]

These industrial giants buy up huge blocks of timber acreage with heavy debt financing, often at a discount of as much as 40% below retails prices. They promptly place a very high fair market value on the timber. On cutting it they realize capital gains on the difference between their low cost and the high market value. In order to pay off the banks who financed the timber purchases, the timber is cut under accelerated and unrestrained cutting programs with little regard for sound conservation and reforestation practices. Subsequent manufacturing and selling operations are often conducted at a substantial loss, in view of the artificially high values assigned to the timber. These same high levels, however, measured against the bargain-basement prices paid for the timber, produce huge capital gains taxed at the preferential rate.[26] As a result, the Treasury found, the overall effective tax rate of fifteen large companies in the timber, plywood, and paper industries, each of whom had assets ranging from $25 million to $250 million, was one-half to one-third less than the average rate paid by other United States corporations.

During the Senate Finance Committee Hearings on the 1969 tax bill, Senator Vance Hartke reminded the Nixon administration of these appalling statistics:

SENATOR HARTKE: You are acquainted with the fact that the capital gains treatment [for timber] is allowed for the taxpayer whether he practices conservation methods or not, are you not?

MR. COHEN: I am indeed, Senator.

SENATOR HARTKE: You do know that there is a distortion here in favor of just a few companies, about five companies really, throughout the United States. In fact, one of them accounts for the biggest portion of this revenue loss to the Treasury as a result of this preferential treatment which is given to timber companies, is that true?

The response was that the administration was concerned about it but had not had time to study it in detail.[27]

Wealthy investors and investing syndicates are using this same tax loophole to have a tax-avoidance field day. While acquiring enormous timber tracts, mostly with borrowed funds, and using the operating losses from manufacturing operations to reduce their income tax liabilities on other sources of income, they are pocketing huge capital gains on timber cutting taxed to them at capital gains rates.[28] One well-known tax service urged business executives in the high ordinary income tax brackets to take advantage of this bonanza as follows:

Towering Tax Breaks—*First of all,* your investment constantly grows in value—tax free. There's no tax at all until there's a cutting or disposition of the timber. You can almost see those dollars growing on the trees. You can set things up so that you get *capital gains* treatment when the timber is cut. You can *deduct* the current maintenance and operating costs against your *current* tax eroded executive income. And, you can deplete—or offset—the capital cost of your timber investment against your sales proceeds.[29]

During the Kennedy administration the Treasury proposed in effect that the capital gains treatment for timber be eliminated for all except small farmers and other holders of small timber interests.[30] However representatives of the lumber, paper, pulp, and plywood industries descended on the Congressional committees in droves to register their opposition, and the proposal, like so many other tax reforms suggested at the time, was killed.[31]

Proliferation of Depletion Allowances

Just as the preferential capital gains treatment for certain types of transactions has mushroomed over the years as the result of Congressional favoritism, so the loophole of the depletion allowance has been opened wider and wider to admit additional "natural resources" to its tax shelter. Percentage depletion for oil and gas was introduced under the Revenue Act of 1926 as a substitute for the so-called discovery depletion allowance that had previously been permitted, and under the Revenue Act of 1932 it was extended to cover many additional types of minerals and metals in varying percentages.[32]

As spokesmen for one industry after another succeeded in persuading Congress to grant allowances for percentage depletion, the producers of other substances clamored for similar or even more favorable treatment. Between 1940 and 1954 the tax benefits of percentage depletion were extended to cover many substances not previously favored, including a number whose qualification as scarce "natural resources," limited in supply, and difficult to discover, and the production of which warranted special tax inducements in the national interest, were, to say the least, doubtful. Such additional objects of Congressional tax bounty included ball clay, china clay, and sagger clay (15%), brick and tile clay (5%), gravel (5%), mollusk shells (including clam shells and oyster shells) (5%), peat (5%), sand (5%), shale and stone (with certain exceptions) (5%), and slate (15%).[33]

The infectious spread of the depletion allowance was underscored in the following colloquy during a Senate Finance Committee hearing a few years ago:

SENATOR DOUGLAS [to Professor C. Lowell Harris of Columbia University, a witness before the Committee]: Do you approve the depletion allowance on clam and oyster shells which this body put through in 1951, as a wasting natural resource?

MR. HARRIS: No, Senator, not after the amount deducted exceeds the owner's investment.

SENATOR DOUGLAS: What?

MR. HARRIS: No.

SENATOR DOUGLAS: Or sand and gravel?

MR. HARRIS: No, though if it is given in one case then if there are materials that are compatible and the—

SENATOR DOUGLAS: Exactly so. You start with a loophole and it becomes a truckhole, exactly so.

SENATOR GORE: Repetitiously.

SENATOR DOUGLAS: That is right. It spreads out.[34]

The pressure of special interests to obtain the benefits of percentage depletion reached such proportions that one senator warned his colleagues that unless certain products made in his state were included, he would propose the elimination of the allowance for materials produced in many other states. The threat, needless to say, resulted in the quick adoption of a measure that included the senator's pet industry.[35]

Mercifully Congress was persuaded to put some limit on the almost boundless spread of percentage depletion, and specifically excluded from participation the following:

(A) Soil, sod, dirt, turf, water or mosses; or
(B) Minerals from sea water, the air or similar inexhaustible sources.[36]

Nevertheless, even though water, soil, and sod are expressly excluded from enjoying the benefits of percentage depletion, it has been held that a seller of soil and a landowner using ground water for irrigation purposes were entitled to a depletion deduction based on cost.[37] And recently, although the dissenting Justices asserted that this was "depletion run riot," a firm that used underground steam from nearby geysers to drive electric generators was held by the Tax Court to be entitled to the same generous depletion allowance as oil and gas, on the theory that underground steam was "a gas." [38]

Probably anticipating powerful resistance in the House and Senate, the administration has hesitated to launch a bold frontal attack on depletion allowances in general. Even the relatively modest reforms suggested in the past by the Treasury have, for the most part, been rejected by Congress.[39] While reductions in depletion allowances have been incorporated in the Tax Reform Act of 1969, they have been largely token in nature. The Act provides for the reduction of the allowance for oil and gas from 27½% to 22% [40] and for minor changes in the allowances for other minerals and "natural resources." [41] However, major surgery in the depletion allowance area still remains to be accomplished.

11

Keeping Income in the Family and Saving Taxes at the Same Time

Family Income Splitting

If an individual whose income places him in a high tax bracket can divert some of that income to other members of the family who are in lower tax brackets, considerable tax savings will result for the family unit as a whole. This situation has led to the familiar device of income splitting within the family.[1] It is facilitated by an ineffective gift tax structure with rates that are substantially below estate tax rates, and by overly generous gift tax exemptions and exclusions that encourage programs of inter-family giving to minimize or avoid gift taxation altogether.

Since the federal income tax is progressive, with the rate increasing as taxable income increases,[2] a couple with a taxable income of $100,000 after deductions does not simply pay twice as much tax as one with a taxable income of $50,000, but closer to three times as much. But it does not follow that taxpaying *families* with higher incomes pay at progressively higher rates. On the contrary, it is quite common for a family whose members collectively have a much larger income than a similar family unit, to have a smaller total tax liability.

In one family consisting of a married couple and five dependent children, the entire family income may consist of the father's $50,000 salary as a corporate executive, or his $50,000 earnings from a privately owned business. His federal income tax liability on his and his wife's joint return would be $11,300,[3] since all the income is taxed in the father's relatively high tax bracket. In another family of similar composition the family receipts aggregating $60,000 consist of the father's $30,000 income from a family partnership, $15,000 received by the oldest son working with his father as a partner, and $3,000 income received by each of the five children from separate trust funds set up by the father for them over a period of years. Their total federal income tax liability, despite an annual income which is $10,000 greater, will be in the neighborhood of $10,300. It is $1,000 less than that of the first family because the tax is levied on *individuals,* and the amount of tax depends on the income level and applicable tax bracket of each individual. The annual receipts of the *family unit* as such is irrelevant.

The Use of Outright Gifts

The simplest and most common device for diverting income from family members in the high tax brackets is the use of gifts. By giving away income-producing property to children, grandchildren, and other family members, a father may successfully channel income taxable to him at a high rate to others to whom it will be taxable at much lower rates or not taxable at all.

Take the case of H, a well-to-do taxpayer with five children, who is in his early fifties. In addition to a yearly salary of $120,000 as a corporate executive, he receives $60,000 income each year from a $750,000 portfolio of investments. He is in a 66% tax bracket; on their joint return he and his wife are liable for about $76,000 in taxes.[4]

A simple expedient available to H is to initiate an annual gift program for his five children. The gift tax law allows one to make tax-free gifts up to a total of $30,000 ($60,000 with the consent of one's spouse) during one's lifetime. In addition, in any calendar year, gifts up to $3,000 each ($6,000 with the consent of one's spouse) may be made to any number of persons.[5] If H diverts $60,000 worth of income-producing property to his children immediately, and thereafter makes annual gifts of $6,000 to each of them, at the end of ten years he will have disposed of $360,000 of his securities without having to pay any gift taxes. As a result, H's income tax liability will have decreased each year until at the end of the period his and his wife's income tax bill will have declined to approximately $62,000. While it is true that the five children will soon have portfolios of their own yielding separate incomes subject to taxation, the size of their incomes will place them in relatively low income tax brackets; even at the end of the ten-year period their individual tax rates will be relatively low.

At the end of the ten-year period, instead of all the H family income of $180,000 being payable and taxable to the father, it will be split between the father and his five children with the following income tax consequences:

H, the father

Executive salary	$120,000
Dividend income at 8% from his remaining $390,000 securities portfolio	31,200
Total income	$151,200
Federal income tax on joint return [6]	$ 62,000

H's children

Income of each child: dividends from $72,000 of securities at 8% return	$ 5,760
Federal income tax liability of each child [7]	$ 750
Federal income tax liability of five children	$ 3,750

The total family income tax liability at the conclusion of the gift program will be $65,750 per year, or $10,250 per year less than it was originally. By splitting his own income with other family members in lower tax brackets, H has substantially cut the total family income tax bill, and has managed to do it without having to pay any gift taxes. In addition he has diminished the size of his eventual estate, thereby substantially reducing possible estate tax liabilities.

The Use of Trusts, Including Multiple Accumulation Trusts

Suppose that H's children are minors, to whom he is reluctant to make outright gifts. In that case he can accomplish almost precisely the same income-splitting results by making the gifts to his children in trust. The income can be accumulated or paid out to the children while they are under age, and any accumulated income can be transferred to them, together with the trust principal, when they reach twenty-one.[8] He can even make himself or his wife the trustee and continue to manage the trust investments. The trust of each child will be in a relatively low income tax bracket; moreover the first $100 of each trust's income will be tax-exempt.

Some exceedingly well-to-do people, in order to effect significant reductions in their own income tax rate, are obliged to give away to family members even larger amounts of assets.[9] When very large amounts are donated each year, or when the property given is of a type that increases steadily in value and income-yield (such as growth stocks or valuable real estate), the resulting incomes of the children and other gift beneficiaries may, notwithstanding their lower tax brackets, involve them in substantial income tax liabilities. But until recently there was a remedy available even in this type of situation, namely, the creation of multiple accumulation trusts. A number of trusts were created for each family member with a provision that the income would be *accumulated* for the beneficiary instead of being paid out to him each year. This device permitted substantial portions of the income of wealthy families to escape taxation altogether.

Instead of setting up a single trust for each of his children, a parent could have created say four *separate* trusts for each child, each with a separate trustee, a separate bank account, and separate records.[10] In this way he could have given away the same amount of securities, but by quadrupling the number of trusts, the securities portfolio of each trust and its annual income would be one-fourth as large. Each trust would automatically be in a much lower tax bracket under the progressive income tax rate schedule, and each trust would be entitled to the $100 exemption. As long as the parent did not retain substantial incidents of ownership and control over the trust property,[11] each trust could provide that the income be accumulated for the benefit of the child and be paid out to him or her only after specified intervals of years.[12] As a result the annual income tax liability of each trust was substantially reduced.

For example, a father wishing to donate $200,000 to each of his four children, could establish four separate trusts for each child and transfer $50,000 to each trust. Assuming an 8% return, each trust would have had an income of $4,000 a year and have paid an income tax of $670; the four trusts would have paid a total tax of $2,680. If a single trust of $200,000 had been set up for each child, it would have been liable, on its 8% return of $16,000, for an annual income tax of $4,300. The multiple trust device saved in taxes about 10% of the income for each child, and for all four children the annual income tax saving amounted to more than $6,400.

Another example of the use of an accumulation trust to minimize taxes was the creation of a trust by a husband for the benefit of his wife. The income was accumulated for her benefit for a period of years, then distributed to her, and the principal was returned to the husband. If the trust had an income of $5,000 per year and expenses of $400, the yearly tax to the trust was $800. If the couple had an income of $76,000, they would have been liable for an annual income tax of $2,668 on the trust income if it had been distributed to the wife rather than accumulated for her. By the accumulation device the couple saved over two-thirds of the tax otherwise payable on the trust income, not to mention the possibility that the wife may have paid little or no tax when the accumulated income was finally distributed.

During Congressional hearings some years ago on the subject of tax evasion and avoidance, it was disclosed that six families had evaded a total of almost $1.9 million in income taxes by means of 98 separate accumulation trusts. One taxpayer had on a single day created 64 trusts, with his wife and three children as beneficiaries, and had transferred 277,500 shares of Pan American stock to the trusts. The stock was immediately sold by the trusts, and by having 64 trusts instead of just four, a $485,000 reduction in the capital gains tax was achieved. In another instance four separate related grantors had created 56 accumulation trusts, and saved $701,227 in income taxes over a three-year period.[13]

As a result of these revelations Congress enacted legislation imposing partial limitations on the tax-free accumulation of income in trusts,[14] but, in addition to other shortcomings, the provisions placed no restrictions on the creation of multiple trusts for a single beneficiary. It was not until the Tax Reform Act of 1969 that the use of trusts for the accumulation of income, including the multiple variety, was finally sharply curtailed as a tax avoidance loophole.[15] The Act generally provides that the beneficiaries are to be taxed on the distributions in substantially the same manner as if the income had been distributed to the beneficiary when it was earned by the trust.

The Reversionary Short-Term Trust

A wealthy taxpayer can effect a tax-saving shift of income-producing property to other family members in lower income tax brackets and even arrange to get the property back later. The device is the handy reversionary ten-year trust. The property given in trust reverts to the father when the trust ends. If the trust is irrevocable and is to last for at least ten years, the trust income is taxable to the beneficiary, and not to the father.[16]

A father in a 60% income tax bracket may set up a trust of $100,000 of his property; the income will be irrevocably payable to one of his children, who has no other income, for ten years, at which time the property will be returned to the father.[17] If the trust produces dividend income of $6,000 a year the federal income tax payable each year by the child will be only $815.[18] If the father had continued to receive it, the $6,000 additional income would have cost him $3,600 in taxes. The net income tax saving of $2,785 a year amounts to $27,850 over the ten-year trust period, not to mention possible additional savings in state and local income taxes.

If this trust is an initial gift, there will be no gift tax; with his wife's consent, the father can use part of their joint $60,000 gift tax exemption. The gift of an income interest for 10 years will be valued at about 30% of the principle, or about $30,000.[19]

In this manner a father can reduce his high tax liabilities almost without limit, by diverting income to other family members in low tax brackets. He can set up any number of trusts for minor children, grandchildren, in-laws, and other family members, with substantial overall income tax savings, taking full advantage of the liberal gift tax exclusions and exemptions available to himself and his wife so as to reduce or eliminate any gift tax liabilities. At the end of ten years, perhaps when he is retired and is in a much lower income tax bracket, the property and its income will again be available to the father.

Income-Splitting for Future Generations ad Infinitum

Wealthy families can even provide for tax saving income-splitting for the benefit of future generations. A wealthy taxpayer may during his lifetime, or by his will, create a series of trusts for the benefit of his children or grandchildren that provides that the income of the trust property is to be distributed to his descendants according to the discretion of the trustee. The trustee may be given the right to distribute the income among the children and grandchildren *as a class,* equally or unequally, apportioning it among one, or more, or all of them in whatever manner he deems advisable, according to their needs and desires.

Years later the trustee, in consultation with the family, can apportion larger shares of income to descendants in the lower tax brackets and smaller shares to those whose other resources place them in higher income tax brackets, thereby effectively minimizing the aggregate family income tax liabilities. Such so-called "sprinkling trust" provisions are widely used. Their use as a potential tax avoidance device deserves serious consideration by Congress.

Splitting Income through Family Partnerships and Corporations

Suppose a taxpayer is the sole proprietor of a successful manufacturing business, the net income of which, in spite of its relatively small capital investment, is growing so rapidly that he soon finds himself in the 70% bracket for income tax purposes. His income tax payments are so large that, after meeting his family obligations and living expenses, he can hardly repay the balance of a loan made when he started the business, much less save funds for expanding the business itself. At the same time his married son, studying engineering, and a son-in-law preparing to teach school, are earning little or nothing, and in fact the father furnishes part of their support. One handy vehicle available is the creation of a "family partnership."

The husband and wife can use their combined marital gift tax exemption and annual exclusions to transfer, over a period of years, a one-fourth interest in the business' manufacturing plant and equipment and other capital to each young man. The son and son-in-law, in turn, can contribute this interest as they receive it to a newly formed partnership with the father, in return for which, each will receive a 25% interest in the partnership. While a father cannot, simply by making gifts of half of the partnership's capital, arrange to have all or most of the partnership income and profits diverted to his son and son-in-law, they may each be given jobs with the new firm, draw a salary, and participate as 25% owners in the profits.

As long as provision is made for reasonable compensation for the father's continued services, and for his sharing in half the profits, the other two may share the remaining profits.[20] In businesses in which capital is a significant income-producing factor, it is immaterial that the contributions of the son and son-in-law to the partnership were obtained by means of gifts from the father.[21] The result, of course, is a substantial overall saving in income tax liabilities of the family, since all the growing business income previously taxed to the father at the highest tax rate, will now be split between him and other family members in much lower tax brackets.

Very much the same result can be accomplished by the formation of a "family corporation," with gifts of the stock to family members. The corporate form in fact provides an even more certain manner of dividing shares of a business and distributing them among the family. Though the use of a corporation will involve an additional income tax payable by the corporation, even this disadvantage can be avoided by the use of a so-called small-business corporation.[22]

Other Family Income Splitting Expedients

There are numerous variations of these family income splitting devices. For example, the father-proprietor of a flourishing business, whose sons or sons-in-law already have substantial incomes of their own, might reduce his own high tax bracket business income, and effect even greater overall family tax savings, by creating a partnership with trusts for his numerous grandchildren as limited partners. He can supply them with the necessary capital contributions to the partnership through a programmed series of gifts to the trusts, largely or entirely without the payment of any gift taxes. A substantial part of the partnership's business income will then be divided among the many trusts for the grandchildren, each of which will be in a relatively low income tax bracket. Further tax savings can be achieved by resorting to other gimmicks.[23]

It should be mentioned parenthetically, that one of the most effective income-splitting devices involves nothing more than acquiring a wife or a husband, since married couples automatically have the advantage of "splitting" their income if they choose to do so. Many authorities consider the tax bonanza of income splitting effected by marriage another inequity that undermines the progressive income tax rate structure.[24]

Widening the Loophole in 1969

Perhaps without intending to do so, Congress has recently made the use of income-splitting devices more inviting than ever. The Tax Reform Act of 1969 reduced the tax rates for single individuals and increased the size of the individual standard deduction. As a result, splitting a sizeable amount of income otherwise taxable to a parent and diverting it to a number of children will have the effect of reducing the combined family tax bill even more than before. Tax practitioners have already taken note of this and it can be anticipated there will be a new surge in the use of income-splitting devices.

12

Generation-Skipping and Other Means of Avoiding Estate Taxes

The federal tax on estates, like the federal income tax, has a progressive rate structure; it ranges from 3% on estates in excess of $60,000 to a maximum of 77% on those in excess of $10 million. One would expect, therefore, that estate taxes would absorb a much higher percentage of the assets of an affluent man with a fortune of $10 million than of a man with $500,000. Unfortunately the reverse is often true.

Under the estate tax rate schedule an individual worth $10 million, by no means an exceptionally large amount by current standards,[1] would be expected to be liable eventually for a tax of more than $6 million. In all likelihood the tax ultimately payable will be only a small fraction of that amount because of the many loopholes enabling wealthy families to minimize the impact of estate taxes on their fortunes.

Avoiding Estate Taxes through Trusts

The most popular method of minimizing or entirely avoiding estate taxes for three and sometimes four generations is often referred to as "generation skipping" through the use of trusts. Leading banking officials acknowledge that by placing family wealth in trusts instead of making outright gifts or bequests of property, well-to-do families can avoid the payment of estate taxes for more than one hundred years.[2]

The difference between a gift or bequest of property in trust and an outright gift or bequest may be illustrated as follows: T, Sr., desiring to make a gift to his son, may simply transfer to him the title to a piece of real estate, securities, or other property. T, Sr., no longer has any interest in the property, which is now owned by the son. Or instead of making a gift during his lifetime, T, Sr., may choose to bequeath similar property to his son by his will. In the former case the father has made an outright gift, in the latter an outright bequest.

But suppose that instead of transferring ownership outright, T, Sr., during his lifetime or by his will, gives the real estate, securities, or other property to a trustee who will hold it and pay the income over to the son as long as the son lives. On the son's death the trust will end, and the trustee will divide the property and distribute it among the son's children. Although the trustee is the legal owner, the beneficial interest in the property transferred belongs to the son and grandchildren. The son is called the life beneficiary, and the grandchildren, to whom the property will ultimately be distributed when the trust terminates, are called the remaindermen.

A gift made during one's lifetime, outright or in trust, may be subject to gift tax if the gift is large. But gift tax rates are much lower than estate tax rates; moreover, the generous lifetime exemption and the limitless annual gift tax exclusions will minimize the amount of gift tax liability or may eliminate it altogether.[3] Similarly, a bequest in a will may be outright or in trust, and a federal estate tax is payable if the estate is sufficiently large.[4]

By making a gift or a bequest of property in trust rather than outright, the T family will achieve a significant tax saving and avoid a second estate tax when the interest in the property passes from the son to the next generation. For example, suppose that T, Sr., gives or bequeaths securities or other property *outright* to his son, T, Jr., who enjoys the income during his lifetime and bequeaths the property or its equivalent to his own child. If the amount of the property involved is sufficiently large, a substantial estate tax will have to be paid by the estate of T, Jr. If, however, the original gift or bequest by T, Sr., to his son is *in trust,* with the latter receiving only the income during his lifetime, and with the remainder distributable on his death to his children, no additional estate tax will be due when T, Jr., dies. And this is true no matter what the value of the property was originally, or how greatly it may have appreciated during the lifetime of T, Jr.[5]

Of course trusts sometimes serve worthwhile purposes apart from their employment as tax-saving devices. For example, by leaving property in trust for an infant, or an adult child whom a father fears may dissipate the principal if it is left to him outright, the parent can protect a descendent from his own profligacy, or from the demands of creditors. Then, again, the use of a trust will often enable a parent to control more effectively the apportionment of income and principal among his descendents than if the property were left outright. However, the widespread popularity of trusts since the enactment of the estate tax law has been caused largely by their role in the reduction and avoidance of estate taxes.

Generation Skipping Almost ad Infinitum

A trust is not limited in its duration to the life of a single beneficiary as in the foregoing examples. There can be any number of beneficiaries, with the trust continuing on and on through the span of many lives. The only limitation is the Rule Against Perpetuities, which has been adopted in one way or another by the various states. It specifies that a trust, while it may continue throughout the lives of many persons, cannot continue longer than twenty-one years after the death of the last person named in the trust instrument who was alive when the trust was created.[6]

For example, John J, Sr., desiring to provide for the welfare of his son, his grandchild, his great grandchild, and even his great great grandchild, not yet born, may by his will create a trust which provides that the trustees are to pay the income first to his son John J, Jr., during the latter's lifetime, and thereafter to his grandson John J III as long as he lives. After John J III dies the income is to be paid to his great grandchild, John J IV; and on his death the trustees will continue to pay the income for twenty-one years to John J V, the great great grandchild. Only at the end of the twenty-one-year period will they distribute the property held in trust to John J V.

Under our laws an estate tax is incurred when the creator of the trust dies, but no estate tax is due thereafter as beneficial ownership passes from one generation to the other, not even when the trust finally terminates. Only when John J V, five generations removed from the creator of the trust, eventually dies, sixty or seventy years after the trust ends, will a second estate tax have to be paid. Thus one hundred and fifty years may pass without any estate tax being paid on a family's fortune. Moreover, by his will, John J V, may start the process all over again by creating trusts for his descendents which will exempt the family fortune from estate taxes for another one hundred to one hundred and fifty years.

Trust Beneficiaries' Powers Over Trust Property

It may be thought that by using the trust device, the successive generations of beneficiaries are seriously limited in their enjoyment of the trust property. On the contrary, under our liberal tax laws, the beneficiaries may enjoy all the trust income, act as co-trustees, and participate in the management and investment policy of the trust without risk of estate taxation. They may also be permitted to dip into the trust principal for their emergency needs, or even to support themselves in their accustomed standard of living. In fact for all practical purposes, the trust instrument can give the trustee discretion to hand over to the beneficiaries principal for almost every conceivable purpose—to refurnish a winter home in the Caribbean, to acquire an ocean-going yacht, or any other luxury.

And this is not all. For many years opinions differed as to whether a trust beneficiary should also be given the right to determine the persons who would enjoy the trust property after him, and the proportions in which they would participate without incurring an additional estate tax liability.[7] But in 1954 Congress gave further encouragement to estate tax avoidance by providing that, without causing the imposition of an additional estate tax, a trust beneficiary may receive and exercise a so-called special power of appointment, whereby he can determine the subsequent disposition of the trust property; the only substantial restriction is that he cannot direct its transfer to himself, his estate, or his own creditors.[8]

With such broad and virtually limitless powers of enjoyment and management of the trust property, and even of its ultimate disposition, to all intents and purposes the successive generations of trust beneficiaries may possess almost the same rights and privileges as if they had been given the property outright.[9] Yet, as long as the trust device, frequently embellished by powers of appointment, is employed, estate taxes may be completely avoided as the family property passes from one generation to another.[10]

It is small wonder that this tax immunity has been severely criticized by legal scholars, such as Professor Griswold of the Harvard Law School who wrote:

This discrimination, which in practice operates in favor of large estates, should be eliminated by imposing a tax on the death of those who have control of the property whether that control is called ownership or power.[11]

Avoiding Estate Taxes by Lifetime Gifts

When the estate tax law imposing a tax on transfers of property at death was passed in 1916, it was obvious that the tax could easily be avoided by giving away property during one's lifetime. Congress therefore supplemented the tax on estates with a tax on gifts. But since gifts are taxed at a rate that is only 75% of the estate tax rate,[12] a floodgate was opened permitting people to escape the more burdensome estate tax by transfers during their lifetime. In addition to the liberal lifetime and annual exemptions,[13] under the gift tax law one-half of all gifts made to one's wife are gift tax-free,[14] and gifts to children, with one's wife's consent, are treated as having been made one-half by the husband and one-half by the wife.[15]

The effect of these provisions is twofold. In the first place, because of the gift tax exemptions and exclusions, very substantial amounts can be given to any number of family members gift tax-free, especially where regular annual gift-making programs are followed. But even more important, the split treatment of gifts by a father to his children with his wife's consent (one-half being considered the gift of each spouse) effectively lowers the tax rate on gifts in excess of exemptions and exclusions. Splitting the gifts in half puts them in a lower bracket in the progressive gift tax scale. When gifts of millions of dollars are involved, gift taxes may be reduced by as much as a million dollars.

By dividing his gifts between gifts during his lifetime and transfers by will, a taxpayer can cause the family fortune to fall into a lower estate tax bracket, resulting in huge savings in estate taxes. For example, an individual with a $20 million fortune can give away $10 million by lifetime gifts taxable at the lower gift tax rate, and later leave another $10 million by his last will. If the entire $20 million had been transferred at death, the estate tax would have been approximately $6 million on the first $10 million, and $7,700,000 on the second $10 million, or a total of about $13,-700,000.[16] But by giving away half during his lifetime and leaving the balance by will, the gift tax will amount to approximately $4,500,000 and the estate tax to approximately $6,000,000, for a total of about $10,500,000, a saving of more than $3 million.

The Marital Deduction

The greatest estate tax benefit to wealthy people is to be survived by one's husband or wife. In 1948 Congress adopted the "Marital Deduction" provisions,[17] which in effect permit one-half of a person's estate to pass tax-free to one's spouse. If a man leaves one-half of his property to his wife and one-half to his children, the wife's share is not taxed in his estate, but on her death it will be taxed in her estate as though it had never been connected with her deceased husband's estate.

The significance of this theoretical split of the husband's property in two for tax purposes is that it places both the husband's and the wife's estate in lower tax brackets than otherwise would have been the case. As a result of the marital deduction an estate that would have otherwise been taxed in the 60% or 70% bracket may be taxed in the 30% or 40% bracket.[18]

Other Devices for Avoiding or Minimizing Estate Taxes

Life Insurance

As long as certain simple precautions are taken, if the ownership of a life insurance policy has been transferred more than three years before the death of the insured, the proceeds of the policy, payable to a wife, children, or other named beneficiaries, will not be included in or taxed as part of his estate, even though he himself has paid all the premiums on the insurance.[19]

This extraordinary loophole in the estate tax structure has been severely criticized;[20] it is based on the narrow legalistic technicality that since the ownership of the policy had been transferred prior to death, it cannot be part of the insured's estate. But this view completely ignores the practical economic realities of life insurance. Unlike the gift or transfer of a piece of real estate, securities, or other property, the transfer of an insurance policy is essentially testamentary in character, designed to take effect only on death. A man who takes out insurance on his life and continues to pay the premiums does so for the purpose of enriching the beneficiaries with the proceeds that become payable on his death.

Yet the escape hatch remains[21] and there is no limit on the amount of insurance that can be left tax-free in this manner. The policy can be for $1,000 worth of insurance, or for $10 million. The provisions of the Internal Revenue Code apply not only to conventional life insurance but to group insurance policies given by corporate employers to their executives and other employees as well.

Death Benefits from Corporate Pension and Profit-Sharing Plans

Frequently corporate executives are participants in company pension and profit-sharing plans that provide for the payment of substantial death benefits to members of the executive's family. But as long as such benefits are payable to someone other than the estate of the deceased, they pass to family members free of all estate tax liability.[22]

Transferring the Family Business Below Its True Worth

Another device for avoiding estate taxes involves the transfer to the next generation of interests in the family owned business.

For example, a taxpayer and his two sons own a family business conducted by a corporation which they control as stockholders. They enter into a stockholders' agreement which provides that in the event of the death of any stockholder the corporation will purchase the stock at a value substantially below its true worth. If at the time the agreement is made all the family members are in good health, so that it can be shown that the agreement was not made in contemplation of death, the arrangement will usually be upheld. In this way a family business can be passed on to children with a minimum of estate tax impact.[23]

Paying Estate Taxes in Advance

When a man dies his estate will pay the estate taxes with money that is itself subject to tax. If he leaves a $20 million estate that is liable for $6 million in estate taxes, the estate is valued for tax purposes at $20 million, even though $6 million will be subtracted from it and paid to the government. There can be a big saving in paying part of the estate tax in advance.

Here is the way it works: A wealthy man, obviously near death, is advised to make a substantial present gift to his children in much the same manner as he has already provided for them in his will. A gift tax will have to be paid, if the gift is sufficiently large, because it is an immediate transfer. But since the gift is obviously made because of his approaching death, the property will also be included in his estate and subject to estate tax.[24] Since the law does not require one to pay tax twice on the same transfer, the gift tax paid or payable may normally be credited against the estate tax due, and in addition is allowed as a deduction for estate tax purposes. In short, the amount of the gift tax paid escapes the estate tax.

For example, a man with a net taxable estate of $1 million makes a gift of $750,000 in contemplation of death. A gift tax of approximately $175,000 is paid or payable. When he dies, instead of leaving an estate of $1 million, he will be deemed to have left $825,000. The estate tax on it will be about $260,000, less the $175,000 gift tax paid, or about $85,000. The estate tax on $1 million would have been about $325,000. This gimmick saves approximately $65,000 in taxes.

Fortunes Multiply through Gifts and Trusts

The R Family

In 1968 James R possessed a fortune of about $20 million. He and his wife were both 67 years of age and had a son, James R, Jr., 46, a grandson, James R III, 25, and a great grandson, James R IV, who was two years old.

R, Sr., placed one-half of his $20 million with his wife's consent in trust for the lifetime of R, Jr., giving his son the right to appoint the income and principal to anyone but himself, his own estate, or his or his estate's creditors. Under the "split gift" provisions of the gift tax law, one-half of the $10 million in the trust was deemed to have been donated by R, Sr., and one-half by his wife. The split gifts fell into a lower gift tax bracket and the result was a combined gift tax of about $3,688,000. Had the gift been treated as being made solely by R, Sr., who actually provided the money, the tax would have been about $4,566,000. The wealth of R, Sr., reduced by the $10 million transferred to the trust and the $3,688,000 gift tax, amounted to approximately $6,312,000.

In 1971 R, Sr., passes away. In his will, however, he had taken full tax advantage of the marital deduction and left one-half of his remaining estate, or approximately $3,150,000, outright to his widow, and the other half, after the payment of estate taxes, to his widow in trust, with the income payable to her for life and the principal on her death to be added to the trust previously created for the son, R, Jr. Under the will of Mrs. R, Sr., who dies the following year, the $3,150,000 left to her outright by her husband is also contributed to her son's trust.

The combined estate taxes and administration expenses on the estates of R, Sr., and his wife will be approximately $2,900,000; the original family fortune of $20,000,000 will be reduced by this sum and by the gift tax of $3,688,000, leaving approximately $13,400,000 in trust for the benefit of the son, and generating a handsome income.[25]

The approximately $13½ million left in trust will probably increase substantially in value, even using a reasonably conservative rate of capital appreciation of 5% per year. At that rate the trust corpus will double every fourteen years; by 1986 it will be worth approximately $26,800,000.

R, Jr., exercises the power of appointment granted him under the trust and directs that after he dies the trust shall continue during the life of R III, and confers upon his son a power of appointment over the principal and income identical to the one which his father had given to him. In the year 2000, when R, Jr., dies at the age of 78, the trust principal will be worth about $53,600,000, and will yield an income more than sufficient to provide for the needs of R III and his family.

R III dies at the age of 71 in the year 2014, after having exercised his own power of appointment, as his father had done before him, over a trust fund now grown to approximately $107,000,000. He directed that the income of the trust be paid to his own son, R IV, and granted the latter a special power of appointment over the remainder. By the time R IV dies at the age of 76 in the year 2042, the corpus of the trust will be worth more than $428,-000,000.

At his death R IV leaves a son, R V, who is 50 years of age, and a grandson, R VI, 25. Since R IV is the last descendant who was alive at the time when the original trust was created, the trust can continue under the Rule Against Perpetuities for an additional twenty-one-year period only. By his will R IV exercises his power of appointment and directs that the trust shall continue with the income payable to his son, R V, or in the event of the latter's death, to his grandson, R VI, for an additional twenty-one years.

R V dies in the year 2056 at the age of 64, before the expiration of the twenty-one-year period, and thereupon his son, R VI, becomes the income beneficiary of the trust, now grown to some $857,000,000, for an additional seven years. In the year 2063, ninety-five years after the trust was originally established, the trust finally terminates and R VI receives outright the principal that had been held in trust all those years. However, there is still no additional estate tax to be paid. Not until R VI dies in the year 2098 at the age of 81, when the value of the family property, conservatively estimated, will have increased to more than $7 billion, will another estate tax be payable.

Thus on a fortune enjoyed by a man's son, grandson, great grandson, and great great grandson, and which grew to more than $7 billion, only about $6 million, somewhat under .1% of its ultimate value, was expended in estate and gift taxes over a period of 130 years. In the meantime the successive generations of the family were able to enjoy the more than ample income, dip into principal when necessary, designate the succeeding beneficiaries, and to all intents and purposes, enjoy all of the advantages of owning the property.

The W Family

Take, by way of contrast, the hypothetical case of the moderately successful Charles W, with a wife and three children, who has managed to accumulate property worth about $200,000. Such a fortune will normally not warrant establishing trusts since the income yield will be insufficient. Nor does W have sufficient wealth to make substantial gifts during his lifetime. He will wish to retain what he possesses for the support of his wife and family and to take care of personal and business emergencies, and will normally leave his entire estate to his wife for her support and emergency needs. Even with the benefit of the marital deduction, the estate taxes will be about $4800, leaving his widow with a net estate of approximately $195,000.

If W and his wife had been living on an income of $30,000 a year, it will probably be difficult for Mrs. W to reduce her expenses much below this amount and she will have to dip into capital. If her husband's estate produces an income of 5% a year, and if the capital appreciates at a rate of 5% annually, in the first year she will have to withdraw about $10,000, leaving $185,000 of the principal remaining. During the next three years, she will be obliged to continue to invade principal, each year to a greater extent, as the amount of capital is depleted. Four years after the death of her husband the principal will have shrunk to approximately $147,000.

At this point, if Mrs. W dies, her estate will be subject to a tax of approximately $14,000. There will be even less justification for the creation of income trusts for her children with the remaining $133,000. In the ordinary course, the $133,000 that she will leave to her children outright will be expended by them over the years in order to meet their normal everyday cost of living. Thus W's original assets of $200,000 will have been spent during his children's lives, with about $18,800, over 9%, being consumed by estate taxes. Compare this percentage with the .1% the R family paid in estate and gift taxes on its expanding fortune!

The Hearst Estate

William Randolph Hearst, Sr., the so-called Lord of San Simeon, left a fortune estimated at hundreds of millions of dollars. His fortune was placed in a family trust that will probably continue well into the twenty-first century. While a substantial estate tax was surely paid on his death in 1951, it is likely that no additional estate tax will be due on this enormous wealth as it continues to appreciate, at least until the year 2050, and probably later than that. As a recent article on the Hearst dynasty put it:

The trust terminates on the death of the last surviving son and/or grandchild who was alive at the time of the death of the first William

Randolph Hearst, which, with normal life expectancies, should get it past the year 2000. By that time the corporation should be worth—at a guess and barring cataclysms—quite a few billions of dollars. Enough, to say the least, to make it again one of the greatest American fortunes —perhaps the greatest.[26]

It seems fair to assume, therefore, that by the use of generation-skipping trusts and other tax-saving devices, great fortunes such as the Rockefeller, Mellon, Ford, and duPont holdings, in spite of the enormous amounts donated to charity and other worthy causes, are growing larger and larger, rather than shrinking in size.

Tax-Saving Devices Available Only to the Wealthy

While theoretically the use of substantial lifetime gifts to family members, trusts for future generations, transfers of insurance policies, and other expedients for avoiding estate and gift taxes are available to all taxpayers, Treasury Department surveys indicate that these devices are employed for the most part by the very well-to-do.[27] Most taxpayers, even those who are moderately well off, wish to keep up their present standard of living and cannot afford to make substantial gifts of property while alive. The possibility is always present that they may need it for their own use if their economic situation deteriorates. A man with a moderate estate who wishes to provide for his wife, children, or grandchildren will usu-aly give or leave his property to them outright rather than in trust, since trust beneficiaries depend basically on income, and unless the assets placed in trust are very large, the income will be insufficient to maintain the previous standard of living. Such taxpayers, too, will generally find it prudent to retain ownership and control over their insurance policies, which may have to be borrowed against for personal requirements or to finance the needs of a business.

On the other hand, the affluent taxpayer worth several millions can afford to make substantial gifts of securities, real estate, or stock in his business corporation to his children or grandchildren, taking full advantage of gift tax exclusions and of the more favor-able gift tax rates, without seriously diminishing his own standard of living or jeopardizing that of his widow. He can create trusts for his family and descendants with large assets that he can comfortably spare, which will yield more income than his heirs will ever need. The trusts will continue from one generation to the next, insulating them from the impact of estate and gift taxes, or at the very least substantially diminishing such impact. Life insurance policies in large amounts can be safely transferred to family members without impairing his financial or credit position. Treasury Department surveys amply support these conclusions.

Are the Purposes of Estate and Gift Taxes Being Realized?

Two purposes have been most frequently claimed to be the objectives of estate and gift taxes. One is to discourage the growth of economic dynasties through the transfer of expanding family wealth from generation to generation. The second is to raise tax revenue for the government. While leading tax authorities have for years differed as to which purpose is the more important, there seems to be general agreement that neither is being effectively accomplished under the present tax structure.[28]

That estate and gift taxes fail to prevent the creation of economic dynasties by the passing of family fortunes from one generation to another is obvious. As to their revenue raising accomplishments, they now produce approximately $3 billion a year, approximately 2% of total federal tax receipts.[29] Placed in proper prospective, it is totally inadequate. In 1955 Louis Eisenstein advised a Joint Committee of the House and Senate that:

While this tax [federal estate and gift tax] helps to support many lawyers it does relatively little to support the government.[30]

The billions of dollars of such taxes that have been avoided by wealthy taxpayers for so many years must be raised from other taxpayers far less able to afford them.

The desire to minimize or entirely escape estate taxes frequently has adverse sociological side-effects. Taxpayers making dispositions of their property are not motivated solely by love and affection and the desire to provide for family needs, but often simply to save taxes. Fortunes are tied up in elaborate trusts, by fathers who, but for the tax savings, would have preferred to leave their property to their children outright. Conversely, large lifetime gifts are made, often ill-advisedly, for the same purpose. A wealthy father, widowed, and advanced in years, enjoying his country residence with its comforts and pleasant memories, is persuaded to give it away to a son or daughter, simply because it will mean substantial savings in estate taxes. Not infrequently, the transfer having been made, he finds himself, to his regret, beholden to a child who is now in possession, and who permits him to visit what was once his own property only when it suits the child's convenience, or perhaps not at all.

Proposals for Reform

Leading tax experts agree that the revision of our entire federal estate and gift tax structure is long overdue.[31] A stubborn adherence to narrow legal technicalities instead of the recognition of economic realities has caused this country to lag far behind others in this area. In England, for example, where the trust concept originated, Parliament decided during the reign of Queen Victoria that it was time to put a stop to the avoidance of estate taxes through the creation of generation-skipping trusts, and imposed an inheritance tax whenever a person succeeded to the beneficial ownership of property held in trust.[32]

The circumvention of estate taxes through use of multiple generation-skipping trusts, powers of appointment, and lifetime gifts are major loopholes that must be closed. The discrepancy in rates between gift and estate taxes, as well as the overly generous gift tax exemptions and exclusions that encourage minimization or avoidance of the estate tax impact, must be dealt with by reducing or eliminating the differential. The closing of minor loopholes, such as the immunity from estate taxation of life insurance and pension and profit-sharing death benefits, should follow as a matter of course.

A more comprehensive approach for eliminating present loopholes in the form of a unified estate and gift tax law is favored by many of these authorities.[33] One such proposal [34] suggests a single integrated tax covering all transfers from generation to generation while permitting tax-free transfers between husbands and wives. The differential in rates between estate and gift tax would be reduced or eliminated entirely, and the rates themselves would be reduced. The net effect would be that eventually the entire estate of a wealthy man would be subjected to taxation at a rate appropriate to its overall size. All transfers for the benefit of the next generation would be taken into consideration to prevent individual transfers made at separate times from being taxed in lower brackets or not taxed at all.[35]

This proposal was incorporated in essence in the tax reform package submitted to Congress by the Treasury officials of the departing Johnson administration in February 1969. It did not become part of the Tax Reform Act of 1969, but Chairman Mills said he would take it up at a later time. The Treasury suggested combining the separate estate and gift taxes into a single uniform transfer tax, with one $60,000 exemption, which would be applicable to both lifetime and death transfers. The rate schedule would be about 20% less than present estate tax rates and would be revised to make it more evenly "progressive" as the size of the estate increased. Transfers between husbands and wives, whether by lifetime gift or at death, would be tax-free, and tax avoidance by means of "generation-skipping" trusts would be prevented by taxing, under a substitute rate schedule, transfers of wealth by the creation of trusts when such enjoyment passes from one generation to the next.

Whether reform is to be accomplished by retaining the present tax structure after eliminating the loopholes, or by the enactment of a single integrated gift and estate tax along the above lines, there can be little doubt that a thorough review and revision of the present estate and gift tax law can no longer be postponed.

13

Tax Abuses of Corporate Pension Plans and Similar Arrangements

Pension, profit-sharing, and stock bonus plans established by corporations are intended to provide retirement income and other benefits for employees and their families as a supplement to Social Security payments. Accordingly the federal government has granted advantageous tax treatment to such plans. Employers are permitted to deduct contributions for tax purposes; the income on these funds is free of tax; and lump sum distributions to covered employees were formerly taxed as capital gains.[1] (Although not still so highly favored, they are generally taxed at reduced rates). Furthermore the creation of such plans and the extent of the coverage and benefits they provide are entirely within the discretion of the corporate employer,[2] a situation that opens up a great potential for favoritism, inadequate coverage, and tax avoidance.

Pension Plans for the Benefit of Insiders

Frequently a company pension plan, though ostensibly established for the benefit of its employees, is really a one-sided arrangement conferring most, and sometimes practically all the benefits on a few officer-stockholders who control its affairs.

Take the case of a fictitious soft goods firm, B Apparel Corporation, which sells ladies' garments manufactured in the South by its affiliate, B Manufacturing Corporation. Both companies are owned and controlled by two brothers. The apparel corporation has a sales office in New York City where the brothers, three stenographers, two bookkeepers, and a telephone operator-receptionist are employed. B Manufacturing Corporation runs a large plant in South Carolina and employs 1500 persons. The employees in the New York office and at the southern factory are paid relatively modest wages and are covered by Blue Cross-Blue Shield and by state workmen's compensation and disability insurance. The brothers, both in their 50s, draw salaries of $75,000 a year from the New York corporation, but to their distress, they find that after taking care of their own and their families' substantial living expenses and taxes, it is virtually impossible for them to put aside any money for retirement or outside investments.

A non-contributory corporate pension plan provides just the right solution for their problem. The employees do not contribute to the plan; the entire expense is borne by the corporation. The plan does not have to include their 1500 employees at the southern plant, but can be set up for the apparel corporation and cover just the two brothers and their six New York office employees. Furthermore, no benefits will have to be paid until retirement, and if the office workers should leave before retirement age they will not have to be paid any benefits at all.

Accordingly a B Apparel Corporation non-contributory pension plan is adopted. The annual contributions made to the plan by the corporation, all of which are tax deductible, are determined by an actuary engaged by the B brothers for this purpose. He bases his computations on the number of employees to be covered, their salaries, and the length of service; and makes certain assumptions as to how long the average employee will live, how many are likely to leave the corporation before they reach retirement age, and how much the fund is likely to earn on its investments. The Internal Revenue Service generally approves of such plans on the basis of determinations and assumptions of this sort, even though the plans are heavily weighted in favor of the owners and are sometimes not completely sound financially.[3]

The B Apparel Corporation plan will provide for a contribution of $100,000 a year by the corporation to a pension trust.[4] Because of the age of the B brothers, their length of service (each having worked for the corporation for thirty-five years), and their high salaries, it is perfectly permissible for them to derive as much as 90% of the plan's benefits. The other six employees, because of their youth, relatively small salaries, shorter period of service, and the likelihood of their leaving their jobs before retirement, will be provided with only minor benefits. If an employee dies before retirement a small part of his accumulated benefits will be paid to his family. But if he is fired, changes his job, or stops working altogether before he reaches retirement age, he will receive nothing, since there is no requirement under the law that benefits that have accrued to employees vest, or belong irrevocably to them, after any period of time.

The plan may also provide that the company take out life insurance policies for the benefit of the employees, including the B brothers, with the pension fund paying the premiums. Again, since the two brothers receive the highest salaries and occupy the most important positions with the company, most of the insurance coverage will be for their benefit.

Assuming that the pension fund earns a little more than 5% on its investments and that the $100,000 annual contribution is made at the beginning of each year, after ten years the plan will have accumulated some $350,000 in income and $1 million in contributions, or a total of $1,350,000.

By that time the B brothers will have reached retirement age since they are the oldest; retiring first, they will have first call on all monies accumulated in the pension fund. The other six employees will not have reached retirement age or will have left for other jobs. Accordingly the B brothers can use $1,200,000 of the pension fund to pay themselves $600,000 each, the lump sum payment provided for them under the pension plan upon their retirement, and sell the business to new owners, who may terminate the pension plan at that point. Although the balance of about $150,000 left in the fund will theoretically take care of the remaining employees, some of them may never receive any retirement benefits. Just because a pension plan has been adopted, there is no guarantee that the employees covered will receive pensions.

Because of overly optimistic and unsound assumptions by the actuary, the amounts contributed under the pension plan may be insufficient to ensure payment of the benefits envisaged for those supposedly covered. The plan may have only dubious and ephemeral benefits for the rest of the employees but it has distinct monetary and tax advantages for the B brothers as owners and chief executives. In the first place, all expenses of the plan, including the $100,000 annual contribution, are deductible by the corporation on its income tax returns. Thus in effect the federal and state governments will be paying about 55% of these costs, while the B brothers, as owners of the business, will be paying only 45%, or $450,000.[5]

Furthermore, the brothers can obtain unwarranted tax benefits for their company by juggling these deductions to their own advantage. When their corporation has very profitable years their actuary can modify his assumptions so as to call for greater contributions to the plan, thereby increasing the amount of the deduction and saving taxes on otherwise taxable corporate income. In lean years the actuary may make still other assumptions justifying smaller contributions to the pension fund or terminating them altogether, thereby jeopardizing the employees' pension benefits and weakening the financial soundness of the pension fund.

The earnings of the pension fund are tax-free to the corporation;[6] and the brothers pay no income tax on the contributions made by the corporation each year for their own benefit, nor any tax on the accrual of earnings of the pension fund from its investments, most of which accumulate for their benefit.[7] Should they die before retirement age, their benefits, payable to their wives or other family members, are exempt from estate taxes.[8] While the other employees are theoretically entitled to the same tax advantages, from a practical standpoint, these tax benefits will make little if any difference in their case.

Moreover, until recently, under both pension and profit-sharing plans, lump sum retirement benefits were taxable at capital gains rather than at ordinary income rates. Accordingly, the $600,000 lump sum benefit that the B brothers had provided for themselves, and which was payable to them on retirement after ten years, was taxable to them at the more favorable capital gains rates,[9] and they were obliged to pay only $150,000 in federal income taxes. Thus at a cost to their company of $450,000 over ten years,[10] the B brothers netted combined retirement benefits totaling $900,000 after taxes.

Group Term Life Insurance and Other Benefits

In addition to a pension plan, the B brothers can arrange to have the corporation provide group term life insurance, major medical expense insurance, and a health plan for themselves and the other employees. Under each of these plans, because of their higher salaries and executive positions, the brothers again will be assured most of the benefits. The group term life insurance policy, for example, taken out by the corporation, can cover each of them with $50,000 worth of insurance while allocating only $2000-$5000 worth for the other employees.

All these benefits are tax-free to the B brothers and other employees, including the $50,000 worth of life insurance coverage, since the premiums paid each year by the corporation to maintain the policy for their benefit is, under another liberal provision of the tax law, not considered income to them.[11] Furthermore, by merely filling out a simple assignment form, they can make the insurance proceeds payable on their death to their wives or children exempt from estate taxes as well.[12]

Alternate Company Plans

Profit-sharing plans and qualified stock bonus plans are other arrangements for providing employees with compensation on retirement or termination of employment. However, from the point of view of the B brothers and employers similarly motivated, these plans are less attractive than pension plans.

Under a typical profit-sharing plan the employer sets aside a part of the profits of the business each year and contributes this sum to a trust for the benefit of the employees.[13] The amount of the benefit each employee is entitled to is usually based on the size of his annual salary. Again the lion's share of the profits will be set aside for the owners of the business. However the Internal Revenue Service does not permit profit-sharing plans to be so heavily weighted in favor of the owners and against the other employees. Employees under profit-sharing plans are assured of receiving some benefits, since the account of each employee is credited with certain amounts each year, and the employer is required to pay a substantial part of the accrued benefits to a worker who leaves before retirement age.

Attempts to Correct Abuses

In 1963, in connection with other reforms suggested in the capital gains area, the Treasury Department proposed to Congress that lump sum distributions from pension, profit-sharing, and stock bonus plans, such as the $600,000 distribution to each of the two B brothers, be treated as ordinary compensation taxable at ordinary income tax rates rather than as capital gains.[14] The Treasury emphasized that lump sum payments, often amounting to huge sums in the case of highly paid executives,[15] were essentially nothing more than deferred compensation for services that should be taxed the same way as other compensation; and that treating them as capital gains was in effect a discrimination against other taxpayers who were obliged to pay taxes on their salaries and wages at ordinary rates. The participants in corporate pension and profit-sharing plans, it was claimed, received enough of an advantage by virtue of the fact that any tax on the contributions made by employers for their benefit, as well as on the accrued earnings of such contributions, was deferred. When eventually the benefits were paid out to them in lump sums, they should pay taxes on them on an ordinary income basis.

At the same time the Treasury advocated the elimination of the special tax advantage received by highly paid executives through tax-free group term life insurance taken out for their benefit. The practice, according to Treasury data, had produced widespread abuse, with some corporations providing their top executives with "jumbo" insurance coverage of almost $1 million, all of it income tax-free, with the proceeds on their death passing to their family beneficiaries free of estate tax.[16] The Treasury emphasized that executives and other employees covered by such policies were in reality receiving a tax-free income each year to the extent of the value of this insurance coverage.[17]

Except for an amendment in 1963, which limited to $50,000 the amount of tax-free life insurance which an employer could provide under group life insurance plans, Congress declined to accept these proposed reforms. Finally in the Tax Reform Act of 1969, Congress provided that that part of lump sum distributions from pension and profit-sharing plans representing contributions made by the employer would be taxed at ordinary income rates as though received over a seven-year period, and not as capital gains.

The Need for Pension Plan Reform

For a long time economists, representatives of the Treasury Department, and members of Congress have had serious doubts as to whether pension plan legislation, the administration of such plans by employers, and supervision by the Treasury Department provided adequate safeguards.

Critics have focused their concern primarily on two areas not adequately covered by legislation or by Internal Revenue regulations and rulings. First, the law does not require that benefits accruing to employees of non-contributory pension plans vest in the employees so that some pay-out of benefits must be made to an employee even though he changes his job or otherwise terminates his service with the employer before retirement age. Secondly, economists and other experts question whether the plans now in operation are financially sound. Do the plans provide assurance that the pension fund will have sufficient monies on hand to pay the pensions or other retirement benefits to covered employees when they retire should the employer encounter financial difficulties or go out of business altogether? As the number of pension plans and the employees covered by them have proliferated, this concern has steadily mounted. In this connection Senator Russell Long, Chairman of the Senate Finance Committee, stated:

Pension trust funds hold millions of dollars of assets which makes them significant factors in the nation's economy. In this area, as with any large concentration of wealth, we must see that any abuses or excesses are curbed. The most serious matters concern the problem of vesting, that is, the fixing of the right of an employee to his pension even if he changes jobs, and the problem of financial security, that is, the assurance to the employee that the money will be in the pension fund when the time comes for him to collect his pension, even if the employing company folds or the employee loses his job through no fault of his own.[18]

Worst of all is the fact that the law permits pension plans to be weighted in favor of employer-stockholders and other insiders. Coupled with the obvious income and estate tax advantages that such plans make possible, it only serves to encourage the establishment of non-contributory pension plans that are neither fair nor financially sound. As early as 1942 the House Ways and Means Committee recognized the dangers implicit in the operation and administration of corporate pension plans, and issued a report in connection with proposed pension plan legislation, which stated in part:

This provision [permitting corporate employers to take as income tax deductions amounts set aside in a pension trust for employees' pensions or other retirement benefits] has been considerably abused by the use of discriminatory plans which either cover only a small percentage of the employees or else favor the higher paid or stockholding employees as against the lower-paid or non-stockholding employees. Under the present law, it is contended the officers of a corporation may set up pension plans for themselves and make no provision for the other employees. Such actions are not in keeping with the purpose of this provision.[19]

At that time Randolph Paul, on behalf of the Treasury, urged Congress to enact specific safeguards to insure early vesting of employee benefits, and to limit to specified maxima the size of pensions that could be paid to favored executives and others.[20] However, Congress failed to adopt this eminently sound advice. As a result the pertinent provisions of the Revenue Act of 1942,[21] in very general and vague language, merely purported to prohibit pension plans that discriminated in favor of officers, stockholders, and supervisory and other highly paid employees. This woefully inadequate legislation failed to insure fairer and more soundly based pension plans or to close the tax loopholes favoring highly paid corporate insiders.

Proper safeguards were incorporated in the legislation authorizing pension plans for professionals, self-employed businessmen, and others,[22] as distinguished from corporate employees. Under the legislation permitting such plans, only a reasonable amount may be set aside each year toward retirement. All employees who have worked a reasonable length of time must be covered, and after they have worked for a short period their pension rights must become vested, so that if they should leave the employer, the funds accrued for their benefit are not used to the advantage of the owner, but are paid to the employees. Finally, when pension benefits are distributed upon retirement in a lump sum, instead of such payment receiving the preferential capital gains treatment, it is taxed at ordinary income tax rates subject to certain appropriate averaging provisions.

However, the vague and inadequate laws applicable to corporate pension plans, including the tax loopholes permitted by them, still remain uncorrected. Only recently has the adequacy of corporate pension plan legislation received renewed attention. A special report of a presidential committee on corporate retirement plans has been submitted to Congress, but it has yet to be acted upon.[23] Among other things the report deals with the need for vesting requirements and the financial security of corporate pension plans.

At present there is no requirement for any vesting with respect to non-contributory pension plans.[24] It should be mandatory in any pension plan that a certain minimum amount of an employee's accrued benefits irrevocably vest, so that they are not lost when the employee leaves his employment. Perhaps it should be required that at least 10% of an employee's benefits should become irrevocably vested for each year of employment, as is presently required in the case of profit-sharing plans.

All pension plans should have to be properly funded and financially sound, so that employees supposedly covered by them are assured of receiving the benefits promised when they retire. Far too much discretion and latitude is allowed under present law to corporate employers and their actuaries in setting up pension plans and in the assumptions, calculations, and actuarial criteria on which their operation is based. Frequently insufficient funds are set aside to take care of future retirements and demands upon the fund in twenty or thirty years when younger employees will retire. Under the present law, employers are permitted, by manipulation of actuarial assumptions, to vary the amount of contributions to the plan from year to year to suit their own tax advantage.

Finally, the present tax loopholes, so costly to the Treasury [25]— the freedom from income tax of as much as $50,000 worth of group life insurance coverage, and the exemption from estate tax of the proceeds of such life insurance and lump sum pension payments— should be eliminated.[26]

14

Loopholes That Are Tailor-Made—The Special Bill

A cynical commentator on the American tax system observed that:

> Our taxes reflect a continuing struggle among contending interests for the privilege of paying the least; [and] a changing product of earnest efforts to have others pay them.[1]

That our tax laws provide so many escape routes benefiting upper-income taxpayers and other favored groups is bad enough. But worse still, Congress frequently goes so far as to single out individual taxpayers for tax relief in the form of special or private bills.

In the case of most tax benefits that favor certain groups of taxpayers, such as those flowing from the ownership of tax-exempt municipal bonds, oil and gas properties, executive stock options, and other property accorded privileged treatment, the public, although ignorant of the details, has some idea that these preferences exist. But when a Congressional committee quietly, even surreptitiously, agrees to confer on individual taxpayers special favors in the form of private tax bills at the urging of some influential legislator or lobbyist, the public is completely in the dark. Such a bill often takes the form of an amendment to a tax law, and ostensibly covers all taxpayers, but is actually tailored to the situation and requirements of a particular individual without naming him. Probably no one knows how many pieces of legislation of this kind have been enacted in the last thirty years on the initiative of some congressman or senator eager to provide special benefits or relief for an influential constituent. Surely they number in the hundreds, if not in the thousands.

Many of these special enactments involve individuals of relatively humble means or small business organizations that have suffered some hardship, or otherwise find themselves in a predicament because of ignorance or lack of knowledge of some legal technicality. In such cases the names of the beneficiaries and the reasons for the tax relief afforded them are usually set forth in the bill. On the other hand, many wealthier and more influential taxpayers are relieved of substantial taxes and penalties imposed on them as the result of neglect, mistakes by their lawyers, or faulty tax planning, by custom-made bills masquerading as provisions applicable to the general public. But even when the beneficiaries are the victims of unfortunate circumstances and merit sympathy, the fact is that there are thousands of other taxpayers who find themselves in the same situation, and it is only those with the necessary Congressional connections who receive relief.

Probably the most notorious of these special bills is the so-called Mayer Amendment, which, it has generally been assumed, was enacted in 1951 for the benefit of Louis B. Mayer and another executive of Loew's Incorporated, a major motion picture company. It saved Mayer about $2 million in income taxes.[2] Mayer, who was in charge of the Metro-Goldwyn-Mayer studio, had a contract with Loew's Incorporated that provided that he receive a percentage of the net proceeds of every picture made from 1924 until he left the company. On retiring in 1951, Mayer surrendered his rights under his contract in return for a $2¾ million payment. Under the existing tax law payments made to an employee on retirement were treated as ordinary income. Since Mayer's income placed him in a tax bracket of approximately 90%, he was faced with the prospect of paying a huge tax on this money. Fortunately for Mayer he had access to persons in Washington who succeeded in inducing one of the tax-writing committees to slip through a provision [3] that the $2¾ million would be treated as a capital gain with a maximum tax of 25%.

Although couched in general language as an act relating to the "Taxability to Employee of Termination Payments," the enactment actually covered the situation of no one but Mayer and his fellow executive. Its application was specifically limited to a person who had been employed for over twenty years, and who possessed an employment contract, in effect for at least twelve years, which gave him the right to receive a percentage of the future profits or receipts of his employer for life or for a period of at least five years after termination of his employment. These were conditions that obviously no one but Mayer and his associate would ever be able to meet. No other person taxable at a very high rate—whether a movie director, actor, writer, singer, or professional athlete—could possibly take advantage of the provision. When the matter came before the Senate Senator Humphrey opposed it, but to no avail. He pointed out that the amendment could apply to only one specially favored taxpayer:

> I believe this is a patently discriminatory and unjustifiable provision. . . . How many persons can possibly benefit from this provision? How many can there be who today fit its particular limitations? I know of none, but there must be at least one, or [the representative of the U. S. Chamber of Commerce] would not have suggested it. I am wondering if the Committee would tell me how many taxpayers would be affected by this provision.[4]

Two articles in the Harvard Law Review [5] and Philip M. Stern's book on tax loopholes [6] review the whole unbelievably sordid spectacle of special bills enacted for the benefit of influential taxpayers during the years following World War II. Through it all runs the recurrent theme of Congressional influence obtained through campaign contributions and other favors, the tireless activities of lobbyists, the inordinate power of members of the tax-writing committees of Congress, and the time-honored practice of reciprocal back-scratching. They cite the following examples from among the many pieces of legislation made to order for privileged taxpayers: a bill rescuing a personal holding company from having to pay substantial taxes on its net income which it had been unable to distribute during World War II; a special enactment permitting a commission business in the South, operated as a partnership, to be taxed more favorably as a corporation; a special bill making deductible, as business expenses, payments made by certain coal companies to the pension fund of a labor union, which would not have been tax deductible under applicable law; special provisions granting relief from the impact of the excess profit tax to a television manufacturer, a paper company, and a newspaper publisher; a special bill for the relief of Dupont stockholders exempting them from paying capital gains taxes on billions of dollars worth of General Motors stock distributed by the Dupont company to its stockholders under an anti-trust decree; and a special bill, enacted in 1956 and made retroactive to 1954, which was designed to save the estate of Mrs. Gerard Swope some $4 million in estate taxes. Mrs. Swope, in leaving her husband with a power to appoint her estate either to her children or to charity, had been guilty of faulty estate planning. But the special bill in effect converted the power of appointment to one for charity, thereby enabling the estate to obtain the charitable deduction for which it had not qualified.

Perhaps the best known instance of special relief for a single taxpayer after World War II was the case of the then General of the Army Eisenhower. After selling all the rights to his memoirs for a lump sum payment of $635,000, he was confronted with the unpleasant prospect of having to pay most of it to the government in income taxes. A special Treasury ruling, applicable only to the general and to no other writer, composer, or artist in similar circumstances, averted this result by conferring the benefit of the much lower capital gains treatment to Eisenhower's particular situation.[7]

The proclivity for enacting special bills for the relief of individual taxpayers with powerful friends in Congress continues unabated, and is being pursued today as vigorously as ever. In 1967 a news item disclosed that the Senate-House conferees had agreed on a bill designed to provide tax relief to the stockholders of Financial General Corporation of Washington, D.C. The committee generously tacked on a "rider" that gave a $20 million tax rebate to the American Motors Corporation by permitting that company to carry back net operating losses for five years instead of the usual three, and by amending the law in other ways for its special benefit.[8] Harvey Aluminum Company, another of the country's industrial giants with potent political connections in both parties, also appears to have been the beneficiary of a "rider." In the words of Republican Senator John Williams, it was "tailored" to give it a "$2 million windfall"; the Treasury itself acknowledged the bill would affect no other concern but Harvey Aluminum.[9]

While many special bills submitted by individual legislators are turned down by the Congressional committees to which they are referred for approval, it would seem that if the particular taxpayers or their Washington connections carry sufficient weight they manage to be approved. Obtaining the nod from a member of the House Ways and Means Committee or of the Senate Finance Committee is particularly helpful. As one Senator, a member of the Senate Finance Committee, is reputed to have remarked:

What's the good of being on this Committee if you can't get through a little old amendment now and then? [10]

Even under the Tax Reform Act of 1969, as Senator Kennedy pointed out, a host of taxpayers were singled out for favored treatment. These included Mobil Oil Corporation, Uniroyal, Inc., Lockheed Aircraft Corp., Litton Industries, Transamerica Corp., the MacDonald-Douglas Corp., The Morris and Gwendolyn Cafritz Foundation, half a dozen other private foundations, and nineteen oil pipeline companies.[11] Although the beneficiaries of these special provisions were not always named, most congressmen knew who they were. One provision was hand-tailored to benefit television station WWL, the CBS affiliate in New Orleans, which Loyola University has operated profitably for years. Under the new law, religious organizations are subject for the first time to taxation on income from business that is unrelated to their religious activities.

An exception that only station WWL can satisfy was written into the law at the suggestion of Senator Long of Louisiana. Curiously enough, the draftsmen of the law wrote the exception in such a way that the initial letters of the three necessary qualifications are the station's call letters. The exception reads:

Except . . . in the case of a trade or business . . .
    (A) Which consists of . . .
    (B) Which is carried on by . . .
    (C) Less than 10% of net income. . . .[12]

Stanley S. Surrey, a leading tax authority and assistant secretary of the treasury in the Johnson administration, has suggested that all retroactive tax proposals limited in application to a single taxpayer or to a small group should be presented openly to the House and Senate Judiciary Committees as private relief bills. The two committees should devise rigorous standards and procedures for dealing with them. Every private bill should identify the beneficiary by name and specify the amount of tax benefits involved. Relief should be confined to situations presenting a general problem affecting the taxpaying public as a whole, and denied where only a particular individual is affected, unless the equities for individual relief are overwhelming. In this way, instead of special relief being handed out liberally to taxpayers with powerful political connections and influence, without anyone being the wiser, there would be full publicity and public understanding.[13]

It has been said that the American system of taxation depends for its effectiveness on each individual honestly assessing himself for the taxes he owes.[14] Unless the public feels that the law is being applied impartially and uniformly to all taxpayers, this system of voluntary self-assessment is eventually bound to break down.

15

Tax Windfalls in Real Estate

Tax Advantages Prior to the Tax Reform Act of 1969

The tax avoidance field day that investors in real estate have been enjoying for years [1] will not be quite as exhilarating in the future because of certain limitations contained in the Tax Reform Act of 1969. Until these reforms were enacted investors in any kind of real estate, business or residential, could use excessive allowances for depreciation to convert what would otherwise be ordinary income into capital gains. The key to these tax windfalls lay in the kind of depreciation deductions that were allowed until recently. [2]

The Theory of the Deduction for Depreciation

The cost of an income-producing property, such as a building, machinery, or equipment that wears out or becomes obsolete over a period of years, is usually spread over its useful life by means of depreciation allowances. Each year the allowance is deducted from the property's taxable income to compensate the owner for the decrease in the value of the property. This allowance is only fair, since otherwise a property owner would be paying a tax on the property's income without being compensated for the fact that his investment is gradually becoming less valuable. The theory is that the successive yearly deductions for the property's depreciation, when added up, will equal the property's original cost if it has become worthless, or its original cost less salvage value if it still has some worth. The owner is then able to replace the worn out asset if he chooses, or offset his loss if he disposes of it for less than its original cost.

The amount of depreciation that can be deducted for tax purposes each year depends on the property's estimated useful life. A piece of machinery costing $80,000 may be worthless or obsolete in eight years. Accordingly the owner may deduct $10,000 of depreciation each year, so that at the end of eight years he will have recovered the machinery's cost and be able to replace it. An apartment or office building costing $1 million, apart from the land on which it is built,[3] may have an estimated life of fifty years, so that the owner may deduct $20,000 a year for its depreciation.

To the great advantage of investors in real estate and other depreciable property, depreciation is not limited to the owner's cash investment in the property, but is allowed on the building's total cost, including all amounts borrowed to finance the purchase. Since in most large real estate transactions the mortgage loans from banks or other financial institutions amount to as much as 75% or 80% of the purchase price, the investor gets the benefit of a depreciation allowance applied to all the borrowed funds.

It is important to keep in mind that the depreciation deduction is merely a "paper" or bookkeeping item available to the owner for tax purposes. The amounts he deducts for depreciation are not paid out like cash expenditures for wages, repairs, maintenance, and other operating expenses. If in fact the deductions he is permitted to take exceed the property's real diminishment in value, he receives the benefit of tax deductions for expenses that were never really incurred.

Accelerated Depreciation

The examples previously mentioned illustrate what is known as "straight-line" depreciation; that is, the cost of the machinery or

of the building is depreciated *evenly* over the period of its estimated useful life, with the same amount deducted each year—
$10,000 for the machinery and $20,000 for the building. However, until recently the tax law permitted real estate to be
depreciated or "written-off" more rapidly by a number of accelerated depreciation methods. One such method, the double-declining-
balance method, was allowed for new buildings. It permitted the
owner to deduct twice the *percentage* of normal or straight-line
depreciation each year from the remaining balance. The result
was that twice the *amount* of straight-line depreciation was deducted the first year, but declining amounts were deducted in succeeding years.

In the case of the new office or apartment building that cost
$1 million and was estimated to last fifty years, normal deprecia-
tion would be 2%, or $20,000 per year. Under the double-
declining-balance method the owner could deduct 4%, or $40,000,
for depreciation the first year. In the second year he could deduct
4% of the remaining balance, or $38,400 (4% of $960,000); and
$36,864 in the third year (4% of $921,600). At the end of the
fifty-year period these deductions would total $1 million, just as
the straight-line deductions would. The double-declining-balance
and other rapid depreciation methods simply permitted the largest
deductions to be concentrated in the earlier years; they were offset
by very small amounts near the end of the life of the asset. It was
this "bunching" of depreciation deductions at the beginning of an
asset's life that provided the opportunity for unwarranted tax
avoidance.

Double-Barreled Tax Advantages

PURCHASE OF A $2,100,000 PROPERTY WITH $525,000 CASH

Assume that N, a fictitious taxpayer whose annual income placed
him in a 60% income tax bracket, decided to erect or purchase a
new apartment building in 1955 for $2,100,000. He invested
$525,000 cash and obtained a mortgage of $1,575,000 for the
remaining 75% of the cost. The mortgage was to be amortized

over thirty-five years, and carried 5½% interest. The land was valued at $100,000 and the building at $2 million.

If N adopted fifty years as the building's useful life (with which the Internal Revenue was unlikely to disagree), using the straight-line method he could depreciate the building's cost evenly over the period, by deducting $40,000 (2% of $2 million) from income each year. It is more likely, however, that N would have taken advantage of the tax law's exceedingly liberal depreciation rules and used the more favored double-declining-balance method, which allowed him to deduct twice as much depreciation the first year ($80,000 instead of $40,000) and ever-decreasing amounts in succeeding years.

RESULTS AFTER THE FIRST YEAR

Assume that the apartment building produced a net income, after operating expenses, of $165,000. At the end of the first year, the results of N's investment would have been as follows:

Gross income (rents)	$300,000	
Less operating expenses	135,000	
Net income from operations		$165,000
Interest on mortgage (5½%)		86,625
Net income before depreciation		$ 78,375
Deduction for depreciation		80,000
Net tax loss		($ 1,625)
Amortization payments on mortgage		$ 14,860

After using part of his $78,375 cash flow for the payment on the mortgage debt, N still had $63,515 ($78,375 − $14,860) tax-free cash in his pocket. As a final bonanza, he had a $1,625 tax loss, which he could use to eliminate taxes on $1,625 of income from stocks, bonds, or other investments he held and which would otherwise have been taxable to him at a 60% tax rate. He would have already received a return of more than 12% ($63,515 ÷ $525,000) on his cash investment.

N SELLS AFTER TEN YEARS

N continued in ownership of the property for ten years. During this time increases in rent exceeded increases in expenses, and the net income increased gradually from $165,000 to $205,000 per year. During the last several years, the property showed a taxable profit, which increased each year, as contrasted to tax losses or small tax profits during the earlier years. The profits occurred because the annual depreciation deductions (under the double-declining-balance method) and interest payments on the mortgage were steadily declining. Since N was obliged to pay an income tax at his 60% rate on the building's growing profit, he decided to sell the property to another real estate investor. Since it was a good building, well maintained, and showing an increasing operating profit, and since real estate values had been increasing in an inflationary economic environment, N was able to sell the property for $2,600,000, $500,000 more than its original cost.

N'S BENEFITS OVER THE TEN-YEAR PERIOD

An analysis of N's operations in connection with this investment after ten years would have disclosed that he was able to take a total of $670,335 in depreciation deductions (almost $150,000 more than the amount of his cash investment) and to reduce the mortgage debt by about $190,000. Although his real income was $1,015,000, he reported only $340,000 of taxable income from the property.[4] He was able to use the $670,335 of depreciation not only to offset income from the property itself, but to save himself a 60% tax on part of his income from other sources.

When N sold the building to the new owner for $2,600,000, his gain was computed as follows:

Sale price		$2,600,000
Original cost	$2,100,000	
Less depreciation deductions over 10 years	670,335	
N's adjusted cost basis		1,429,665
Gain on sale		$1,170,335

N's gain on the sale was a long-term capital gain, taxable at a maximum effective rate of 25%; his tax was $292,583 (25% of $1,170,335).

But here is where the nature of the tax-avoidance device is revealed. The significant fact is that $670,335 of N's $1,170,335 gain on the sale, more than one-half of the total, consisted of the recovery of the depreciation deductions which he had taken over the previous ten years, and which he had used to offset and eliminate income that would otherwise have been taxable at ordinary rates. In effect, N was permitted to convert $670,335 of ordinary income taxable at 60% into a capital gain taxable at 25%, netting him a tax windfall of $234,617.

When one considers that tax savings of this and greater magnitude were achieved by thousands of other investors in real estate, it is clear that the total amount of unwarranted tax benefits and consequent loss of revenue to the government was staggering. N's $2 million acquisition was petty compared to the amounts involved in really large real estate investments. When an Empire State Building, a large downtown office building complex in a major city, or a huge apartment or residential development was involved, the purchase prices were so astronomical that the aggregate depreciation deductions and the consequent tax savings ran into the millions in a single transaction.

Some wealthy investors, with very substantial incomes from dividends, interest, and other sources taxable to them at high rates, made investments of this kind in order to build up huge tax losses that offset the tax on their other income. Still others used the large tax-free cash flow generated by excessive depreciation to get back their invested capital tax-free, and many were able to accomplish both objectives.

The Key to the Tax Device—Excessive Depreciation Allowances

The truth is that for the past twenty years the market values of properties like that purchased and later sold by N did not decline. Rather, partly because of an inflationary trend that appears likely to continue in the foreseeable future, and partly because of shortages of desirable apartment houses and office buildings, the value of such investments have generally continued to increase, and sales have been occurring at successively higher prices.

Even when such properties diminished in value over a period of years they certainly did not decline at the accelerated rate used by N. As a matter of fact, in our inflationary economy, because of increases in rental income, buildings such as N's tend to increase in value in the earlier years and to decrease more sharply in the later years, exactly the reverse of the theory underlying accelerated depreciation. Machinery and equipment, and even some factory buildings may become obsolete more quickly, but well located and otherwise highly desirable office buildings, apartment houses, and other prime real estate do not depreciate more sharply in the earlier years. The extraordinary rapid depreciation methods previously permitted under our tax laws, and to some extent still allowed, were not and are not justified.

The fact that N was able to resell the property for more than its original cost is convincing evidence that no decline in value had taken place. Even if part of the increase in the resale price was due to an increase in the value of the land, it alone could not possibly have accounted for the profit on resale. If the land, originally valued at $100,000, had doubled in value in ten years, this increase would still have represented only a small part of the half million dollars that N received over its original cost. N's tax-free windfall of almost $235,000, generated entirely as the result of rapid depreciation sanctioned by the tax law, was based on a theoretical eventuality that in fact never occurred.

Under a proper method of taxation N and others like him would not have been able to realize such preferential tax benefits. If the depreciation rules for real estate had been the same as those applicable to machinery, equipment, and other personal property,[5] the entire amount of N's $670,335 of depreciation deductions, would have been taxable at his ordinary income tax rate of 60% when he recovered it as part of the proceeds on resale. In other words, the tax savings N realized from the excessive depreciation deductions allowed him would have been "recaptured" by the government when he sold the property at a profit.

Tax-Free Depreciation Windfalls Almost ad Infinitum

The former tax benefits of accelerated depreciation did not stop when N resold the property. When the new owner purchased it, again largely with money obtained by a mortgage loan, the process started all over again. While the new owner could not use the double- or 200%-declining-balance depreciation method that N employed because the property was no longer new, he was still permitted to depreciate the entire cost rapidly, using the 150%-declining-balance method. Although his tax-free benefits may not have been as spectacular as N's, they were nevertheless the envy of any ordinary taxpayer. And when eight or ten years later he in turn found it advantageous to dispose of the property, the cycle repeated itself with the third owner.

It is true that the general inflationary trend of the economy since World War II has contributed greatly to the harvesting of these enormous tax-free benefits by investors in real estate. If there had been no inflation, the benefits, though considerable, would have been smaller.

It should be added, however, that not every real estate investment turned out to be so profitable. Even in inflationary times some real estate investors suffered substantial losses. This risk was always present, although the story of real estate in the last several decades has been one of a more or less steady rise in market values. In any event, when a real estate investor with ample income from other sources resold a property for less than its depreciated book value, the loss was fully deductible against his other income taxable to him at ordinary income tax rates up to 70%.[6] It hardly seems fair that when he resold at a profit, assuming he had held the property for at least six months, his gain should have been taxed at the then 25% maximum rate for long-term capital gains. The government bore up to 70% of his losses but received no more than 25% of his profits.

Treasury Reform Proposals

During the early 1960s the use of rapid depreciation methods to convert ordinary income from real estate investments into tax favored capital gains had become so well known that more and more tax-wise investors were taking advantage of this tax gimmick. Accounts of enormous tax-free benefits reaped by real estate investors were reported in the *New York Times,* the *Wall Street Journal,* and other publications.[7] The nature of the use of the tax shelter was epitomized in headlines such as "Real Estate Investors Turn Depreciation Tax Write-Offs Into Gains." One tax service alerted its subscribers to the tempting tax benefits to be derived with an article entitled "How To Parley Real Estate and Stock into Ready Cash Plus a Tax Shelter." [8]

In 1962, 1963, and 1969 the Treasury Department urged Congress to do something about the situation that was making these tax-avoidance schemes so attractive. It recommended that all accelerated depreciation methods should be done away with entirely for real estate investments, and only normal straight-line depreciation allowed. If an owner sold a piece of real estate for a profit, the Treasury proposed that the portion of his gain that represented the recovery of all depreciation, even at normal rates, previously deducted, should be taxed at ordinary income tax rates rather than at the capital gains rate.

Probably sensing that Congress might be cool to this proposal to close the loophole completely, in 1963 Treasury Secretary Dillon offered a compromise suggestion. Instead of requiring real estate investors who had reaped extra tax benefits by excessive depreciation deductions to surrender those benefits in full when they resold the property, the government, he said, would be satisfied to let them keep some of the benefits, and even all of them under some circumstances.[9]

The Treasury's case was overwhelmingly persuasive, supported as it was by statistical data and case histories from the Treasury's files. It was shown that accelerated methods of depreciation were distorted and unrealistic as applied to real estate; that the amortization methods generally used by banks and other mortgage lenders (whereby repayments of the mortgage loan are relatively low at the beginning of the loan period and gradually increase thereafter, the very opposite of the accelerated methods being used by real estate investors) were a more realistic measure of the rate at which real property declined in economic value, if indeed it declined at all; that the fallacy of accelerated depreciation methods was recognized by the real estate business community itself; and that even the straight-line depreciation method was overly generous in permitting similar though less extreme tax avoidance results.

The practice of taking excessive depreciation deductions, the Treasury pointed out, permitted investors not only to pay off their mortgages with tax-free funds, but also to realize substantial tax-free cash returns on their investments. Some of them were able to show a book loss on the property year after year, which they could use to offset other income otherwise taxable at ordinary rates.[10]

Furthermore the investors who were realizing the greatest benefits from the device had no real concern with the property's actual loss of value. After the cream of ultra-liberal depreciation allowances in the earlier years had been skimmed off, they would sell the building to another tax-motivated investor who would commence the rapid depreciation cycle afresh, basing his excessive deductions on the increased purchase price he had paid. At the same time the former owner would use the sale proceeds to purchase a new piece of property, and begin the process all over again.[11]

Among other evidence furnished the House Ways and Means Committee was an analysis of the prospectuses issued in connection with public stock offerings by eleven large real estate corporations. The Treasury pointed out that

seven of the eleven corporations project losses for income tax purposes. The eleven corporations as a whole will have available $26,672,000 in cash for distribution, yet their income for tax purposes will be only 3.5 percent of that amount, or $936,000. In addition, these corporations will increase their equities in properties by making mortgage amortization payments of $14,217,000. Their $936,000 taxable income will be only 2.2 percent of the $40,890,000 total of their cash available for distribution plus their mortgage amortization payments. The reason why these companies can provide a cash flow which is 96.5 percent tax-free and also make substantial principal payments on mortgages lies in their tremendous depreciation deductions, which will amount to $35,-366,000.[12]

In other words, 96.5% of the profit of these companies was tax-free to their stockholders.

Apparently the opposition of the real estate lobby was too potent, and even the Treasury's compromise suggestion was rejected. Instead Congress adopted a further watered-down proposal. It not only permitted the uninhibited use of the double-declining-balance and other rapid depreciation methods as before—rejecting out of hand the suggestion that such excessive write-offs be eliminated—but drastically cut down the amount that the government could "recapture" as ordinary income out of the tax windfall when the property was resold.[13]

Former Assistant Secretary of the Treasury Stanley S. Surrey stated not long ago that the gap in the current law, permitting excessively rapid depreciation write-offs, was costing the government $750 million a year in tax revenue, by conservative estimates.

The government and low-income tenants of urban residential development projects, he said, "would both be better off if action were taken to recapture some of the $750 million of lost revenue now being used for building and to apply it in a direct and affirmative way toward the low-income housing we so desperately need." He pointed out that according to a recent Treasury study, a number of real estate investors were not only getting a tax-free 10% return on their equity, but their interest and "unreal" depreciation deductions were so great that they could apply real estate "losses" against more than half of their other taxable income (such as salaries), which could be written in six figures.

One real estate operator, according to Surrey, was enjoying almost $1 million a year in income from real estate and other sources, but because of depreciation deductions was paying on the average only 11% of it in income taxes—about the same effective rate paid by a married worker with two children who earned $10,000 a year.[14]

New Limitations on the Depreciation Loophole

While the Tax Reform Act of 1969 did not put an end to the real estate tax shelter, it eliminated some of its advantages. Most real estate investors are now barred from using the extreme accelerated depreciation methods previously permitted, including the double-declining-balance and the sum-of-the-digits methods. When buildings other than residential housing are sold at a profit, the government now "recaptures" the tax on the difference between straight-line depreciation and the amount that the investor had previously used to reduce income taxes. The recapture is accomplished by taxing the amount of such excess depreciation recovered in the sales price at ordinary income rates, rather than at capital gains rates. If a residential building is sold within 100 months of its purchase, there is full recapture; thereafter the recapture is reduced by 1% for each month over 100 months that the property is owned.

Nevertheless, under the new law all the old favored accelerated depreciation methods, including the double-declining-balance method, are still applicable to new housing, and investors in old apartment buildings with useful lives of 20 years or more are permitted to use a 125%-declining-balance method. Investors in other types of new construction of any kind are permitted to deduct depreciation according to a 150%-declining-balance method.

Finally, in spite of the new recapture provisions referred to above, when real property is sold there is no recapture of the amount of straight-line depreciation that is recovered in the sales price. Unlike other taxpayers, investors in all kinds of real property are still able, to this extent, to convert ordinary income into capital gains.

The new reforms, therefore, do not go far enough. In the case of personal property the depreciation tax loophole was eliminated in its entirety a number of years ago,[15] and there appears to be no justifiable reason why different rules should apply to real estate. Clearly, as a number of writers in the tax field have suggested, the remaining avenues of tax avoidance in this area should be closed.[16]

16

The Tax Abuses of Philanthropy Curtailed

Inducements to Charitable Giving

Our laws have always, quite properly, encouraged people to give to churches, hospitals, colleges, and other charitable institutions by permitting the contributions to be deducted for tax purposes. This liberal tax treatment of philanthropy has been a reflection of a broad consensus that religious, educational, and other charitable organizations perform services and functions that are useful to society and that otherwise the government would have to finance or provide.[1]

For federal income tax purposes individuals may now deduct up to 50% of their adjusted gross incomes for most charitable donations,[2] and contributions that in any year exceed this limit may usually be carried over and used during the five succeeding years.[3] Furthermore gifts to most charitable causes are deductible without limitation for both federal estate and gift tax purposes.[4]

This liberal tax treatment is based on both practical and moral grounds. If a taxpayer is to be encouraged to give up part of what he may otherwise enjoy himself for a worthy cause it seems only fair that the resources he sacrifices for the benefit of others should not be burdened with a tax. If a taxpayer with a $25,000 a year income, whose family status and permissible deductions place him in a 30% income tax bracket, gives $1,000 of his cash savings to charity he would not only be making a generous donation, but he would be paying a 30% tax on the donation as well. The allowance of the deduction reduces the net cost of the charitable gift by $300; from another point of view the government reimburses him for 30% of his donation.

In the case of well-to-do taxpayers in high income tax brackets the actual cost of their philanthropy is far less, with the government in effect reimbursing them for as much as 70% of their contributions. In view of the well established public policy to encourage wealthy people to support charity, this is, as a general rule, entirely proper. However, while most charitable donations have no doubt been prompted by generous impulses, until recently loopholes in the tax laws have led to philanthropy less altruistically motivated, which resulted in the abuse of the charitable deduction. Too often, though charity was benefited, the donors reaped unwarranted tax advantages, and in some cases actually profited as a result of their gifts. Cynics charged and many people eventually came to believe that the well-to-do were "making money by giving it away." Innumerable tax avoidance devices were invented for combining philanthropy with tax savings. The charitable, religious, and educational organizations themselves not only winked at these practices, but openly encouraged them. The result was a wave of indignation on the part of the public, the Treasury, and members of Congress that impressed even the House Ways and Means Committee; and in the Tax Reform Act of 1969 most, though not all of these loopholes were swept away.

The Former Abuses—Gone But Not Forgotten

Tax reformers in the Treasury Department have long been uneasy about the practices that ingenious taxpayers and their lawyers had evolved in order to minimize or avoid their tax liabilities. But the churches, colleges, museums, and other beneficiaries understandably opposed any change in the tax laws that might diminish donations, and they represented a powerful voice in the community. Nevertheless, early in 1969 the Treasury included among its tax reform proposals a long list of changes with respect to the tax treatment of charitable contributions.[5] Most of the Treasury's loophole-closing proposals were incorporated in the Tax Reform Act of 1969, which eliminated the following tax avoidance devices, among others:

Bargain Sale of Appreciated Assets. Taxpayers were previously able to sell to charity stock or other property that had risen in value over the years for the amount of their original cost, donating only their profits. They not only recovered their original investment, but received a large deduction for income tax purposes, avoided paying any capital gains tax, and netted little less than if they had sold the stock on the market and kept the proceeds instead of giving them away.

Making a Profit From the Sale of Appreciated Property to Charity. High bracket taxpayers who had short-term gains in securities or other property could sell the assets to charity at their original cost, thereby giving away the profit, and be better off, after using the charitable donation to reduce their income taxes, than if they had sold the property on the market and kept the after-tax proceeds.

Gifts or Trusts of Appreciated Property in Return for a Life Income Contract. Through such arrangements, wealthy taxpayers could obtain life-long incomes for themselves with a rate of return that was almost twice as large as they would receive if their securities or other property had been sold and the money invested in a commercial annuity contract.[6] This was possible because of a combination of income, capital gains, and estate tax savings. While such annuity arrangements are still permitted under certain circumstances, the rules have been substantially tightened to prevent abuse.

Gifts to Charity of Income From Property. The charity would receive the income for a certain period of years, and then the property devolved upon members of the family. The donors were sometimes able to make an overall net profit from the gift because of the various tax benefits [7]

Gifts of Merchandise Resulting in a Profit. The donation by businessmen of merchandise inventory that they would normally have sold often resulted in an overall net profit.

The Unlimited Charitable Deduction

Perhaps the most criticized tax law provision in this area, now eliminated by the 1969 reforms, was one that enabled some exceedingly well-to-do persons to take income tax deductions for their philanthropy without any limitation at all. Although for most individuals the deduction for contributions to charity was previously limited to 30% of adjusted gross income, this limitation did not apply to those whose charitable contributions, added to their income tax payments for the year, exceeded 90% of their taxable income for eight out of the ten preceding years.[8] This privilege enabled most of these taxpayers to escape paying any income tax whatsoever on their multi-million dollar incomes; and those who did pay some tax, paid only a fraction of what they would have paid without the privilege.

One would have assumed that they were turning over their incomes to charity. But that was not the case. They were able to retain their incomes and avoid paying any tax because their annual contributions to charity consisted for the most part of securities or other property that had grown enormously in value since originally acquired, and they were permitted to deduct, for income tax purposes, the full appreciated value of the property. What is more, by giving the property to charity they avoided paying any capital gains tax on their profits, although they utilized the profits as charitable deductions to offset their tax liability on millions of dollars of other income.

In a single year, for example, one taxpayer used contributions to charity of securities having a market value of about $21,600,000, but whose original cost was only about $460,000, to offset almost $20 million of other income. As a consequence he paid no income tax at all; if not for the special privilege of an unlimited charitable deduction, his income tax liability for that year would have been $6,200,000. During the 1958–60 period, twelve taxpayers claiming this privilege escaped paying any income taxes whatsoever because their contributions of securities had increased in market value over the years. Several of these taxpayers had incomes as high as $20 million, and one had an income of almost $50 million. In a single year fourteen wealthy individuals saved an average of $1.1 million each in income taxes by charitable donations of property valued at more than thirty-two times the original cost, as a result of which the government lost $15.7 million in tax revenue.[9]

In 1963 the Treasury Department requested that Congress eliminate the unlimited charitable deduction provision, but was unsuccessful. Treasury Secretary Dillon pointed out that as a result of the privilege, a person of great wealth could receive $1 million a year in dividends, make charitable contributions equal to only a fraction of the amount by which his multi-million dollar securities portfolio or other property holdings had increased in value during the year, and pay no income tax at all. At the same time he could enjoy a large tax-free income, and wind up with assets worth more than they were the year before. The Treasury felt, Secretary Dillon added,

that while this was a very good thing probably for charity, because most of these people give . . . to good charities nevertheless that everybody just as a moral principle should pay taxes.[10]

Contrary to what one would suppose, many top bracket taxpayers could enjoy the unlimited charitable deduction privilege without making particularly large donations to philanthropy. The test that they had to meet to qualify for the privilege was merely that their charitable gifts, added to their income tax payments, exceeded 90% of their *taxable* income. If their *taxable* income was relatively small (though their gross income was enormous) it did not take very much philanthropy to meet the requirement. For example, millionaire investors in the highest income tax bracket, though they possessed large annual gross incomes from oil and gas operations, were frequently able to use their drilling expense allowances and deductions for percentage depletion to reduce their *taxable* incomes to comparatively little. Others, who had a large part of their fortunes invested in tax-exempt municipal bonds that yielded very large gross incomes but no *taxable* income whatsoever, were in a similar position.[11]

An Important Loophole Remains

The Tax Reform Act of 1969 failed to deal with the tax advantage derived from giving to charity certain types of assets that have appreciated in value.

Other than occasional gifts of clothing and household articles to thrift shops and charity bazaars, most charitable donations, particularly by taxpayers in the lower and medium tax brackets, are in the form of cash. Wealthy individuals in the higher brackets, on the other hand, frequently make their contributions in the form of stocks and other securities that have appreciated greatly in value since they were originally acquired. The reason is that gifts of such appreciated property can be effected at much lower out-of-pocket cost than gifts of cash.

Suppose taxpayer O, with a six-figure income, which places him in the 70% income tax bracket, owns a block of Xerox stock worth $50,000, but which he bought years before for only $10,000. O wants to dispose of his investment in this "glamor" stock that pays relatively little in dividends and whose market price is highly volatile, and invest the proceeds in more conservative securities. At the same time he is contemplating making a gift to his Alma Mater.

If O sells the shares he will have to pay a capital gains tax of about $14,000 on his $40,000 profit (35% of $40,000), which will leave him with only $36,000 to reinvest. If O gives the shares to his college, he is allowed a charitable deduction on his income tax return for their current market value ($50,000) that will offset $50,000 of other income taxable to him at 70%, and result in a cash saving of $35,000 (70% of $50,000).

The result is that by giving $50,000 worth of stock to charity, O escapes the capital gains tax and is only $1,000 poorer than if he had sold the stock and reinvested the proceeds ($36,000 — $35,000).

This device of obtaining tax benefits by giving away the profit on appreciated securities and other property without paying a tax on the profit has been under fire from critics for years.[12] As one writer put it, the arrangement "provides incentive for charitable gifts, but it is doubtful that sound public policy should allow both charity and the donor thus to profit at government expense.[13]

About thirty years ago the House Ways and Means Committee suggested that when appreciated property was given to charity the charitable deduction should be limited to the amount of the donor's cost, but the Senate Finance Committee disagreed.[14] It would seem only fair either to limit the deduction or to compel the donor to pay the capital gains tax on his profit.

While it is true that the 1969 law placed some restrictions on the device of giving away appreciated property to charity, donors continue to enjoy all the tax advantages of gifts of securities, real estate, and other property held for more than six months, as long as the donation is made to a recognized publicly supported charitable organization such as a university, a church, or a hospital, and the donations are not in excess of 30% of adjusted gross income.

Another means of tax avoidance that has come into great favor in recent years with the well-to-do is the gift of paintings and other works of art to museums, foundations, and other public or private charitable institutions. The House of Representatives sought to close this loophole, but the provision was eliminated by the Senate in response to claims by museums representatives that if this proposed reform were enacted their sources of valuable art works would dry up. Wealthy art collectors are still able to obtain charitable deductions in the amount of the fair market value of their donations even though the present value is many times the original cost.

The House Ways and Means Committee sought at least to dilute the tax advantage of giving away appreciated property by providing for a minimum tax and requiring that deductions be allocated between taxable and tax-free income, with only the portion allocated to taxable income being deductible. However, this salutory proposal was deleted by the Senate Finance Committee.

Although colleges, universities, churches, hospitals, and other beneficiaries of charitable giving insist that the removal of the tax deduction for gifts of appreciated securities and other property would have a crippling effect on their fund-raising programs, this loophole—and it is a sizeable one—should be eliminated entirely.

17

Tax Favoritism Based on Marriage, Age, or Family Status

There still exists considerable discrimination between taxpayers who are otherwise in similar economic circumstances because of differences in marital status, age, and other factors. Two may not live as cheaply as one, but they certainly pay a lot less in taxes.[1]

Today two young bachelor friends, each making the same amount of money, other things being equal, will pay the same amount of federal income tax. But if one marries, he automatically achieves a substantial income tax saving, while the one who remains single continues to pay the same tax as before. In effect our tax laws penalize a man simply because he chooses to spend his money in other ways rather than on a wife.

The origin of this curious state of affairs goes back about twenty years. Before 1948 a married couple residing in California or one of seven other so-called community property states (where under state law all income belongs equally to each spouse)[2] ordinarily paid less in taxes than a married couple with the same total income residing in a so-called common law state. The first couple's income, even if it were all earned by the husband, was divided for tax purposes between husband and wife, and taxed in a lower tax bracket than the income of the couple in the common law state, where, if it was all earned by the husband, it was taxed at a much higher rate.

Moreover, in common law states a married couple whose income consisted of money earned entirely by the husband paid substantially more in taxes than a couple with an equal income derived from earnings of both spouses; the reason was that when the husband earned all the income, it was taxed in a higher rate bracket than that applicable to the same amount of income divided between two individuals.

These obviously discriminatory rulings, and especially the favored position of couples residing in the eight community property states, created so much dissatisfaction that in the Revenue Act of 1948 Congress attempted to put all married couples on an equal footing by permitting them all to file joint returns and split their income for tax purposes.[3] But in allowing income splitting for all married couples, Congress eliminated one inequity and created another, namely, the discriminatory tax treatment of single persons. The Tax Reform Act of 1969 has only partially alleviated this situation. Married people are still given a substantial advantage. They pay up to 20% less than single persons with the same income. A married couple with a taxable income of $24,000 pays a tax of about $5,660, or about 17% less than the $6,790 paid by a single person with the same income.[4]

Furthermore, married couples receive these advantages even though they may have fewer children or other dependents relying on them for support than single persons with the same income, and even if they have no children or dependents at all. An unmarried man with a taxable income of $20,000 who is obliged to support a widowed sister in a boarding house and an incapacitated brother in a nursing home pays almost $850 more in income taxes than a married couple with two children and the same taxable income. Even if the couple have no one but themselves to support they still pay about $450 less in taxes than the bachelor with his considerably greater support burdens.

This one-sided treatment is not only unfair to single people, but it also discriminates between one married couple and another. By far the greatest benefits from income splitting are enjoyed by married people in the middle- and upper-income brackets, while those with the lowest incomes benefit very little. At the $5,000 income level, income splitting saves a married couple approximately $90 a year; on an income of $150,000, the saving is over $11,000. Income splitting thus operates to reduce the relative tax burden of the wealthy and further undermine the principle of progressivity.

Furthermore, income splitting has greatly reduced federal income tax revenues. In 1959 a well-known tax authority estimated that income splitting for married couples cost the Treasury about $4 billion a year in taxes.[5] Today, with incomes at substantially higher levels, the tax loss is undoubtedly much greater, so that the situation was actually aggravated by the Tax Reform Act of 1969.

Instead of forthrightly eliminating income splitting between married couples, the 1969 act narrowed the gap between the married and unmarried by reducing the rates for single persons. The inevitable results will be a large loss in tax revenues without eliminating the inequities in the comparative tax treatment of people with differing family responsibilities.

Pros and Cons of Income Splitting

Those who justify the present tax advantage of married people point out that single persons generally are not required to live on the same economic scale as married couples. Most single people benefit from economies such as sharing a home with a parent or with another single person, or living in a boarding house; whereas the married status generally requires a larger expenditure for a home for the couple and its family. It is said, too, that eliminating the tax advantage of married couples would have adverse sociological and economic side-effects. It might force more married women to seek jobs, thereby displacing some male jobholders, cause married men to ask higher salaries to offset their higher taxes, which would have an inflationary effect, and might even discourage marriage and promote divorce.[6] Finally, they claim that in most marriages, while the husband may have more income than the wife, and may even produce all of the family income, whatever he makes is shared between them, and that therefore they should be taxed no more than two single persons with equal incomes.[7]

On the other hand, most commentators regard the comparative tax treatment of single persons as basically unfair.[8] They point out that marriage in itself may actually produce economies not available to single persons. For one thing a husband enjoys the imputed income of the services performed in the home by his wife on which he pays no income tax, while the single person has to use taxable income to pay for the same services performed by a maid, a cook, or both. (However it must be admitted that as a practical matter it would be most difficult to measure these economies enjoyed by married couples at different income levels; and even if they could be measured it would be hard to work out a rate schedule for taking them into account for tax purposes.)

As for the argument that married couples should be taxed more leniently because of their greater expenses in raising and providing for a family, critics of the preference emphasize that couples without any children at all enjoy the same advantages from income splitting as those with large family responsibilities.[9]

Pity the Poor Head of a Household

The situation of widows and widowers with children and of single persons supporting relatives was so patently inequitable compared to the tax treatment of married couples that Congress felt that it had to do something, if not to eliminate the disparity altogether, at least to mitigate it somewhat. So in 1951 Congress created a new category of taxpayer called the "Head of Household," [10] which granted widows, widowers, and other unmarried persons with dependents some tax relief. In effect, although the head of a household does not enjoy the same tax advantage as a married couple with the same income, he is allowed about half of that advantage.

Apart from the fact that heads of households receive only half of the tax benefits of married couples even though their burdens of caring for dependents may be as great or greater, the head-of-household provision has other serious objections. The greatest benefits are again derived by those in the upper income brackets, while those in the lowest brackets, who need it most, benefit not at all. Then there is the prerequisite that the dependent relatives, unless they are parents of the taxpayer, must reside in the taxpayer's abode. If for one reason or another an old grandparent, uncle, aunt, brother, or sister whom he supports is unwilling or unable to live in the good-hearted taxpayer's own home, he may not qualify for the head-of-household tax relief, although the cost of support in a separate residence will usually greatly increase his financial burdens.

In 1954 the House of Representatives was prepared to permit heads of "families," such widows and widowers, to split their income for tax purposes like married couples, but the Senate declined to go along, and ultimately only minor changes were made in the provisions applicable to heads of households.[11]

Under the Tax Reform Act of 1969 as passed by the House, widows and widowers with dependent children would have been allowed to split their incomes and get the same tax rate as married couples, but this concession to greater equity was deleted by the Senate.

A Better Life at 65

Rich or poor, sick or well, persons over 65 years of age are given a number of tax benefits whether they need them or not. Every person upon reaching 65 automatically receives a double personal exemption ($1,250 instead of $625), and a married couple twice the exemptions of a younger couple ($2,500 rather than $1,250).[12] It does not matter how much wealth a couple over 65 possess or how much income they may have from other sources. Even if they receive $40,000 or $50,000 a year in dividends and interest on a $1 million securities portfolio, $2,500 of their income, twice the exemption for couples under 65, is automatically tax-free. In addition, those who have income from interest, dividends, wages, and other taxable sources are entitled to a retirement income credit.[13] The credit is reduced by Social Security, Railroad

Retirement benefits, and other tax-exempt income, and by any earned income over $1,200.

The complicated tax provisions for the elderly have been characterized by Stanley S. Surrey, a former Harvard professor and assistant secretary of the treasury, as a "crazy quilt," under which half of the benefits go to older retired people whose incomes exceed $10,000 and virtually none to poorer people who have to supplement their meager resources by working.[14] Moreover these special tax privileges cost the Treasury about $2.3 billion a year.[15] It may be proper to provide additional tax relief for people in the lower brackets, but it hardly makes sense to grant even greater relief to taxpayers who do not need it. It makes even less sense to favor those who are comfortably situated and whose income is *unearned,* while we penalize the 75% of the aged who are obliged to work to support themselves by deducting part of their *earned* income from their retirement income credit.[16]

There are some who challenge altogether the propriety of special tax benefits for those who have no other claims to such treatment than that they have attained the age of 65. There is considerable evidence that the living expenses of an older couple are less than those of younger married couples with similar earnings, especially the newly married who must incur the expenses of setting up a household, paying for a home, buying furniture and appliances, and raising young children, expenses that retired couples no longer have to meet. On the other hand it is urged that elderly persons find it more difficult to obtain employment and are physically less able to work when and if they find jobs. However there are many other groups in society, such as the physically or mentally handicapped, who are even more disadvantaged than older people and who receive no special tax advantages. The blind, like the aged, receive an extra personal exemption, but no other type of handicapped person is so favored.

In 1963, and again in 1967, when the administration proposed amendments designed to remedy these obvious shortcomings of the tax provisions for the elderly, Congress flatly rejected them.[17] The Treasury renewed its recommendations in this area, as part of the tax reform package submitted to Congress in February 1969,[18] but the Tax Reform Act of 1969 failed to remedy this situation.

Inequities in Exemptions for Dependents

Every taxpayer is allowed a dependency exemption for each child he supports. Even if the child has a separate income of his own, the parent does not lose the exemption if the child's income does not exceed $600 a year. If the child is under nineteen or is a full-time student, the parent retains the exemption no matter how much separate income the child has, provided he furnishes more than one-half of the child's support.[19] Under the new law the exemption is $625 for 1970, $650 for 1971, $700 for 1972, and rises to $750 in 1973.

Whether the child's income arises from earnings or from interest, dividends, rents, or other unearned income is immaterial. This results in widespread income and estate tax avoidance since it encourages parents to shift income from themselves to their children by gifts of money, bonds, stocks, or other income-producing property.[20]

In effect, allowing parents whose children have separate earnings or income to disregard that income for tax purposes amounts to giving them a double dependency exemption. The first is the exemption that the parent takes for the child as a deduction from his taxable income. The second arises from the fact that $625, and in some cases more, of the child's separate income is tax-free. This clearly discriminates against parents whose children do not have such additional income either because they do not have time for part-time jobs, or because the parent does not have sufficient wealth to permit programs of yearly gift-giving to his children. In view of the number of children in this category, the untaxed earnings and other incomes of dependent children results in a substantial loss of revenue to the Treasury.

Those who justify exempting the separate earnings of children from tax claim that as a matter of sound public policy children should be encouraged to earn their own money by outside work.

They also claim that children's *unearned* incomes should not be taxed on the ground that it is in the public interest to encourage children to save. However a number of commentators view as unwarranted the automatic exemption of $625, and more in some cases, of the income of dependent children.[21] Any benefits that the public derives from children working or saving their money are, in their view, outweighed by the discrimination involved and the loss in tax revenue that they engender. It has been suggested that a parent who wishes to take advantage of a dependency exemption for a child who has an additional income of his own, whether that income is earned or unearned, should be required to include most if not all of it on his own income tax return.[22]

Another inequality arises because parents are permitted to take a dependency exemption of $625 (which will rise to $750) for a child who is a full-time student. Provided that he furnishes at least one-half of the child's support, the parent obtains the advantage of the tax deduction regardless of the child's age or how much earned or unearned income the child happens to receive. While admittedly the exemption encourages students to earn extra money, it seems unfair to those parents whose full-time student offspring are either too busy with their studies to undertake outside work, or are unable to obtain jobs. Worse still, the exemption favors the more affluent taxpayer and discriminates against the poorer family in most need of the advantage of any tax savings. The student child of a poor family is more likely to have earnings that furnish more than one-half of his support, thereby causing the parent to lose the benefit of an exemption for the child as a dependent. In a wealthier family the student may earn as much or more, but the living standard of the family will be higher and the child's earnings are less likely to provide more than one-half of his support.[23]

The Need for Review

The rate schedules, exemptions, and deductions of married couples, single persons, heads of households, and the aged are in large measure so arbitrary and unfair that, at the very least, this entire area merits further examination by Congress.

The Treasury's proposals for thorough revision of the tax treatment of persons over 65 should be speedily adopted. Any reforms proposed that impinge on the present tax advantages of married couples will undoubtedly encounter stubborn Congressional opposition just because married couples substantially outnumber single taxpayers among the electorate. But most commentators seem to agree that the income tax rates applicable to married couples are disproportionately advantageous compared with those for widows, widowers, and single persons providing support for children and dependent relatives, and that the separate rate schedules for these groups should be thoroughly revised.[24]

One leading writer has suggested replacing the three separate rate schedules for married persons, single persons, and heads of households with a single schedule applicable to all taxpayers. Everybody's taxable income would be subject to the same graduated rate scale, but before applying the rate certain exemptions or deductions would be permitted depending on the number of taxpayer's children, dependents, or other responsibilities of support.[25]

Any overall review of these matters by Congress should take into consideration not only the extent to which tax revenues may be affected, but must focus on the social and economic effects of revising the tax liabilities of persons whose family status or domestic circumstances differ.

18

Tax-Free Benefits That Do Not Meet the Eye—Imputed Income

There is a considerable amount of income, although the average person does not think of it as such, that completely escapes the net of the tax collector. Sometimes referred to as "imputed income," it provides substantial economic benefits to large segments of the population, but it is tax-free because it is not considered to be taxable income in the strict sense of the word. None the less, the benefits it confers add to the resources of those who enjoy them no less than the receipt of money or property customarily treated as taxable income.

Tax Advantage of Home Owners

Taxpayers, whether they are city dwellers, suburbanites, or farmers, receive a distinct tax advantage from owning and occupying their own homes, as compared to those with comparable economic incomes who are tenants.

Take, for example, A and B, each of whom own $50,000 worth of stock that yields an income of 5½%, or $2,750 a year. A uses his $2,750 to pay for the rent of a house or an apartment. B sells half of his securities in order to purchase a $25,000 home, and thereafter receives only $1,375 income from his shares, half as much as he did before. But B uses $1,000 of that income to pay local real estate taxes on his new home, payments which he may take as a deduction on his income tax return to reduce taxes on his salary or other taxable income.

Meanwhile A, who continues as a tenant, is obliged to include and pay taxes on his $2,750 of securities income, which he uses to pay his rent, and has no corresponding tax deduction to offset against his own salary and other income subject to tax.

Although B, the home owner, is allowed the $1,000 a year paid for real estate taxes as an offsetting tax deduction, the value that he and his family receive every year from the investment in the home they occupy—a non-cash benefit equal to the house's rental value—does not have to be reported. In short, the rental value is tax-free to B. By contrast, every dollar of value received by A in the form of dividends or interest from his investment in securities must be reported and is taxable to A.

Taxpayers who do not have sufficient funds to enable them to buy a home for cash can usually obtain a mortgage loan to finance the major part of the purchase price. They are then able to obtain the tax advantage of home occupancy, i.e., the enjoyment of the home's rental value, without paying a tax on it. In such cases the taxpayer can deduct not only his real estate taxes, but the interest he pays to the bank holding the mortgage loan as well. Not only are home owners occupying their own homes treated more equitably under the tax laws than tenants, but there is tax discrimination between individual home owners, since the one who has the resources to purchase the largest and most expensive home enjoys the largest tax-free benefit from his occupancy.

A number of authorities in the tax field have recognized the favoritism enjoyed by taxpayers owning their own homes, and believe that principles of equity require taxation of this income imputed to home ownership.[1] Some think that complete equity of treatment between tenants and home owners not only requires inclusion of the occupancy value of a home as income, but the disallowance of deductions for mortgage interest and real estate taxes.[2] Although these tax advantages undoubtedly encourage home ownership, generally assumed to be a worthwhile social objective, the question still remains as to whether the merits of such a goal are outweighed by equity considerations.

Admittedly such taxation would cause a number of problems. While the imputed income from home occupancy has been subject to taxation in other countries and would undoubtedly raise very large amounts of tax revenue, there would be enormous opposition from vast numbers of home owners who might regard taxing them on the theoretical rental value of their homes as unduly harsh.[3]

Furthermore, where do you draw the line? If the imputed value of home occupancy is taxable, why not the benefits that accrue to the owner of an automobile, camping trailer, or swimming pool, contrasted with the comparable disadvantage of the taxpayer who instead rents his car or trailer, or pays for the use of a cabana at a beach club? The difficulty of determining which of such imputed benefits should be taxable, and which not, has persuaded many to take the view that the "enjoyment value" of property purchased by taxpayers should be free of tax.

Untaxed Benefits from Life Insurance Ownership

Another item of invisible income that escapes taxation arises in connection with the ownership of the typical life insurance policy.

When a person decides to insure his home or his car, he thinks in terms of an annual premium, which he pays to the insurance company as the cost of the insurance protection. The premium can, and often does, change from year to year because of increases or decreases in the cost to the insurance company of providing such coverage. When a person buys life insurance however, he is offered two alternatives. He can make an annual payment which just covers the cost of the insurance for the year, and which increases over the years as the probability of mortality rises. This is called "term" insurance. Or he may buy "straight life" insurance, which carries a constant premium. At the beginning the premium is much larger than the premium for term insurance, but as a person grows older, the cost of term insurance increases and becomes larger than the constant premium for straight life.

When an individual buys a straight life policy he is really doing two things: He is paying for protection for the year involved, and he is giving the insurance company money to hold and invest, and to use later to defray part of the annual cost of insuring him when he is older. Basically this is the same as if he had bought term insurance, paid the year's premium, and put additional money aside, either by purchasing stocks or bonds, placing it in a savings bank, or making any other form of investment.

Each year the individual who has a straight life policy receives a dividend from the insurance company, which is partially attributable to its success in its investments. While interest from savings bank accounts, dividends from stock, and interest from bonds are taxable, the dividend on life insurance policies is not. Thus, although he has chosen to invest his money with a life insurance company in the form of the purchase of a straight life policy, rather than purchase term insurance and invest his money separately, the straight life policyholder receives tax-free income. Accordingly a number of authorities question whether this tax-free income should be permitted and suggest that some form of tax should be imposed on it.[4]

Even assuming for the moment that the income from investments in insurance policies should not be taxable, certainly where the policy is used as collateral for loans in excess of the policy holder's investment in the policy, consideration should be given to taxing the earnings on the policy as ordinary income to the extent of such excess. For when the policy holder borrows on his life insurance he is in effect obtaining a cash benefit, attributable to the policy's earnings, in the form of a loan, which should be treated as a realization of income.

But taxation of the benefits from investing in certain types of life insurance policies should not be confined to situations where the taxpayer borrows on the security of the policy, because some taxpayers have resources that enable them to enjoy the tax advantages of an insurance investment without borrowing and using their policies as collateral. The most equitable solution, therefore, would appear to be the elimination of the tax advantage of investments in life insurance by taxing all the earnings of such policies.[5]

In fact the freedom from income tax of the investment increment of life insurance has been characterized as a major factor in the growth of life insurance as an investment medium for persons seeking ways to minimize their taxes; and the fact that the interest credited by life insurance companies on policies is not subject to income tax during the policy holder's life or at his death, is viewed by some as a special form of tax favoritism enjoyed by the life insurance industry.[6]

The Value of the Non-Working Wife

There is a considerable difference in the economic situation of a married couple where only the husband works and another couple where both spouses are employed. While both couples may enjoy the same total combined income, the first couple enjoys an economic advantage to the extent of the imputed income arising from the wife's services in the home. Strict equity therefore would suggest that the second couple be taxed at a lower rate. Indeed the working wife usually has travel expenses going to and from work, lunches, and other costs related to her job, and may, in fact, have so little time left over for her household duties that she may have to hire a part- or full-time servant to perform services that the other couple obtains tax-free.

It would be exceedingly difficult to set up standards and regulations for measuring or placing a value on the domestic services of the non-working wife in individual cases, not to mention the complicated problems of administering them. According to one authority, the only practical method of overcoming the tax advantage of one married couple as compared to the other would be to allow a certain percentage of gross income to be deducted by married couples where both spouses work, with a maximum dollar limitation.[7] An analogy supporting such treatment is the child care deduction permitted in some cases where a spouse is hospitalized or deceased.[8]

Tax Advantages of Farmers

Farmers are also a privileged group who derive special tax advantages from income not recognized and taxed as other income is taxed. Many farmers own their own homes and derive the advantage of the untaxed imputed income from the value of home occupancy. In addition, much of the food they consume and some of their fuel is produced on the farm and is not reported as income, whereas non-farming taxpayers who use their salaries and other sources of income to purchase food at the supermarket or grocery, use dollars on which they pay a tax in order to make such purchases.

Again as a practical matter, it would be extremely difficult to set up standards and criteria for measuring the value for tax purposes of food and other items produced on farms and consumed by farm families; and the problems in administering such a system, even if it could be worked out, would be almost insuperable.[9] Still it seems unfair to allow such obvious economic benefits to go untaxed when the butcher who takes home sides of beef and other meats for his family's consumption and the owner of an appliance concern who transfers a television set or refrigerator from stock to his own home are obliged to report the value of these items on their tax returns.

Imputed Income Should Be Reviewed

It seems clear that apart from the loss to the Treasury in tax revenue,[10] the escape from taxation of certain types of economic benefits enjoyed by certain classes of taxpayers, such as benefits from insurance policies, owner-occupied homes, home-grown products consumed by farm families, and the services of non-working wives, is an inequity that conflicts with the principle of subjecting all economic benefits impartially to income taxation. While these inequities can theoretically be redressed by taxing these benefits in one form or another, doing so would involve serious practical difficulties of measurement and administration. Nevertheless the problem of imputed income is one that deserves careful consideration by Congress as a necessary part of any program for overall tax reform.

19

Tax Windfalls for Banking Institutions

Mutual savings banks, savings and loan associations, and commercial banks have enjoyed and continue to enjoy a privileged tax status. While most manufacturing companies paid an effective tax rate of 43.3%, mutual savings banks were paying only 5%-6%, savings and loan associations 15%-16%, and commercial banks 22%-23%.[1] If these banking institutions had been taxed on their economic income at the rates applicable to other business organizations they would have been paying in the aggregate well over $1 billion more in income taxes each year.[2]

Excessive Reserves for Bad Debts

The most important of the preferences conferred on banks is the special treatment of bad debts. It was originally based on the view that banking institutions, most of whose funds were invested in loans to businessmen and home buyers, required favored tax treatment to protect them against the kind of catastrophic losses on mortgage and other loans that occurred during the great depression of the 1930s.[3] But the rationale that may at one time have justified this and other kinds of special treatment no longer obtains. Their losses have not been exceptional, and certainly not catastrophic. The overly generous tax treatment of banking institutions served merely to present them with tax windfalls of major proportions every year.

Unlike other business taxpayers, banking institutions have been permitted to reduce their taxable income by setting aside reserves for bad debts that exceed by far their actual bad debt losses. Their reserves were not based on their past or current loss experience, but on special formulas.[4] Commercial banks, for example, were able to use bad debt reserves that were three times the amount needed to cover their losses over the twenty-year period that included the years of the great depression, the period when banks suffered their most devastating losses in modern history.[5] When they report the amount of their income to their stockholders, their bad debt reserves are substantially less than that set aside for tax purposes. Virtually all their surplus and reserves have been accumulated tax-free.[6]

There never was any justification for treating thrift institutions and commercial banks in a manner different from other taxpayers. Rather, like other business and industrial corporations, they should have been required to use their current loss experience as the basis for establishing their reserves for bad debts, and if they had underestimated the amount set aside for this purpose, they could have resorted to loss carryovers and carrybacks to obtain appropriate tax relief.

The Tax Reform Act of 1969 imposed stricter limitations on some of the special tax privileges of banking institutions. Commercial banks will be required to restrict their deductions for bad debts to amounts based on actual experience. This provision does not become fully effective until 1988; in the interim the former advantages of the banks will be gradually reduced.

Although mutual savings banks and savings and loan associations will no longer be allowed to deduct as large bad debt reserves as before, they will still be permitted fictitious deductions for bad debt reserves in excess of their actual loss experience, deductions that are not available to other taxpayers.

Preferential Treatment of Capital Gains and Losses

Another area in which banking institutions were specially preferred involved the tax treatment of certain of their capital gains and losses. In effect commercial banks, mutual savings banks, and savings and loan associations could invest in U.S. government and other bonds on a "heads I win, tails you lose" basis. Under a special provision of the tax law, they enjoyed favorable long-term *capital gains* treatment on their profitable bond transactions, while being permitted to deduct their losses from such investments from *ordinary income.*[7] This preference, granted in 1942, was designed to encourage banks to purchase government securities during World War II. There was no justification for continuing it after the war. Apart from the obvious tax favoritism involved, it encouraged buying and selling of such bonds when market conditions produced favorable tax benefits without really changing the overall size of the banks' government bond portfolios.[8]

The Tax Reform Act of 1969 eliminated the favoritism previously extended to all types of banking institutions in connection with their sales of U.S. government and other bonds. Gains and losses are now treated and taxed as ordinary income, but a number of other tax loopholes were left untouched.

Purchase of Tax-Exempt Securities with Borrowed Funds

Banking institutions are very substantial holders of tax-exempt bonds. Of $118 billion of tax-exempt state and local government bonds outstanding in 1968, commercial banks held $52.6 billion and mutual savings banks $206 million.[9] Other taxpayers are not allowed to use borrowed funds to purchase tax-exempt securities and deduct, for tax purposes, the interest paid on such borrowings,[10] but banks are permitted to do so. It hardly seems equitable to permit commercial banks, which obtain about one-third of their real income from such investments, the funds for which are borrowed from their depositors, to retain this privilege.

A substantial share of the operating expenses of commercial

banks are obviously attributable to their dealings in tax-exempt securities, which represent such a large part of their income. Yet expenditures for the salaries of employees engaged in tax-exempt security trading and the cost of the space and other facilities involved may be deducted by the banks from their other taxable income, thereby reducing it for tax purposes, and compounding the advantage.

Unwarranted Benefits from the Dividends Received Deduction

Ordinarily, corporations that receive dividends from other corporations whose stock they own receive a deduction from taxable income of 85% of such dividends, and in effect pay taxes on only 15% of this income. This practice is allowed because sooner or later such income is distributed by them to their own stockholders, who will be obliged to pay individual income taxes on such receipts; taxing corporations in full on such dividends would amount to a form of double taxation. However, such corporations may not use the dividends they pay to their stockholders as deductions to reduce taxes on other income. Nevertheless some banking institutions are, in effect, permitted to do so.

Mutual thrift institutions are allowed to deduct 85% of the dividends they receive from their investments in the stock of other corporations, despite the fact that having no stockholders, they pay no dividends. All their distributions are made in the form of interest paid to their depositors, which they may deduct in full for tax purposes.[11] As a result they obtain the advantage of the 85% deduction for dividends received, and additionally, in effect, a 100% deduction for the same dividends to the extent that the money is paid out to their depositors in the form of interest. Mutual savings banks have utilized this tax shelter to achieve substantial deductions in their effective income tax rate. The 1969 law has only slightly reduced its advantages. Commercial banks and stock savings and loan associations enjoy the same tax preferences, undiminished by the new law, to the extent that the dividends they receive from investments are part of the income paid to depositors and deducted as interest, rather than becoming part of their net income subsequently distributed to their shareholders.[12]

The availability to these institutions of the 85% dividends received deduction under such circumstances is clearly unjustifiable.

The remaining special tax privileges still available to banks, despite the adoption of recent reforms, cost the Treasury more than half a billion dollars annually in lost tax revenue;[13] these privileges should be eliminated, and these institutions put on the same footing as other taxpayers.

20

Obstacles to Tax Reform

The reforms adopted by the Act of 1969, welcome as they are, represent only first steps in the direction of the kind of overall tax revision that is necessary. The question now is whether the impetus toward reform will continue or will come to a halt. Unfortunately, having given up more ground to the reformers than they expected they would have to, most Congressmen probably now feel that tax revision has gone far enough, perhaps even too far. In spite of all the breast-beating and brave words, public indignation over tax loopholes has largely subsided.

Consequently skeptics are predicting that further tax reform will now be side-tracked, as it has been so many times in the past. The reason for this pessimism is that the complexion of the House of Representatives, where tax laws are initiated, remains predominantly conservative and threatens to become more so; and judging from the way the Senate recently emasculated a number of relatively modest proposals that had been adopted by the House, that body appears to be even less reform-minded. Most lawmakers in Washington, like their constituents, feel that taxes are too high. They are more interested in slashing expenditures and balancing the budget, even at the cost of sacrificing vitally needed federal programs, than in tax revision. To them the needs of the cities and the plight of the urban minorities, the lack of adequate schools and housing facilities, and the monumental problems of water and air pollution are remote. "Law and Order" and "Crime in the Streets" appear to concern them far more. As Senator Russell B. Long, chairman of the powerful Senate Finance Committee, to which all legislation in the upper chamber is referred, observed not long ago:

> Tax reform is change; it is generally controversial, and it is apt to be quite destructive to certain interests. . . . Broad tax reform, though important, just does not possess the air of urgency necessary to seize the concern of the nation.[1]

Lobbyists Galore But None for the Public

It has been estimated that there are some 50 million low- and moderate-income taxpayers, making less than $20,000 a year, whose tax burdens could be reduced if the inequities in our tax system favoring special groups were eliminated.[2] The trouble is that they have no effective means of making their views felt, or of putting pressure on their representatives in Washington.

All the special interests with big stakes in tax legislation, who are concerned with the retention of their privileges and preferences, are represented in Washington by well paid and highly skilled lobbyists. Spokesmen for banks, insurance companies, stock exchanges, oil and gas producers, real estate owners, coal mine operators, timber producers, farmers, ranchers, and their trade associations constantly press upon congressmen and senators their requests and grievances. Even labor and consumer organizations occasionally urge their special concerns before the Congressional tax committees, though traditionally they have been much less influential than the representatives of business.

But there never has been anyone to lobby for the public and the great body of taxpayers whose taxes would be reduced and whose social and economic needs might be better met if the law were overhauled to prevent privileged groups from minimizing their own taxes. Occasionally economists and law professors, generally from the larger universities, and spokesmen for labor unions appear before the tax-writing committees of the House and Senate to point out the public's stake in tax reform, but they do not testify often enough, and when they do, they are vastly outmanned by representatives of business, industry, and other special interests.[3]

Generally it is only the Treasury Department, which from time to time advocates tax reform and defends the integrity of the tax structure before the tax committees of the House and Senate. But in the course of trying to prevent erosion of the tax base by additional exceptions advocated by special interests, the Treasury is obliged to cope with hundreds of tax measures. Often its limited staff is inadequate to the task or has too little time to study the proposals with sufficient care. Usually, when it presents a tax reform program to Congress, in order to secure approval of a few reform measures, the Treasury is forced to compromise on or abandon many others.[4]

Then, too, the nature of the Treasury's reform proposals and the extent of its ardor in defending them depends in large part on the administration for which it speaks and the identity and views of the individual who happens to be the secretary. Moreover, like the Pope, to paraphrase Stalin's remark, the secretary of the treasury has no legions under his command, so that the pressure he can exert, assuming he wishes to do so, is limited. The Treasury proposes, but Congress in the end disposes.

Tax legislation, and especially those special bills so dear to the heart of legislators seeking to advance the economic interests of important constituents in their home states, are often so involved and complex that the average lawmaker may not be fully aware of the hidden preferences they contain or realize their broader economic implications. Deluged as they are with lobbyists and representatives of private interest groups, it is frequently difficult for congressmen and senators, even those with an objective attitude toward tax legislation, to get a balanced view of where the public interest lies.

Strains on Objectivity

The pressures exerted on legislators in Washington, particularly on those who are members of the important tax-writing committees, are enormous. The story is told of the Congressman who was a staunch and loyal spokesman for Tammany Hall, the old New York City Democratic organization. As he was approaching the end of a lengthy and eloquent speech in the House of Representatives in opposition to a certain bill, and was about to conclude his argument detailing the deficiencies of the proposed law and the awful consequences that would ensue were it to be approved, his legislative aide rushed into the House Chamber. He handed him a telegram, freshly arrived from his political boss in New York, instructing him to vote *for* the bill. After pausing for a moment, with great aplomb the congressman adroitly reversed his field, and continued, "Now, Mr. Speaker, that is what I would have said were I against this bill. . . ." [5]

Most members of Congress feel it is their duty to promote and protect the economic interests of their more influential constituents by voting for bills that favor them and against those that affect them adversely. But the interest of a well-to-do taxpayer or of a local industrial group in obtaining special exemptions or exceptions frequently does not coincide with that of the general body of taxpayers in the country, or even of those in the legislator's home state. Unfortunately it is those individuals and business interests, who have the biggest stake in tax legislation, whose voices are heard the loudest in Washington. They can afford the lobbyists, trade associations, and spokesmen capable of exercising maximum pressure on our legislators, whereas medium- and low-income taxpayers are without the organization or resources needed to present their point of view effectively.

Under our loose and inadequate conflict-of-interest laws the objectivity of many congressmen and senators is often questionable. Many are members of or have financial ties with law firms that receive substantial legal fees from wealthy individuals and large corporations for handling their tax and other problems, and since it is the well-to-do private individuals and large business interests in his home state that are the chief sources of campaign funds, the average legislator tends to view their financial problems with special concern. Moreover many legislators themselves have financial interests, often of a very substantial nature, in insurance companies, savings and loan associations, oil and gas producers, radio and television stations, real estate companies, and other businesses that have a large stake in tax legislation. For example, it recently came to light that Senator Long, chairman of the Senate Finance Committee, and members of his family received several million dollars of income from oil and gas producers, much of it exempt from federal income tax; but the oil and gas holdings of many of his senatorial colleagues remain undisclosed. Since the prevailing code of ethics for members of Congress is so pathetically weak, there is no requirement that these ties and financial interests be fully disclosed and the public is none the wiser. With all these pressures, influences, and temptations, it is a rare member of the House or Senate who is capable of a single-minded devotion to the public's interest in tax reform.

During the administration of President Eisenhower an incident occurred that cast a revealing light on morality as it is interpreted on Capitol Hill. Senator Case of South Dakota disclosed, to the acute embarrassment of the president and many of his fellow senators, that a prominent oil company with a vital interest in legislation then under consideration, which was of utmost importance to the petroleum industry, had been lavishing gifts or campaign funds on some senators. A committee of the Senate was promptly summoned to inquire into the matter. But the committee did not focus its investigation on the oil company in question or on the senators involved. Rather it was Senator Case, who had refused these gifts out-of-hand, and who had had the courage to call attention to the scandal, who was put in the dock and subjected to the most rigorous cross examination by his fellow lawmakers.

The Hurdles of the Congressional Tax-Writing Committees

One of the formidable roadblocks to tax reform derives from the very manner in which tax legislation is traditionally handled. All tax legislation originates in the House of Representatives. Proposals first come before the powerful Ways and Means Committee for consideration. If the committee report is favorable the entire House will debate and vote on the bill. After the lower house has passed it, the bill goes to the Senate. There it is taken up initially by the Finance Committee, and if approved, it comes to a vote on the Senate floor. If the Senate proposes amendments the difference between the two versions of the bill are ironed out by a House-Senate conference committee.

Unless a tax proposal or an amendment to a tax bill has received the prior blessing of the House Ways and Means Committee and the Senate Finance Committee there is virtually no chance of its being accepted on the floor of either chamber. The make-up of these two powerful committees is rigidly controlled by the leaders of both parties in the House and Senate. They have generally been able to arrange it so that membership is confined for the most part to tax conservatives. Since any proposal for tax reform must run the gauntlet of these two committees, it is here that reform measures generally die.[6]

Drew Pearson, a sharp critic of Congressional lobbying by special interests, claimed that for years the privilege of the oil depletion allowance was protected on Capitol Hill by the late Sam Rayburn, Speaker of the House, who controlled appointments to the Ways and Means Committee. "No one was admitted to this select circle," according to Pearson, "who couldn't give Rayburn the right answer to one question: 'Do you favor the oil depletion allowance?' " Although Rayburn had been dead for years, Pearson insisted that his "influence still haunts the Ways and Means Committee." On the basis of interviews with members of that committee, Pearson concluded that they had no intention of materially diminishing this seemingly sacrosanct tax privilege.[7]

As for the Senate Finance Committee, we can only imagine the kind of reception that proposals to reform the oil depletion allowance encountered in that body from Chairman Long's remarks in 1968:

One thing I don't think is tax reform—and that is any cut in the 27½ percent depletion rate for oil and gas. . . . If percentage depletion were reduced or eliminated for oil and gas, that is when discrimination would occur.[8]

Past Failures and Recent Accomplishments

Until recently proposals for tax revision have not fared very well at the hands of the lawmakers. On occasion reform measures have been adopted, such as the repeal of the dividend credit in 1964, and the elimination of a few years earlier of foreign tax havens, in the Bahamas and elsewhere, for dummy corporations used as repositories for corporate profits that escaped taxation. But usually major reforms have been voted down by Congress or amended beyond recognition.

A significant tax reform effort was made by the Kennedy administration in 1963 when the secretary of the treasury presented to Congress a number of essentially modest proposals designed to eliminate a few of the most glaring tax abuses. An all-out attack on many of the worst loopholes, such as the oil depletion allowance and the tax-exempt status of interest on municipal and local bonds, was not even ventured. Indeed the administration offered as an inducement for the acceptance of its reform program "a carrot," in the form of a substantial tax cut, especially for the higher-income taxpayers and the business community. But Congress' response was to approve the tax cut and to reject most of the reforms, causing Senator Douglas to observe:

> You see, we had hoped that the prospect of cuts might sweeten and reduce the opposition to reform. Now we find people very enthusiastic about taking cuts, but they reject reforms. The molasses does not make the castor oil go down any better, and if you have to take castor oil without molasses, then the chances for reform are even less. . . .[9]

The 1963 hearings on the administration's tax proposals were interminable, 4,000 pages of testimony before the House Ways and Means Committee and 2,700 pages before the Senate Finance Committee. Hundreds of witnesses testified or offered written statements, which were incorporated into the enormous record. All but a few were spokesmen for business groups—the oil and gas industry, the mining industry, the stock exchanges, real estate investors, cattle, coal and timber interests—and virtually all were vociferous in their opposition to the relatively modest corrections of tax abuses that the administration sought to have adopted.

What went on behind the scenes, the buttonholing of congressmen and senators by lobbyists both in Washington and in their home states, can only be conjectured. The handful of legislators, such as Senators Douglas and Gore, who called for thoroughgoing reform, were lone voices crying in the wilderness. The prevailing mood of Congress was established at the outset of the hearings before the Ways and Means Committee, when Congressman John W. Byrnes of Wisconsin warned that "the greater part of the proposed structural reforms had better be put in deep freeze if we are going to get a tax bill this year." [10]

The arch conservatives, who were not only opposed to all reform but who viewed the present tax laws as too confiscatory, were well represented, as they always have been. A representative of the Investors League, Inc., attacked the graduated income tax, the capital gains tax, and other features of the tax laws as a threat to economic growth, asserting that according to Karl Marx's *Communist Manifesto* the goal of the Communists was to destroy private property by a "heavy progressive or graduated income tax" and by the "abolition of all right of inheritance." [11]

George Meany, head of the AFL-CIO, who can hardly be considered a radical, was one of the few witnesses testifying in support of the reforms. He had the temerity to tell the House committee that Congress should not only close some of the more obvious tax loopholes favoring wealthy taxpayers, as the administration proposed, but it should add amendments for the benefit of lower-income taxpayers, such as an increase in personal exemptions and higher credits for dependents. He was even so bold as to suggest that Congress might consider restoring the "earned income credit," which had been eliminated in the 1940s and which gave to wage and salary earners and entrepreneurs working for a living a modest credit not accorded to the recipients of dividends, interest, and other passive income.[12] Representative James B. Utt of California greeted this testimony by inferring that Meany was promoting the doctrines of Marx and Engels, and proclaimed that "the graduated income tax is probably the greatest weapon in the hands of the Socialists directed at the heart of capitalism." [13]

The net result was that the relatively mild dose of tax reform proposed by the administration was rejected.

In 1969 the reform forces were more successful. Early in the year the Johnson Treasury presented Congress with a formidable tax reform package, and President Nixon, prodded by the public outcry against recent revelations of tax avoidance by wealthy individuals, committed his administration to the accomplishment of meaningful tax reform.

But the opponents of serious reform for the most part gave ground grudgingly. As in the past, trade association spokesmen and other representatives of the real estate interests, Wall Street investment firms, banks, oil and gas industry, and other interested parties bombarded the tax-writing committees with their voluminous prepared statements and requests to be heard; and their lobbyists worked overtime both in and outside the halls of Congress.

But this time, even relatively conservative members of the House Ways and Means and Senate Finance Committees knew that the tax bill on which they were laboring would, in the end, have to include some major concessions to the reformers. Even Representative Byrnes, the ranking Republican on the house committee, who had spoken so scornfully of the need for structural reform five years before, had been reading his mail, and now sang a different tune.

The foundations, reconciled to adoption of the Treasury's proposals in their area, confined themselves to trying to avoid even stricter limitations on their right to contribute to what they regarded as socially useful projects. The real estate lobby, knowing that the use of excessive depreciation as a tax shelter was bound to be curtailed, fought a rear-guard action designed to soften the blow. Charitable organizations, including colleges and universities, admitted that some of the more glaring abuses of the use of charitable donations had to be done away with, and in the end had to content themselves with the fact that the tax advantages flowing from gifts of appreciated property had not been seriously impaired. The savings and loan associations and savings banks had to be grateful that the preferences they had been enjoying were merely reduced, rather than entirely swept away.

In the end a significant measure of tax reform is contained in the new act, despite the fact that almost every reform proposal adopted was whittled down to some degree by the time it had run the gauntlet of the House and Senate conferees. Nevertheless the worst tax loopholes still remain. Percentage depletion and write-offs for intangible drilling expense for the oil and gas industry emerged from the battle virtually unscathed. A strong challenge to the tax-exempt status of state and local government bonds was successfully beaten back when scores of state and municipal officials descended on Washington to protest. Proposals to eliminate entirely the preferred tax treatment of capital gains in securities, real estate, and other property were substantially softened. Many other major escape hatches, including the exemption from income taxation of capital gains accruing on death or as the result of gifts, and the avoidance of estate taxes by the use of generation-skipping trusts still remain to be dealt with.

Present Prospects for Reform

The chances of a major revision of the tax structure that will eliminate the remaining loopholes and inequities are far from bright. The advocates of drastic tax reform in the House and Senate are still relatively few in number, and even they are wary of the organized pressure in their home states by business interests opposed to serious reform. They have learned that the support of tax revision does not pay off politically—witness the defeat in 1966 of Senator Paul Douglas, one of its most outspoken champions. They know that the opponents of tax reform are politically powerful, well organized, and amply supplied with funds. Therefore, after its brief period of popularity in 1969, tax reform is no longer being emphasized as a major issue by progressives on Capitol Hill.

Perhaps most important, in spite of the recent flurry of publicity about tax avoidance by the well-to-do and other privileged groups, the public is generally poorly informed about the nature of the tax structure and its inequities. Its attention is now focused on other issues, so that again there is little effective public pressure for an overhaul of the tax structure.

Finally, the tax laws are exceedingly complex and technical. The average lawmaker, not to mention the average citizen, is baffled by them. On the other hand the lobbyists, tax lawyers, and other spokesmen representing special interests are enormously knowledgeable and highly skilled at taking advantage of every loophole and escape hatch. Confronted with a variety of powerful pressures and influences, members of Congress tend to log-roll for the business and financial interests in their home states when it comes to tax legislation, and the public is generally none the wiser.

Perhaps what is needed more than anything else before a campaign for drastic tax reform can be launched successfully is a public that is better informed as to the inequities inherent in the present tax structure, so that it will become sufficiently aroused to exert relentless pressure for tax reform on its representatives in Washington.[14] The outlook for major tax reform in the immediate future is discouraging. New efforts will surely be made, but that they will succeed is doubtful. One is inclined to share the pessimism of Senator Douglas at the 1963 tax hearings when he reminded Treasury Secretary Dillon how often the administration's promises of reform had failed to materialize:

SENATOR DOUGLAS: The President said in 1961 there was going to be a thoroughgoing program in 1962; 1962 came along and the delay— it was not your fault, I agree, it was the fault of the House.

There was some reform in 1962, but there was going to be a thoroughgoing bill in 1963. Now 1963 came in and very frankly there isn't much reform. Mr. Williams [Senator Williams of Delaware] asked you about 1964. You replied that is an election year. Then 1965. How long, Oh Lord, how long?[15]

21

Ideologies, Principles, and Dogmas

What Constitutes a Tax Loophole?

This book has dealt primarily with the major "loopholes" in our tax laws, particularly those favoring people with large incomes that are either shielded from taxation or that benefit from special allowances or deductions. The result of these preferences is to distort the progressive rate structure and the principle of taxation according to "ability to pay."

But there are many categories of income that escape taxation that are received by those in the lower ranges of the income scale— Social Security payments, unemployment compensation, contributions to employees' health and accident plans, and other fringe benefits, to mention only a few. Since they also represent economic benefits not now taxed, they must likewise be characterized as "loopholes" which, under a comprehensive and strictly neutral tax system, should be "closed."

It has often been said that "one man's loophole is another man's divine right," which is another way of emphasizing that whether a particular tax provision is an inequitable preference or a sound and justifiable exception depends on the person making the judgment. To the investor in an oil property, the deductions he is permitted for intangible drilling expense and percentage depletion serve vital national objectives. The wage earner or salaried employee regards such special allowances as flagrantly discriminatory, while at the same time he looks on any proposal to tax his own fringe benefits as an affront to elementary justice. Yet under a rigorously comprehensive system of taxing all income impartially, both types of income should be subject to tax under a progressive rate schedule.

What Is Income?

The average person has a rather simplistic impression of what constitutes "income." He conceives of it as confined to tangible cash items that he can see—wages, salary, interest, dividends, or the earnings of a business. But there is a whole array of benefits that people enjoy, beyond these more obvious categories, that fall within a strict income concept.

The classic formulation, the so-called Haig-Simons definition, describes income as the sum of goods and services consumed by a person plus (or minus) the increase (or decrease) in the value of his assets during a given interval of time.[1] Under such a comprehensive definition every conceivable benefit, whether it consists of the receipt of cash, services, or payments in kind, or results from enjoyment or use, as well as every increase in the value of one's property is encompassed; and under a neutral "no preference" approach all are to be treated alike. Not only would such notoriously favored sources of income as interest from state and local bonds and capital gains be taxed in full, but many receipts not now subject to taxation, such as gifts and bequests, damages received in personal injury cases, unemployment insurance, strike benefits, and welfare payments would be included.

Indeed under a strict, comprehensive definition, a host of noncash benefits would be considered income. Among other items, the imputed value of owner-occupied homes, the household services performed by a non-working wife, the advantage of a tuition-free public education, and the benefit to a farmer of an irrigation or soil conservation program carried on by the government on his own or adjoining land would be taxable.

What Kind of Income Tax?

At one time government revenues were raised through head taxes; every person, regardless of his wealth, was assessed an equal amount. The first tentative steps toward taxing according to an individual's means were based on rough approximations of comparative wealth, such as the number of window panes in a citizen's house.

According to the eighteenth century doctrine of laissez-faire, as expounded by Adam Smith and his followers, government should interfere as little as possible with private enterprise. Taxation should be kept at a minimum so as not to interfere with or discourage the profit motive, production, and the incentive to invest. While the taxes on factory workers, agricultural laborers, and other poor persons were burdensome and difficult for them to pay, they were tolerated on the theory that the economy as a whole benefited, in that such imposts discouraged indolence and encouraged industry, and prompted the poor to work harder to improve their lot. On the other hand, according to the same doctrine, the levying of large taxes on people with substantial incomes or great wealth would discourage the incentive to save and invest, thereby impeding the growth of the very capital whose continued investment in business and industry was indispensable for the creation of jobs. In short, high taxes on substantial incomes or accumulated wealth would damage the poor by depriving them of employment.[2]

However during this century, and especially in recent years, as the functions and services performed by federal, state, and local governments have expanded, the need for funds to defray the huge cost of national defense, education, housing, urban renewal, job training, and other services has become greater and greater. There is no longer any dispute that vast amounts of revenue have to be raised. The only question is what kind of taxes shall be imposed and who shall pay them.

There are several possible approaches for the levying of income taxes on individuals. One might be to tax people on the basis of how much goods and services they consume. The trouble with this theory is that if you tax a well-to-do person only on what he consumes rather than on his income, the largest part—what he saves—will escape taxation.

Another method would be to tax people according to the benefits they derive from public services, such as police and fire protection, public health services, education, and welfare, or from government expenditures made to encourage certain types of technological research and development. But this approach involves numerous problems: Some types of governmental expenditures confer the greatest benefits on private industry; wealthy people with larger and more elaborate residences probably derive greater advantages from police and fire protection than lower income groups; poorer people undoubtedly benefit more in the area of health, education, and welfare. In any case it is often difficult, if not impossible, to evaluate the amount of benefit individual taxpayers receive from various governmental expenditures or public services, or the extent to which their contributions to the cost of government should offset those benefits. How can one measure the individual benefits flowing from expenditures for police and fire protection or national defense, or from government laws and regulations that enable business to raise capital necessary for expansion or encourage economic growth and stability?

A third alternative would be to tax people on the basis of their respective capacities to contribute to the cost of government, on their "ability to pay." [3]

There are no clearly established scientific formulas for arriving at a proper tax structure, nor are the arguments for any one philosophy without counter-arguments.[4] In our democratic society taxation according to the principle of ability to pay has received wide acceptance as the most equitable method of raising revenue.[5] Indeed it is generally thought to be fundamental to the progressive tax structures from time to time adopted by Congress, though in practice it does not always work out that way.

There is also general agreement that the income tax must be fair and equitable—a concept based on two requirements: that "people in equal position should pay equal amounts of tax," and that "people in unequal position should pay different amounts related in a meaningful fashion to difference in position." [6] Under the first principle, sometimes referred to as "horizontal equity," A and B, each with the same amount of income and similarly situated (e.g., each with a wife and two children), should be required to pay the same amount of income tax. The second principle, often referred to as "vertical equity," requires that C, who also has a wife and two children, but who enjoys an income four times as large as A and B, should be required to pay substantially more than the other two. How much more C should pay will depend on society's view as determined by Congress.

Equity and a Progressive Rate Schedule

The difference in the taxes that should be paid by C, with the same family responsibilities as A and B but with four times as much income, is a matter of controversy. One possibility is to have all three pay the same percentage of their incomes in taxes. If we assume a tax rate of 20%, and if A and B have incomes of $20,000, and C an income of $80,000, A and B would each pay an income tax of $4,000 a year and C $16,000 a year. A and B would each be left with $16,000 after taxes, while C would be able to keep $64,000 to support a family of the same size. This method of taxing each in the same proportion is generally viewed as unfair because it conflicts with the equitable principle of "ability to pay."

Ever since the passage of the first federal income tax law in 1913, the consensus of the American electorate, as voiced by their representatives in Congress, has been in favor of the principle of "progressivity." Progressivity in taxation presupposes that the rate or percentage of income taxed will rise as taxable income increases. Under the progressive rate schedule, C, in the example above, would pay a tax about six or seven times the amount that A or B would pay, even though his income is only four times as much. At C's level of income his proportionately larger tax bill is no more burdensome than the smaller percentage that A and B pay on their lower incomes.

Progressively higher rates applied to ascending levels of income are designed to achieve vertical equity by subjecting those with higher incomes to roughly the same hardship or sacrifice in discharging their heavier tax liabilities as lower income taxpayers are confronted with in meeting their lesser tax burdens. Accordingly, our rate schedules consist of a graduated series of rising percentage rates, starting with 14% for a married couple with a taxable income up to $1,000, and increasing to 70% for a couple with a taxable income of $200,000 or more.

If our income tax rate schedules were truly progressive, and if all sources of income were taxed uniformly, the tax structure could not be criticized as lacking in equity. The trouble is that all income is not taxed uniformly: some types of income, such as the interest on state and local bonds are not taxed at all; other kinds, long-term gains on the sale of securities, for example, are taxed at a preferentially low rate; and still other categories receive the benefit of special deductions, such as the depletion allowance for oil and rapid depreciation for certain real estate investments.

It is these various departures from uniformity, sometimes called preferences, exceptions, special provisions, or loopholes, that are responsible for the fact that our tax system does not tax "all income alike" at progressively graduated rates.

Every Loophole Has Its Own Rationale

Every preference, exception, and special provision has its own theoretical justification. Those opposed to them generally refer to them as inequitable, while those who enjoy their advantages insist that they are not inequitable at all—on the contrary they have been sanctioned by Congress in order to accomplish some public policy objective of overriding national importance, such as contributing to economic growth and stability, the incentive to invest, the maintenance of a high standard of living, or the national defense. Or, it is claimed, the effect of the tax preference is to allocate more efficiently manufacturing and other capital or human resources, reduce unemployment, provide jobs, and increase purchasing power.

The late Louis Eisenstein, the eminent tax scholar, contended that every group enjoying a tax preference or concession has its own ideology, each with

its own style of thought, and its own collection of platitudes. These are repeatedly echoed as if they were divinely inspired.[7]

Every preferred group rationalizes its own position in terms of certain values, which are expressed as

dispassionate principles rising above partisan preferences. The desires of the particular interest are transformed into a profound and impartial concern for everybody. What is good for the group is good for the country.[8]

"Equity," as understood by the beneficiaries of tax-favoritism, consists largely of two principles:

special relief for certain taxpayers who are differently situated from all other taxpayers . . . [and] the privilege of paying as little as somebody else. Since someone is always paying less, it is always possible to ask for equity.[9]

The oil investor insists that the depletion allowance is needed to encourage the search for oil, which is indispensable to the nation's security. The holder of tax-exempt bonds claims that elimination of the exemption of the interest they yield will curtail state and local programs for construction of highways, bridges, schools, and hospitals. The forestry industry and agricultural interests in turn warn that terminating the special capital gains treatment accorded their activities will threaten the very existence of the country's national resources of timber. That the particular preference applicable to their business activity gives them a special tax advantage is merely incidental to the substantial indirect benefits to the country at large.

It is therefore extremely difficult to select the particular economic activities that should be encouraged by tax preferences or incentives. Moreover each exception begets others, and each new preference that is granted further erodes the tax base and increases the taxes that others are required to pay.

Ideologies of Capital Gains

As befitting a preference of such overriding importance,[10] the tax treatment of capital gains has probably been accompanied by more ideological discussion than any other provision of the tax law. The defenders of the favored treatment argue that a higher tax or greater restrictions on capital gains transactions will discourage and possibly immobilize entirely the incentive to invest, augment the role of tax considerations in investment decisions, and reduce capital available for new and productive enterprises. Holders of securities and other property that have substantially appreciated in value will be frozen in their holdings and deterred from disposing of them in favor of other investments, thereby diminishing economic activity and the flow of capital into new businesses. Some have even contended that "capital gain," i.e., the profit a man realizes when he disposes of an investment, is not really "income" at all, though it may to some extent be analogous to income.[11]

But most authorities today insist that the profit from capital gains is no different from other types of income;[12] and one commentator, scoffing at those who suggest otherwise, has written that if capital gains are not income then they "are a means of becoming wealthy without realizing any income."[13] Many believe furthermore that the deterrent effect of the capital gains tax on new investments is overrated.

Accordingly there is broad support for placing greater limitations on the transactions that qualify for the preferential capital gains tax rate, with criticism focusing especially on the six-months holding period. Today if a taxpayer sells an investment after holding it for 5 months and 29 days, he is "a speculator," and will be taxed on his profit at full ordinary income tax rates up to 70%; whereas if he holds on for another day or two and sells after six months, he is regarded as "an investor," and his profit will be preferentially taxed as long-term capital gain. Consequently some tax authorities feel that the requisite holding period for capital gains treatment should be lengthened from six months to at least a year, and that there should be a sliding rate scale, with larger percentages applicable to assets transferred after shorter holding periods, and smaller percentages applied to those held longer.[14]

Analogous ideological arguments are advanced in connection with proposals to impose a capital gains tax on the appreciation in value of assets that are the subject of gifts, or that pass to heirs on death, transfers which now entirely escape such taxation.[15]

Supporters of such proposals point to the beneficial effect such a tax would have in "unlocking" investments that have risen in value, especially when they are owned by wealthy investors in their advanced years. Elderly investors are reluctant to sell because they count on escaping all tax on the appreciated value if they hold the investments until they die. If these investors knew that a capital gains tax on their appreciated holdings would be payable on their death, they would, it is argued, be more likely to sell and make other investments, thereby stimulating the flow of capital into new ventures, now artificially held back by tax considerations.

But opponents claim that this would be a form of double taxation, adding a capital gains tax on death to the present estate tax. A better way to encourage sales by investors who are disinclined to sell because of the capital gains tax they would have to pay, is to reduce the rate of the capital gains tax. Then, they say, investment and reinvestment decisions would be determined solely by economic rather than by tax factors, leading in turn to a more efficient allocation of investment capital, and perhaps to an increase in tax revenues.

A somewhat related proposal advocated by many is the so-called roll-over investment account whereby no capital gains tax whatever would be due as long as the proceeds of sales of investments are reinvested in other property. Only if the proceeds of a sale were consumed rather than reinvested would there be a tax on the gain at ordinary income rates. But if the proceeds of investment sales are continuously invested and reinvested, all taxation of the net gains would be postponed until death, at which time a capital gains tax, in addition to the regular estate tax would be payable.[16]

Tax Preference or Direct Governmental Subsidy

Even if the economic and social arguments in favor of granting economic aid to one group of taxpayers or another are overwhelming, the question still remains whether a tax preference or tax incentive is the most desirable and efficient mechanism for accomplishing this result.

For one thing, the value of the tax preference varies with the tax bracket of the one who enjoys it. To the very affluent man whose substantial income from other sources places him in a 65% tax bracket, each dollar of special allowance from his oil, timber, or other tax-favored income is worth 65¢ (and the Treasury loses the same amount in tax revenue); whereas to the small oil prospector, the average farmer, or the owner of modest timber acreage who does not have other sources of income taxable at high rates, the special deduction or allowance may mean little if anything in tax savings. Frequently, as Wilbur D. Mills, chairman of the House Ways and Means Committee, has pointed out, most of the benefits of tax preferences that are used as incentives to invest in areas the government deems important go to firms that would have made the investment in any case, so that the tax advantage they get is a pure windfall.

Direct governmental expenditures, on the other hand, could be more readily confined to those who would not otherwise have undertaken the activity.[17] It may also be cheaper for the government to pay direct monetary subsidies to those engaged in activities it wishes to encourage, than to grant a tax preference. It would be far less costly, for example, to give direct federal aid to help defray the expenses of those mineral prospectors who need financial aid, than to grant wholesale tax preferences to all prospectors, whether they need assistance or not.

The waste and inefficiency sometimes inherent in the use of a tax preference is demonstrated by the present tax treatment of the elderly. A very large part of the benefits from the special tax exemptions granted to persons over 65, and which costs the Treasury approximately $2 billion annually in lost tax revenues, is enjoyed by older persons in comfortable circumstances. The Treasury itself is now questioning whether the direct distribution of the $2 billion among those aged who most need the assistance would not be infinitely more efficient.[18]

Finally, the cost of a direct monetary subsidy voted by Congress for a stated purpose can be appraised and budgeted in advance, and has the further advantage that the benefits granted are open to public knowledge, scrutiny, and criticism. The indirect benefits conferred by special tax preferences are unpredictable in amount, and hidden from public view—a sort of "back door" method of spending government revenue.[19]

There is, it is true, the counter-argument that subsidies and direct aid have the drawback of more controls and administrative red tape at the federal level, and of increasing federal involvement in state and local affairs. Nevertheless there is a growing consensus that all existing tax benefits or allowances and all proposals for new tax incentives should at least be subjected to a rigorous cost analysis to determine whether, from the point of view of revenue lost to the Treasury, direct government expenditure is not preferable to tax concession.[20]

Tax Credits—A Third Alternative

Recently there has been considerable discussion of the possibility of using another vehicle—tax credits—as a device for compensating taxpayers in whole or part for certain types of expenditures, or for encouraging a variety of socially worthwhile activities and programs.[1] It is now being suggested that the use of the tax credit device, hitherto strictly limited,[22] be expanded to cover college tuition fees, taxes paid to state governments, and expenditures for such projects as air and water pollution control, urban renewal, new factories in ghetto and rural poverty areas, job training for the hard-core unemployed, and underground installation of electric transmission lines.

The difference between the allowance of a tax *credit,* which reduces taxes directly, and a tax *deduction,* which reduces taxable income and only indirectly affects the tax paid, may be illustrated by the following example. At present when a taxpayer makes a gift to charity he may *deduct* the amount from his *taxable income* and so reduce his tax bracket. A charitable contribution of $100 by A, who is in a 60% tax bracket, reduces his tax by $60; whereas a gift of the same amount by B, who is in a 20% tax bracket, saves him only $20. If a full tax credit were permitted for charitable gifts, A and B would derive the same benefit, since each could deduct the $100 donation from the amount of *tax* he has to pay.[23]

At first glance the use of a tax credit would seem fairer since it affects all taxpayers equally, whereas under the present law high income taxpayers derive the greatest benefits from deductions for charitable gifts, medical expenses, and the like. Advocates of the use of tax credits point out that the device possesses considerable flexibility. Congress could from time to time vary the amount of the tax credit, lowering or raising the amount or percentage of the allowance as, in the judgment of the lawmakers, the need for compensating taxpayers for certain expenses or encouraging various social programs diminishes or increases.[24]

However the resort to tax credits presents certain problems, both conceptual and practical. The disadvantages of the device probably outweigh its advantages. If Congress were to allow a tax-payer a partial credit against his federal income tax liability, such as 25% of the sums spent for such purposes as medical expenses or charitable gifts, many taxpayers would be required to defray their federal income taxes with money expended for doctor bills or given to charity. If, for example, a taxpayer in the 60% bracket incurred $4,000 of extraordinary medical costs during the year, and the credit allowed against tax was limited to 25% of this expense, he would be paying a tax at a 60% rate on $3,000, three-fourths of his medical bills. This would be contrary to the principle widely recognized, that one should not be required to pay taxes on money devoted to such purposes, since, having been spent for doctors, hospital care, and the like, the money is no longer available to defray taxes.

If a 100% credit were allowed against taxes for such expenditures, the cost to the Treasury from reduced tax revenue might well be prohibitive. Under the present system, which permits deduction of charitable, medical, and other expenditures from taxable income, the amount of the Treasury loss (and the taxpayer's saving) depends on the taxpayer's tax bracket and can never be more than 70% of the amount spent; and while such personal deductions have an unequal tax value to individuals in different income classes, it is the result of Congress' decision to impose graduated income tax rates.[25]

Finally, the use of tax credits, at least insofar as they are employed to encourage expenditures for college tuition, air and water pollution control, urban renewal, and the like, amount to government subsidies that are hidden, and subject to all the objections of lack of periodic Congressional analysis and review and scrutiny by the public. It is for such reasons that Congressman Mills has indicated his opposition to any wholesale expansion of the tax credit formula.[26]

Is Our Income Tax Really Progressive?

Most people have the impression that our income tax structure *is* progressive, but the late Louis Eisenstein maintained that this progressivism is a myth:

We have devised an income tax which particularly favors those who manage to become wealthy without being very productive. In other words it is felt that in order to make the system work, we must be unusually kind to those who are essentially drones.[27]

In the first place the income tax rate structure itself is not truly progressive or consistent with the principle of ability to pay. The smallest brackets and the steepest increase in rates occur at the bottom of the scale and apply to persons with lower and more modest incomes. The rate for single persons ranges from 14% on a taxable income of $500 to 70% on taxable income over $100,000.[28] The half-way point in the tax rate (42%) is reached at the $22,000-$26,000 taxable income bracket. The second half of the increase in rate (from 40% to 70%) occurs over a much wider spread—as taxable income increases from the $22,000-$26,000 level to the $100,000 (and over) level. It can hardly be said that these rates, 40% for the $22,000-$26,000 taxpayer and 70% for the $100,000-plus taxpayer, are a fair reflection of their comparative abilities to pay.[29]

In any case, even assuming a degree of progressivity in the rate tables, for most of our wealthier citizens the graduated income tax has been only theoretic. Some persons whose six-figure incomes are derived predominantly from executive salaries and other ordinary income sources, have in fact been paying taxes at rates as high as 70%. But the majority of the well-to-do, with incomes from oil operations, tax-exempt bonds, capital gains from securities transactions, and other tax-sheltered sources, enjoy so much income that is either totally exempt, taxed at preferential rates, or subject to large deductions before their tax is computed that their effective rate of tax is shockingly low.

The beneficiaries of substantial income from investments in municipal and local bonds pay no tax whatever on these receipts. Investors in oil properties have the advantage not only of generous deductions for intangible drilling and other costs, but after oil starts to flow, are permitted to enjoy 22% of the resulting income tax-free. Similar tax advantages accrue to the holders of stock options, inventions, and coal and iron royalties; and the preponderance of benefits from the tax-favored treatment of capital gains resulting from the sale of securities and other property are reaped by those at the higher income levels.[30] It is only the unfortunate citizen whose income, large or moderate, is derived from a salary, wages, a business, interest, or dividends, which (apart from a small exclusion) are taxed at full ordinary rates, who pays taxes according to the progressively rising rate schedule.

A table prepared by the Treasury and introduced at the 1963

tax hearings underscored the fact that taxpayers with the largest incomes were paying at lower effective rates than those with much smaller incomes. Persons with annual gross incomes, including capital gains, of $5 million or more were paying at an average effective tax rate of 23.7% (less than half the effective rate of those with about one-tenth of such incomes), while taxpayers with gross incomes ranging from a quarter to a half million dollars annually were actually paying at a rate almost 10% higher than the multi-millionaires.[31] At the same time the average wage earner with a wife and two children, who earned $100 a week, was found to be paying $456 a year in federal income taxes.[32] Subsequent Treasury data disclosed that these same patterns prevailed, and, if anything, were even more pronounced in later years.[33]

From the point of view of horizontal equity, that is, the comparative tax payments of individuals having the same incomes and otherwise similarly situated, the 1963 Congressional tax hearings were equally revealing. For example, in the case of two taxpayers both with annual gross incomes of $300,000, one paid at an effective rate of 71% and the other at 4%.[34]

It is obvious that the overall impact of our tax structure has been far from progressive, particularly on those in the lower- and middle-income groups, and especially when all the other taxes—excise taxes, state and city sales taxes, and other local taxes—that people are obliged to pay are taken into account. While the Revenue Act of 1964 reduced the tax rates of all taxpayers, it is generally acknowledged that the biggest reductions were in the high brackets, especially when increases in after-tax income were taken into account.[35] The 1968 "across-the-board" 10% tax surcharge was still another departure from progressivity, and under the Tax Reform Act of 1969, the ideal of progressivity has been further impaired by substantial cuts in the tax rates applicable to high-salaried executives.

In fact, from 1954 to 1969 the effective tax rates of the higher income groups have been reduced far more than those of the lower and moderate income levels. When changes in the minimum living standard are taken into account, the low-income groups are actually being taxed at a higher rate now than fifteen to twenty years ago.[36] To put it another way, over this period the after-tax income of lower- and middle-income taxpayers has increased only slightly and at a considerably lower rate than the increase in after-tax income of those with larger incomes.[37] The tax rate changes scheduled to go into effect in 1970 and thereafter under the Tax Reform Act of 1969 will only begin to alter this trend.

Some contend that our tax policy is moving further and further from the ideology of progressivism, and that the Democratic Party, once the champion of this principle, now pays only lip service to it. Indeed, when one examines the utterances of Treasury officials and other spokesmen in recent Democratic administrations, there appears to be considerable support for this contention.[38] The traditional position of the Democrats, that the major economic problem was the critical gap between an excessive productive capacity and an under-capacity to consume, and which was based on a progressive income tax rate structure scaled to the ability to pay, has been largely abandoned. In its stead, it is claimed, they seem to have adopted the theories of Andrew Mellon, Secretary of the Treasury in Republican administrations forty years ago, who maintained that low taxes for business and the well-to-do provided the indispensable incentive for initiative, saving, and investment, creating the wealth and prosperity that would eventually trickle down to factory workers, farmers, and small businessmen in the form of full employment, higher wages, and lower prices.

But the gospel of Mellon that the prosperity of the majority depends on lighter taxes for the well-to-do will not, according to the critics, provide the massive governmental revenues needed for better schools, housing, hospitals, highways, environmental controls, and other social improvements. As they see it,

We will not enter the Great Society through the doorway of Mellon.[39]

22

Is an Ideal Income Tax Possible?

Would it be possible to have an "ideal" income tax, a comprehensive system, basically fair and neutral, to which all men of good will could cheerfully subscribe? The consensus of tax scholars seems to be that such a system is practical and possible.[1]

The Comprehensive Tax Base

Comprehensive income tax would of course be based on a far broader concept of income than is used under our present tax law. Using the Haig-Simons definition of income, it would encompass all goods and services consumed by a taxpayer, plus the gain (or minus the loss) in the net worth of his assets during the taxable year. Every kind of income, including many not now subject to taxation, from whatever source it was derived, would be taxed alike.

Thus not only would the more familiar categories of income—wages, salaries, dividends, and profits from a business—be taxed, but all net capital gains from the sale of securities and other property (now taxed at a preferential rate), all interest on state and local bonds (now tax-exempt), and all appreciation in the value of property transferred by gift or at death (now free of income tax) would be included and taxed like ordinary income. All special allowances and deductions from income now permitted, such as percentage depletion in excess of cost for oil and other mineral income and accelerated depreciation for real estate, would be ended.

In addition, a multitude of other benefits and accretions to wealth, cash and non-cash, direct and indirect, would, under such a strict no-preference concept, be deemed taxable, although they are not taxed today and most people do not even think of them as income. Thus most supporters of a comprehensive tax would agree that the following items, among many others, would probably be includible:

Welfare payments and clothing and rent allowances received in cash or in kind

Social Security and Railroad Retirement payments over and above the amount contributed thereto by the employee

Workmen's compensation payments

Unemployment compensation payments

The rental value of owner-occupied homes

The interest or dividends credited to the policy holder on certain types of life insurance policies

Food and fuel from the farm consumed by farm families

Pensions to veterans and compensation for service-incurred illness or disability

Death benefits paid to a family by Social Security or by an employer on death of an employee

Payments received from federal or state governments to encourage soil conservation or reforestation

Premiums paid by an employer on group life insurance for employees

Contributions by employers toward the cost of accident and health plans for employees

Money received for scholarships and fellowships

Borderline Items of Income

There are numerous additional items that many advocates of a comprehensive tax base are disinclined to include, although they may agree that they are "income" in the strict sense of the word.[2]

The gifts people receive and the bequests or insurance proceeds left to them on the death of relatives are "income" in its broadest sense. But many authorities would not subject them to the income tax on the theory that they would bear their proper share of tax under a reformed estate and gift tax law. Damages received by a taxpayer for personal injuries or by his family for his wrongful death would likewise be excluded on the theory that they compensate for pain, suffering, injury, and loss of earning power.

The imputed value to a husband of the domestic services of his non-working wife and the benefit from owning (rather than renting) an automobile, power boat, and other items of personal property are also income, as strictly defined. They would probably have to be excluded, however, as being too difficult to evaluate and as presenting overwhelming administrative problems.

The same reasoning would apply to the benefits of tuition-free public education, the indirect advantage to a farmer from a flood control or soil conservation program carried out not on his own, but on adjoining land, and to a businessman whose store or factory is made more valuable by a public improvement in the neighborhood. They would probably be excluded as non-cash benefits, either because of the difficulty of measuring the extent to which the benefit received exceeded the contribution made by way of taxes, or because the problems of collection would be insuperable, or for a combination of such reasons. The benefits people receive from police, fire, and military protection would be disregarded on similar grounds.

Most authorities would exclude as income the unrealized appreciation in value of securities and other assets as it accrues year by year because of the formidable administrative and compliance problems involved. This accumulated appreciation in asset value would eventually be taxed as capital gain when a gift was made or on death, and interest could be collected then from the time the gain accrued.

Problems and Complications

Of course under a strict no-preference income tax system, the only deductions from income permitted would be business expenses and expenditures incurred in connection with the production or earning of income. None of the usual personal deductions people now take on their income tax returns—such as charitable donations, medical expenses, casualty losses, state and local taxes—would be allowed. However many supporters of a comprehensive tax base would allow deductions for extraordinary medical expenses and casualty losses in excess of a certain percentage of gross income, or under some similar formula.[3] They are also inclined to permit personal and dependency exemptions such as the $625-$750 personal exemption that each taxpayer may deduct for himself and for each child or dependent. They regard the personal exemption as not inconsistent with the comprehensive tax base concept, but rather as a rough method of allowing for differences in ability to pay of families of unequal size. Such allowances are generally justified, and properly so; some differentiation must be made on humane or moral grounds between two taxpayers enjoying the same gross income, one of whom supports a large family, or suffers the calamity of a fire or water damage to his home, or who is saddled with excessive medical expenses, while the other is free of such burdens. There is certainly a legitimate basis for distinguishing between allowances for unavoidable expenses and permitting deductions for voluntary expenditures (for charitable gifts, or for interest on a mortgage loan or on a refrigerator purchased on the installment plan). Some commentators feel that the question of allowing a deduction for charitable gifts will have to be decided by Congress, since in the absence of a tax deduction as an inducement to charitable giving, the government may have to make direct subsidies to charitable, educational, and religious institutions.[4]

The present rate structure and income splitting for married couples is unfair to bachelors and heads of households. Congress will have to decide whether to retain the various rate structures and the present methods of taxing separate family units, as well as the number and size of personal exemptions.[5]

The time when income is received raises difficult problems. If a taxpayer in a high income bracket can split or defer salary payments, dividends, or other items of income to another year when his income level is lower, he will be able to reduce his tax payments. For example, a member of a partnership is taxed currently on his share of the partnership's profits, whether they are distributed to him in the taxable year or not, even if he is unable to have them paid to him because of the restrictions of a partnership agreement. The stockholder of a corporation, on the other hand, even if he is the sole stockholder, is not taxed on the corporate earnings until they are distributed to him in the form of dividends. By the same token, the undistributed income of a trust is not always currently taxed to the beneficiary.[6]

Some commentators feel therefore, that under a comprehensive tax system the separate income tax on corporations should be eliminated and the earnings taxed to the shareholders whether distributed or not; and that the beneficiaries of trusts should be similarly taxed currently on all undistributed income of the trust.[7] Congress will have to decide the question of how the various taxpaying units, partnerships, corporations, and trusts shall be taxed.

Taxpayers who are able to make arrangements for postponing the receipt of income by means of deferred compensation agreements or through payments in annual installments obtain an advantage over other taxpayers who are required to report income at the time the right to it accrues, even though it may not be paid to them until a subsequent year.[8] Even more disadvantaged in this respect is the actor, writer, or professional athlete whose large income may be concentrated in a few years of his career, or the investor whose capital gains are "bunched" within a single year.

In spite of these problems most champions of a comprehensive tax base, while agreeing that ideally all income should be taxed as it accrues rather than when it is received, are prepared as a practical matter to accept the accounting practices and periods commonly used in business as well as the carryback and carryover of losses and other items permitted under present law. They rely on a suitable averaging system, applicable to all types of income, including capital gains, that are concentrated in a particular year, to mitigate the disadvantages suffered by those with an irregular income who are unable to time its receipt to their advantage.[9]

Exceptions to a Comprehensive Income Tax

There are other problems that would arise in connection with formulating a comprehensive tax base along the foregoing lines, not the least of which is how to draw the line between business expenses, which people would be allowed to deduct, and personal expenditures, which they could not. Supporters of such a system frankly admit that while it will not solve every problem, it will solve most of them, and that although departures from a strict income definition will sometimes be necessary, such exceptions will be limited to two types.

In the first place a departure in the form of a tax concession or preference (such as the rapid write-off of expenditures for soil or water conservation, or for certain types of research and experimentation) will be tolerated only if it promotes a major national objective, and provided that a tax concession rather than a direct government subsidy is the most effective and least costly method of achieving it.

Secondly, exceptions will be made to the policy of taxing all income of every kind where the problems of measurement or evaluation or other administrative difficulties make it too costly or otherwise impractical. Typical examples would be the imputed value to a husband of the domestic services of his non-working wife, the value of food and fuel consumed on farms, or the benefits of a free public education.[10]

Critics insist that the exceptions would be so numerous that the so-called ideal income tax would be as complicated as the present tax law. Professor Bittker of Yale, who holds this view, has tartly observed that the enthusiastic supporters of a comprehensive tax base have "a capacious knapsack of arguments to support a wide range of departures" from their theoretically strict income tax concept. Before they are through, he predicts, there will be so many departures from the strict concept of "no preference" and of treating all income alike that the result will be a structure more complex, unwieldy, and no more equitable than the present system with all its imperfections.[11] But the tax scholars who have responded to his attack on the comprehensive tax base concept feel that Bittker exaggerates the problems, most of which, they feel, will lend themselves to a practical solution.[12]

The present tax structure is heavily weighted in favor of those whose incomes are derived from capital gains, state and local bond interest, oil and other minerals, and certain kinds of real estate, and discriminates unfairly against everyone who does not enjoy income of that sort—whether he be a wage earner in an automobile factory, a $175,000-a-year executive, or a successful lawyer, doctor, actor, or small businessman.

Under a comprehensive income tax, if an exception by way of a tax preference or incentive were proposed, Congress would decide in open debate whether the favoring of a particular business or social activity constituted a major policy objective of overriding national importance, and whether the goal might not be more efficiently accomplished by direct government subsidy. Once the slate is wiped clean of the existing preferences, Congress would be more likely to select the direct aid approach rather than that of the tax concession; the former would be open to public scrutiny, its cost easier to estimate and control, and it would be simpler to discontinue when the need for it ends or becomes less acute. The well-known fact that one tax preference leads to another, as each group or interest insists that it is only "equitable" that the preference granted another be granted to it, should have a sobering effect in discouraging the proliferation of loopholes.

There is every reason to believe that under a comprehensive

income tax system present rates could be sharply reduced, with the maximum rate about 50%, without any overall loss in tax revenues.[13] If a national emergency or the urgent demands of enlarged social programs required higher rates, the base on which taxes would be levied would be much broader and more equitable.

Finally the anomalies of the present system—with millionaires paying only a small percentage of their annual receipts toward taxes while other citizens having infinitely smaller incomes pay at much higher rates—would be brought to an end. Not the least important result would be the boost to taxpayer morale. The widespread knowledge that so many of the well-to-do are not bearing their fair share of the tax burden is inducing more and more taxpayers to get into the act of "beating the government" under our self-assessment tax system.

23

Proposals for Reform

No Dearth of Recommendations

The fact that, until recently, major revision of our tax structure failed to materialize was not due to any shortage of reform proposals. From the 1950s on the House Ways and Means Committee and other Congressional bodies were deluged with formal papers, reports, and testimony from economists, law professors, and other experts, on the subject of tax revision, as well as a variety of proposals received from the Treasury's tax staff, The Brookings Institution, and others.

This broad spectrum of expert opinion disclosed a general consensus that reform of our tax laws was urgently required. Suggested modifications included broadening the tax base to cover various types of exempt income, elimination of preferential treatment accorded certain sources of income, reduction in rates, an averaging system for all types of income to avoid the problem of "bunched income" in a single year, an end to double taxation of corporate income (first at the corporate level and then at the shareholder level), and simplification of the exceedingly complicated tax structure.

In 1963 the American Bar Association, an organization that traditionally had not even been found in the ranks, let alone the vanguard, of those urging drastic tax reform, adopted a resolution that asserted that the federal income tax

does not provide for an equitable distribution of the tax burden and for a sufficiently broad base . . . ; . . . because of an accumulation of exceptions and special provisions caused by the impact of excessively high income tax rates, something less than one-half [of the $450 billion annual national income] is subject to income tax. . . . [The structure] is unnecessarily complex and should undergo substantial revision.[1]

For a number of years, and especially since President Johnson's 1967 request for a temporary income tax surcharge to curb inflation and to meet the mounting needs of the government for revenue, a growing number of members of Congress have been adding their voices to the demand for tax reform. They advocated reform either as a companion to a tax increase or as a measure that would produce more than enough additional revenue to make a tax increase unnecessary. Most of these Congressional proposals called for plugging some of the major loopholes favoring wealthy taxpayers. Probably the best known proposal was the bill introduced in October 1967 by Congressman Henry Reuss of Wisconsin on behalf of himself and several other House members.[2]

Some proposals put forth in the guise of tax reform would have accomplished the very opposite. For example, Senator Russell Long, chairman of the Senate Finance Committee, insisted for years that his so-called Simplified Tax Plan would, with a single stroke, achieve the long-sought goal of equitable treatment for all taxpayers. However, upon analysis, it proved to be something less of a boon than its supporters claimed.

The central idea of the Long plan was to induce high-income individuals who paid little or no taxes, because their income was exempt or sheltered by various tax preferences, to surrender these immunities in return for being taxed at an especially low rate. If they would forswear resorting to the various exemptions and preferences available to them because their income was derived from oil, tax-exempt bonds, cattle raising, timber, capital gains from security transactions, and all the rest, and agreed to have all income from whatever source derived subject to taxation, they would have the advantage of being taxed at a rate graduating from 20% to a maximum of 50%.[3] In addition they would be spared all the expenditure of time, money, and energy that they and their accountants, lawyers, and tax advisors customarily devoted to tax planning and tax avoidance; and all this time and effort would be redirected toward more socially useful activities, including the production of income and profit.

But the fatal flaw in the Long proposal was that it was optional and not compulsory. Under its complicated provisions for electing, terminating, and revoking the Plan, resourceful taxpayers could avail themselves of its low rate provisions during periods when it was advantageous, and withdraw from it when it no longer served their purpose, at which time they could go back to enjoying all their former preferences, allowances, and tax-sheltering devices. Furthermore, while one who elected to use the Plan forfeited the privileges of resorting to tax loopholes *for himself,* this restriction did not apply to members of his family, the corporations he controlled, or to his family trusts. Taxpayers choosing the Long Simplified Tax Plan could postpone or accelerate, and otherwise manipulate various types of income and deductions so that they would be subject to or escape the Plan's reach, or shift income or deductions to corporations, trusts, or family members.

In short, the Plan was so flexible and left so much room for maneuver that wealthy taxpayers utilizing the Plan could have the best of both worlds—the advantage of a low tax rate on income they reported under the Plan, and the effective use of all the tax-avoidance devices which they were supposed to forgo.[4]

Reform Program of the Treasury Under the Johnson Administration

In 1968 when Congress finally gave its blessing to President Johnson's urgent request for a temporary 10% income tax surcharge, it exacted a promise from him to submit his recommendations for tax reform by the end of the year. However early in January 1969, on the verge of retiring from office, the president decided against a formal presentation of a reform program on behalf of his administration. Instead he chose to have the Treasury Department, which had been working on a series of tax proposals for some time, submit its studies directly to Congress. A few weeks later this material, which did not carry the former president's endorsement, was turned over to the House Ways and Means Committee and made public.

The Treasury's proposals,[5] which consisted of some 500 pages of detailed statistical data, analyses, and suggested revisions of the Internal Revenue Code, recommended many important reforms, including a minimum tax aimed at very wealthy citizens who were able to avoid paying any taxes;[6] elimination of loopholes in the areas of charitable donations,[7] "gentleman farming" and cattle breeding,[8] multi-corporate organizations,[9] and accumulation trusts;[10] revision of the tax treatment of private foundations [11] and certain tax-exempt religious organizations;[12] imposition of a capital gains tax on transfers at death or by gift;[13] and drastic revision of the estate and gift tax law.[14]

While the Treasury's proposals failed to come to grips, except partially and tangentially, with such major loopholes as oil and mineral depletion, tax-exempt bonds, stock options, excessive real estate depreciation, and the preferential tax treatment of capital gains, they represented real progress toward reform.

The House Ways and Means Committee, after holding hearings on the Treasury's program and other reform recommendations through the spring and summer of 1969, reported out a bill in August 1969, which in some respects went farther than the Treasury proposals. However, when the House bill came before the Senate, that body, with rare exceptions, watered down its provisions, so that the final bill, as signed by President Nixon, proved a disappointment to those who had hoped for more forceful reform measures.

The Tax Reform Act of 1969

The main provisions of the Tax Reform Act of 1969 [15] may be summarized as follows:

Minimum Tax on Items of Tax Preference

Many individuals and corporations with tax-exempt or tax-favored incomes who previously paid relatively little or no income tax thereon are now required to pay some tax on this income.

Among the tax-sheltered or preferred types of income now subject to tax are oil income subject to a percentage depletion allowance in excess of cost, income from real estate operations to the extent that accelerated depreciation exceeds straight-line depreciation, income on the exercise of stock options, and the half of long-term capital gains that ordinarily does not have to be included in income. The tax on ordinary income and the sum of $30,000 are permitted as deductions from the sheltered income, and the remainder is taxed at 10%.

Real Estate

The tax advantages of accelerated depreciation for real estate are reduced. To all intents and purposes accelerated depreciation deductions are confined to investments in apartment houses, and future depreciation deductions in excess of straight-line depreciation will be recaptured as ordinary income on the sale of business real estate properties and apartment houses not held for the requisite period.[16]

Charities

The ability of certain very wealthy taxpayers to minimize or entirely eliminate their tax liabilities by resorting to the "unlimited charitable deduction" will gradually be ended over a period of years. Taxpayers who contribute property that has appreciated in value to other than recognized charities (for example, to private charitable foundations) will either be confined to deducting the original cost of the property, or will have to pay a capital gains tax on the amount of the appreciation in value since it was acquired. Finally, a whole grab bag of previously permissible gimmicks, which enabled donors to achieve large income or estate tax savings or a net profit from the transaction, are now outlawed or substantially restricted. They include "bargain sales" of property to charity, gifts in trust of income or of future interests, and numerous other arrangements.[17]

Capital Gains

Capital gains are still taxed at one-half the ordinary tax rate, but the 25% maximum effective tax on the gain, previously applicable, has been abolished.[18]

Capital Losses

Previously, long-term capital losses up to $1,000 a year could be deducted in full from ordinary income. Under the new law only 50% of the loss up to $1,000 (or $2,000 for a couple) may be deducted from ordinary income.

Pension and Profit-Sharing Plans

Lump sum distributions from pension and profit sharing plans, previously taxed at capital gains rates, are treated and taxed as ordinary income, with a seven-year averaging provision.[19]

Multiple Accumulation Trusts

The beneficiaries of multiple accumulation trusts, who formerly reaped tax advantages from this device,[20] will be taxed on the income accumulated in their trust when they receive it, and with substantially the same tax results as if the income had been paid to them directly as it was earned.

Oil, Gas, and Other Minerals

In addition to other minor changes, the depletion allowance for producers of oil and gas has been reduced from 27½% to 22%, and slightly reduced for some other minerals. A favorite tax-avoidance device, the mineral production payment, has been eliminated by a change in the law. Such transactions are now treated as loans.[21]

Multiple Corporations

After a period of years, organizations that previously were permitted multi-corporate surtax exemptions and other tax benefits intended only for small business enterprises, will gradually be limited to one $25,000 surtax exemption and a single accumulated earnings credit.[22]

Restricted Stock

Key corporate executives in the past have been permitted to treat as capital gain the appreciation in value of "restricted stock" received by them as compensation, and were taxed on this appreciation at the capital gains rate. Now they are taxed on this increment at ordinary income rates.[23]

Farm and Livestock Losses

The preferred capital gains treatment previously accorded certain farming and livestock operations is somewhat curtailed under the new law by provisions for the recapture of depreciation and certain operating losses previously taken when the property is sold. Further limitations are likewise imposed on excessive hobby losses incurred by "gentleman farmers" and others.[24]

Banking Institutions

Over an eighteen-year period commercial banks will gradually be limited in their deductions for bad debts to their actual loss experience, instead of the excessive bad debt deductions permitted under previous law. Mutual savings banks and savings and loan associations are now more limited in their deductions for bad debt reserves, although they are still allowed to deduct sums greater than their actual loss experience justifies.

Banking institutions are no longer permitted to treat their long-term profits on sales of U.S. government and other bonds as capital gains, but are taxed on them at ordinary income rates.[25]

Private Foundations

The chief provisions affecting private charitable foundations are those imposing new restrictions on self-dealing between a foundation and its creator or members of his family, requiring foundations to distribute their income currently rather than to accumulate it, and in general limiting to 20% the interest that they may hold in corporate enterprises.[26] In addition a 4% tax has been imposed on foundations' net investment income.

Tax-Exempt Organizations

In the future religious, educational, and other charitable organizations will be prohibited from acquiring businesses and other property with borrowed funds, while at the same time having their income from the acquired business remain tax-free. The long-standing exemption of certain religious organizations from the tax on their unrelated business income has also been terminated.[27]

Convertible Bonds

"Conglomerate" corporations' widespread practice of deducting interest on bond issues used by them in acquiring other companies has been discouraged. They are now prohibited from deducting such interest if the capital or earnings of the conglomerate are deemed, under special tests, to be insufficient.

In addition, individual taxpayers are not permitted to report their gain on the sale of property under the installment method if they receive in exchange a convertible bond that is readily marketable.

Utility Dividends

Under the new Act utilities are no longer able to pay tax-free dividends by using accelerated depreciation methods for tax purposes.

Tax Reduction

A number of provisions to reduce taxes will become effective at various dates: Personal exemptions will increase gradually to $750; the standard deduction will increase over a period of years to 15% or $2,000, whichever is lower; a new maximum tax rate of 50% is applicable to salaries, wages, and other earned income; and the tax rates for single individuals and heads of households will be scaled-down. Families with an income of less than $1,100 after personal exemptions are exempt from tax. This low-income allowance will be reduced to $1,000 by 1972 to offset increases in the personal exemption.

Further Goals

While the Tax Reform Act of 1969 puts an end to a number of existing inequities, it by no means accomplishes the kind of reform that is ultimately desirable. Rather, it is merely a step, though an important one, in that direction. The "minimum tax" provision, revolutionary as it is in the light of tax reform history, can hardly be described as a "soak the rich" program, since in no event will more than 10% of the tax-free or tax-sheltered income of even the wealthiest individual be collected in taxes. Moreover a number of major loopholes—percentage depletion and intangible drilling expenses for oil and gas, tax-exempt bonds, capital gains at death, and the numerous tax-avoidance devices connected with the estate and gift tax, to mention but a few—have been overlooked entirely or only partially closed.

No tax reform program can be considered adequate unless it deals effectively with the major tax preferences and abuses that still remain, by:

Eliminating percentage depletion in excess of cost for oil, gas and other minerals, as well as the privilege of deducting intangible drilling and development costs from income

Doing away entirely with the tax-exempt status of state and local bonds, including industrial revenue bonds

Imposing a capital gains tax on property transferred on death or by gift

Terminating the capital gains treatment for stock options, for farm income that includes the sale of livestock, for the sale or licensing of inventions, and for royalties and other income derived from the sale of timber, coal, and iron

Minimizing tax avoidance through family income splitting by raising gift tax rates, and reducing gift tax exemptions and exclusions

Preventing the avoidance of estate taxes by imposing an inheritance tax when the beneficial ownership of a trust is transferred, by stricter taxation of "special" powers of appointment, and by taxing certain life insurance proceeds and death benefits under pension and profit-sharing plans. (Eventual comprehensive reform will require the elimination or narrowing of the differential between gift and estate taxes, or a single integrated tax covering all transfers from generation to generation with perhaps tax-free transfers between husbands and wives.)

Subjecting closely held corporations to the penalty of the Personal Holding Company tax unless at least 60% of their income is of the active rather than passive variety

Eliminating the deduction for the appreciated value of gifts of stock and other securities to charity

Ending accelerated depreciation for all kinds of real estate accompanied by the taxation, at ordinary income tax rates, of all previous depreciation deductions recovered on resale

Eliminating the exemption from income tax of group life insurance coverage and the exclusion from estate taxation of the proceeds of such insurance

Strictly limiting private and special tax bills for the relief of individual taxpayers

Revising the special tax exemptions for persons over 65 along the lines of the Treasury's proposals, and bringing into more equitable balance the separate rate schedules for married couples, heads of households, and single persons

Reviewing the immunity from taxation of items of imputed income such as the value of owner-occupied homes and the interest or dividends credited to the owners of certain types of life insurance

Further revising the tax treatment of banking institutions so as to eliminate completely their use of excessive bad debt reserves to reduce their tax liabilities, and ending other special immunities which favor them over other taxpayers

Revising the rate structure to achieve greater progressivity
Eliminating the 50% maximum tax on earned income.

Most important of all, the preferred tax treatment of capital gains should be ended and capital gains should be taxed on the same basis as items of ordinary income.

Not all revisions of the tax law that would result from such a program should be put into effect immediately. Some reform measures would require a transition period during which the effectiveness of substantive changes in the law would either be postponed or be only partially operative. In this way taxpayers who have arranged their affairs on the basis of present law would be given an opportunity to reshape them in the light of the new legislation.

It is difficult to predict how much additional tax revenue such reforms would produce. Philip M. Stern, whose proposals for reform envisaged a virtually comprehensive tax base under which all sources and kinds of income would be subject to a uniform tax, forecast some years ago, that if his program were adopted tax revenues would be increased by as much as $40 billion annually, even if rates were sharply reduced.[28]

Some idea of how much the government is now losing as the result of the tax loopholes that still remain, and of the additional revenue that would be collected if they were eliminated entirely, may be gained from an appraisal made recently by the Treasury Department. In January 1969 the Secretary of the Treasury calculated that the Treasury was losing over $10½ billion in taxes every year as the result of certain enumerated tax preferences.[29] But since his list of loopholes was far from complete, and omits the need for revision of estate and gift taxes, the treatment of intangible drilling expense, and the preferred tax status of capital gains, among others, that estimate must be regarded as most conservative.

The Treasury has stated that the loophole-closing provisions of the House version of the Tax Reform Act of 1969 would initially add about $4 billion annually to tax revenues.[30] It would be a fair guess that another $10 billion would be raised each year if all additional tax preferences and tax-avoidance devices were swept away.

Perhaps the goal of drastic tax reform, a system embodying maximum equity and neutrality, is visionary and impossible to achieve. The influence of those favored under the present tax system may prove too great to overcome. It may well be that the chairman of the Senate Finance Committee was right when he declared that

It is a fact of life of which we are all fully aware, that people and organizations with interests to protect are not going to allow Congress to scrap the present system of taxation for a broad-based, no exception, low rate system that may do some violence to those interests.[31]

Moreover the long-term goal, a truly comprehensive income tax integrated with a revised estate and gift tax law, will take years to accomplish. Nevertheless, and in spite of the numerous problems inherent in evolving such a tax structure, it will be worth the effort in the end.

Notes

The following abbreviations are used in the Notes:

House Hearings on H.R. 8363
U.S., Congress, House, Committee on Ways and Means, *Hearings on H.R. 8363 (President's 1963 Tax Message),* 88th Cong., 1st sess., 1963.

I. R. Code
Internal Revenue Code

Patman Hearings
U.S., Congress, House, Select Committee on Small Business, *Hearings before Subcommittee No. 1.*

Patman Report
U.S., Congress, House, Select Committee on Small Business, "Tax-Exempt Foundations and Charitable Trusts: Their Impact on Our Economy," *Subcommittee Chairman's Report to Subcommittee No. 1.*

Senate Hearings on H.R. 8363
U.S., Congress, Senate, Committee on Finance, *Hearings on H.R. 8363 (Revenue Act of 1963),* 88th Cong., 1st sess., 1963.

Senate Hearings on H.R. 13270
U.S., Congress, Senate, Committee on Finance, *Hearings on H.R. 13270 to Reform the Income Tax Laws, Part 1,* 91st Cong., 1st sess., 4 and 5 September 1969.

Treasury Dept. 1969 Reform Studies
U.S., Treasury Department, *Tax Reform Studies and Proposals,* 91st Cong., 1st sess., 5 February 1969.

Treasury Report
U.S., Congress, Senate, Committee on Finance, *Treasury Department Report on Private Foundations,* 89th Cong., 1st sess., 2 February 1965.

1. Some of Our Taxpayers Have Been Missing

1. U.S., Congress, House, *Congressional Record,* 90th Cong., 1st sess., 12 October 1967, p. H. 13351.

2. *New York Times,* 8 September 1967.

3. H.R. 13490, 90th Cong., 1st sess., 1967. The Reuss bill proposed the elimination of the unlimited charitable deduction, the special tax treatment of stock options, the $100 dividend exclusion, the benefits derived by multiple corporations, the tax exemption of industrial development bonds, accelerated depreciation for real estate, and the payment of estate taxes by the redemption of government bonds. It also recommended that depletion allowances for oil and other minerals be reduced and that capital gains untaxed at death be subject to tax.

4. See Chap. 23.

5. President's Tax Reform Proposals, 21 April 1969.

6. 1 Tax Revision Compendium 538 (1959).

7. U.S., Congress, Senate, Committee on Finance, *Hearings on H.R. 8363 (Revenue Act of 1963),* 88th Cong., 1st sess., 15 October 1963 ff., pp. 140-46, 283, 309.

8. Ibid., pp. 283, 848. Adjusted gross income did not include interest on state and municipal bonds, deductions for intangible drilling and development expense in connection with oil and gas operations, and one-half of all capital gains.

9. Ibid., pp. 279, 284.

10. Ibid., pp. 281-82, 377, 1252-53, 2235-36.

11. Ibid., p. 237.

12. Ibid., pp. 850-51, 2239.

13. U.S., Congress, House, Committee on Ways and Means, *Hearings on H.R. 8363 (President's 1963 Tax Message),* 88th Cong., 1st sess., 1963, p. 606.

14. Drew Pearson and Jack Anderson, "The Tax Gap," *New York Post,* 1 November 1967.

15. *Senate Hearings on H.R. 8363,* pp. 235-36.

16. Ibid., pp. 307-309.

17. Between 1957 and 1966 the number of persons filing returns disclosing adjusted gross incomes between one-half million and $1 million increased from 578 to 1545; and those disclosing gross incomes of $1 million or more increased from 217 to 626. U.S. Treasury Department, Internal Revenue Service, *Statistics of Income 1966—Individual Income Tax Returns,* Table 66, p. 235.

18. *Wall Street Journal,* 20 January 1969. In 1965 the number of millionaires who entirely escaped income tax was even greater. U.S., Congress, House, Select Committee on Small Business, *Report of Sub-*

committee No. 1, 26 March 1968, p. 27 (Congressman Wright Patman, chairman). U.S., Congress, Senate, Committee on Finance, *Hearings on H.R. 13270,* Statement by Assistant Secretary Edwin S. Cohen, 91st Cong., 1st sess., 4 September 1969, p. 639.

19. U.S., Treasury Department, *Tax Reform Studies and Proposals,* 91st Cong., 1st sess., 5 February 1969, pp. 80-84, 89-97.

20. R. A. Musgrave, *In Defense of an Income Concept,* 81 Harvard Law Review, 44, 47 (1967); Horace M. Gray, *Tax Reform and the Depletion Allowance,* 2 Tax Revision Compendium 979 (1959).

21. Musgrave, p. 62; Joseph A. Pechman, *Comprehensive Income Taxation,* 81 Harvard Law Review 63, 65-66 (1967).

22. *Senate Hearings on H.R. 8363,* p. 1252.

23. *Senate Hearings on H.R. 13270,* pp. 697, 698.

2. The Immunities of Religious Property—Little Rendered Unto Caesar

1. O. K. Armstrong, "Tax Churches on Business Profits," *Christianity Today,* 13 October 1961, p. 19.

2. Bishop James Pike, "Tax Organized Religion," *Playboy,* April 1967, pp. 100, 148.

3. Martin Larson, *Church Wealth and Business Income* (New York: Philosophical Library Inc., 1965), pp. 51 ff.; Anson Phelps Stokes, *Church and State in the U.S.* (New York: Harper & Bros., 1950), vol. III, p. 419; Edward B. Fiske, "To Tax or Not To Tax," *New York Times,* 28 May 1967, editorial section.

4. *A Report on Churches and Taxation,* Guild of St. Ives, May 1967, p. 1; Arvo Van Alstyne, *Tax Exemption of Church Property,* 20 Ohio State Law Journal 461-62 (1959); note also *Constitutionality of Religious Tax Benefits,* 49 Columbia Law Review 968-92 (1949); *Time Magazine,* 15 May 1964, p. 53.

5. St. Ives, pp. 9-10; Van Alstyne, pp. 461, 462-63; Willard L. Sperry, *Religion in America* (New York: The MacMillan Company, 1946), pp. 60-61; Judge Reuben Oppenheimer, opinion in Murray v. Goldstein, 241 Maryland 383, 216 Atlantic 2d 897, certiorari denied 385 U.S. 816 (1966).

6. City of Hannibal v. Draper, 15 Missouri 634, 639 (1852).

7. Stokes, p. 421.

8. Sperry, pp. 60-61; St. Ives, p. 1; Van Alstyne, pp. 461 ff.

9. Internal Revenue Code, Sec. 501, 502, 511. Herbert H. Brown and Joseph T. Martin, Jr., *Church and State—Taxation of Religious Organizations,* 5 Villanova Law Review 255 (1959–60).

10. St. Ives, p. 1; Brown and Martin, pp. 269-70.

11. St. Ives, p. 1; Brown and Martin, pp. 271-73.

12. Larson, pp. 56 ff.

13. I.R. Code, Sec. 170(b)(1)(A), (B), (2); Brown and Martin, p. 274.

14. St. Ives, p. 1; 49 Columbia Law Review 968 ff.

15. I.R. Code, Sec. 2055, 2522; St. Ives, p. 1; Helen B. Shaffer, *Editorial Research Reports,* 18 November 1964, pp. 829-30.

16. *Time Magazine,* 1 July 1966, p. 45.

17. Larson, *Church Wealth and Business Income; Tax Exempt Property of Churches in Key American Cities,* Part I (Protestants and Other Americans United for Separation of Church and State, 1964) pp. 8-9; "Tax-Exempt Property In Baltimore," *Church and State,* October 1964, p. 11; "Religious Tax-Exempt Property in Buffalo," *Church and State,* February 1965, pp. 11-12.

18. Another study by the National Council of Christians and Jews estimates that the current assets of all charities, including religious organizations have increased 170% in the ten-year period 1955–65 to a total of $54.8 million, and predicts that they will reach $100 billion by 1975. However Larson believes that this estimate is much too conservative. Larson, *Church Wealth,* pp. 71-72.

19. Pike, p 100

20. Pike, p. 100; St. Ives, pp. 8-9.

21. Edward Zipperstein, "Taxation of Clergymen," *Taxes,* vol. 41 (1963), p. 219; I.R. Code, Sec. 107; Revenue Ruling 62-212, 1962-2 CB 41.

22. Larson, *Church Wealth,* pp. 64-65.

23. Ibid., p. 51; *Real Estate Tax Exemptions in New York City—A Design for Reform,* Citizens Budget Commission, Inc., April 1967.

24. Pike, p. 144.

25. *Christianity Today,* 19 January 1962, p. 26.

26. *Time Magazine,* 15 May 1964, p. 53.

27. Murray v. Goldstein.

28. Robert Liston, "Mrs. Murray's War on God," *Saturday Evening Post,* 11 July 1964, p. 83.

29. 49 Columbia Law Review 968-92; St. Ives, pp. 6-8; Van Alstyne, p. 461; Fred A. Hurvich, *Religion and the Taxing Power,* 35 University of Cincinnati Law Review 531 (1966).

30. Fiske, loc. cit.

31. Shaffer, pp. 823-39; Armstrong, p. 19; James C. Tanner, "Church Business," *Wall Street Journal,* 29 October 1963; Larson, *Church Wealth,* pp. 68-77.

32. The resort to such tax avoidance schemes received considerable impetus from a decision of the U.S. Supreme Court, which held certain

aspects of such transactions to be lawful. Commissioner v. Clay B. Brown, 380 U.S. 536 (1965). The Tax Reform Act of 1969 deprives the participants of the tax advantages derived from these "boot-strap" acquisitions. See Chap. 23.

33. Larson, *Church Wealth,* p. 74.

34. Tanner, loc. cit.

35. I.R. Code, Sec. 511-14.

36. St. Ives, p. 12.

37. Tanner, loc. cit.

38. Armstrong, p. 19.

39. Ibid., p. 19.

40. Tanner, loc. cit.; Larson, *Church Wealth,* p. 75.

41. Larson, *Church Wealth,* pp. 71-77.

42. *Wall Street Journal,* 29 October 1963.

43. Opposition to the tax exemptions enjoyed by religious organizations may be more widespread today than has been generally supposed. A nationally televised program, "CBS Reports: The Business of Religion," 18 June 1968, indicated that, according to a CBS survey, a large majority of the general public, clergymen, and members of the House and Senate favored a full disclosure of church income, and taxation of income-producing property and unrelated business income of church organizations. *New York Times,* 19 June 1968.

More recently a joint statement by the National Council of Churches, representing most Protestant denominations, and the U.S. Catholic Conference urged Congress to eliminate the special exemption for churches on unrelated business income and to close the "Clay Brown" loopholes under which churches and other non-profit organizations could purchase businesses on credit using the tax-free profits of the acquired business to pay the purchase price. The Protestant organizations went even further and proposed that churches pay the local governments their "just share" of municipal, fire, police and sanitation services on a voluntary basis." *New York Times,* 3 May 1969.

44. Eugene Carson Blake, "Tax Exemption and the Churches," *Christianity Today,* 3 August 1959.

45. Ibid.

46. Tanner, loc. cit.; Armstrong, p. 19; *New York Times,* 28 May 1967, editorial; "Churches and Tax Exemption," *Commonweal,* 28 December 1956, pp. 324-25.

47. Armstrong, p. 19.

48. Tanner, loc. cit.

49. Shaffer, pp. 835-36.

50. *Christian Century,* 6 June 1962, p. 707.

51. Pike, pp. 147-48; St. Ives, pp. 14-15.

52. *New York Times,* 28 May 1967, editorial; *Time Magazine,* 1 July 1966, p. 45; *America,* 26 May 1962, p. 288, 12 January 1957, p. 408.

53. Larson, *Church Wealth,* p. 71.

54. *Time Magazine,* 26 April 1963, p. 69; Douglas Bedell, *Wall Street Journal,* 11 September 1967.

55. Bedell, loc. cit.

56. See Chap. 23.

57. *U.S. News & World Report,* 24 August 1959, p. 57; Shaffer, pp. 837-39; St. Ives, pp. 15-18; Pike, p. 93; Larson, *Church Wealth,* pp. 79-82.

58. Larson, *Church Wealth,* p. 79; Mark A. Talney, "End to Tax Exemption," *Christian Century,* 20 October 1965, p. 1297.

59. See Chap. 3.

60. Pike, p. 144; St. Ives, pp. 15-18; Larson, *Church Wealth,* pp. 78-80.

61. Pike, p. 144. Bishop Pike would exempt only that proportion of the value of church buildings which is devoted to charitable and non-denominational community activities (the proportion to be arrived at on a space and time use basis), and tax the rest.

62. Tanner, loc. cit.

63. St. Ives, pp. 16-19.

64. Some clerical opponents of modifying present tax exemptions for religious organizations have, in the course of defending mushrooming church wealth, pointed to the swollen endowments of the wealthier private universities. *America,* 12 January 1957, p. 408.

65. *1966 Corporation Support of Higher Education,* Council for Financial Aid to Education, Inc. (1967), p. 22; *Responsible Giving to Higher Education,* Council for Financial Aid to Education, Inc. (1960), p. 9; Duncan Norton-Taylor, "Private Colleges: A Question of Survival," *Fortune,* October 1967.

66. Norton-Taylor, loc. cit.; Kenneth G. Patrick, "Education and the Business Dollar," *Michigan Business Review,* March 1963; p. 20; Addresses by James R. Killian, Jr. and Keith Spalding, *Symposium on Impact of Federal Aid to Higher Education,* Council for Financial Aid to Education (1967); Roger M. Blough, "What Price College?" Convocation at Millsaps College, Jackson, Miss., 25 February 1967, pp. 2-5; James M. Heister, "The Private University in our Tax Economy," New York University Institute on Federal Taxation, vol. 21 (1963), p. 1.

3. Private Foundation Field Day Comes to an End

1. Subcommittee No. 1 of Select Committee on Small Business. (Hereafter referred to as the "Patman Committee.")

2. U.S., Congress, House, Select Committee on Small Business, *Report of Subcommittee No. 1,* 21 December 1966, p. 1.

3. Lawrence G. Knecht, *Use of the Foundation as a Planning Device,* 20 New York University Institute on Federal Taxation 259 (1962).

4. I.R. Code, Sec. 170.

5. I.R. Code, Sec. 2055, 2522.

6. I.R. Code, Sec. 501 (c)(3).

7. The reports bear the title "Tax-Exempt Foundations and Charitable Trusts: Their Impact on Our Economy," *Subcommittee Chairman's Report to Subcommittee No. 1,* Select Committee on Small Business, House of Representatives. They include reports dated 31 December 1962, 16 October 1963, 20 March 1964, 21 December 1966, 28 April 1967, and 26 March 1968. These reports will be referred to hereafter as "Patman Report," and the hearings as "Patman Hearings" under the appropriate dates.

8. Patman Report, 31 December 1962, p. 5.

9. Ibid., p. 74.

10. Barry R. Peril, "Tax-Exempt Targets: The Patman Report and Private Charitable Foundations," *Taxes,* Feb. 1964, pp. 69-83.

11. Marvin Caplan, "Foundations with Tax Umbrellas," *The Progressive,* Feb. 1963, pp. 27-30; *Business Week,* 25 August 1962, p. 85.

12. Patman Hearings, 4 September 1964, p. 281.

13. Ibid., pp. 282-83.

14. Ibid., p. 283.

15. Ibid., p. 284.

16. Patman Report, 31 December 1962, p. 17.

17. Ibid., 16 October 1963, p. 1.

18. Ibid., pp. IX-XI.

19. Peril, pp. 69-83.

20. The Treasury Department found that the investment assets of all private foundations at the end of 1962 had a value of $16.3 billion; U.S. Congress, Senate, Committee on Finance, *Treasury Department Report on Private Foundations,* 89th Cong., 1st sess., 2 February 1965, pp. 82-83 Committee Print (hereafter referred to as "Treasury Report"). In its 1968 report, the Patman Committee found that the assets of 596 foundations studied by it had a value of $15.1 billion at the end of 1966, compared to $10.2 billion at the end of 1960. Patman Report, 26 March 1968, p. 1.

21. Patman Report, 16 October 1963, pp. 1-2; 21 December 1966, pp. 1, 3.

22. Patman Hearings, 21 July 1964, pp. 144-52; Patman Report, 31 December 1962, p. 81.

23. William C. Golden, *Legislative Proposals Concerning Private Foundations,* 41 Indiana Law Journal 555, 560 (1966).

24. Patman Hearings, 21 July 1964, pp. 146-51.

25. I.R. Code, Sec. 503.

26. *Colleges, Charities and the Revenue Act of 1950,* 60 Yale Law Journal 851, 866 (1951).

27. Victor H. Frank, Jr., "Organizations and Aspects of the Patman Report," *Taxes,* Jan. 1964, pp. 36-41; Kenneth L. Karst, *Tax-Exemption of Donor-Controlled Foundations,* 25 Ohio State Law Journal 183, 190-94 (1964).

28. Frank, pp. 851, 869.

29. Treasury Report.

30. Ibid., pp. 21-23.

31. John E. Riecker, *Foundations and the Patman Report,* 63 Michigan Law Review 122-25 (Nov. 1964).

32. Bernard Wolfman, "The Treasury Report on Private Foundations," New York University Conference on Private Foundations, vol. 7 (1965), p. 191; Ernest L. Folk, III, "Regulation of Charitable Foundations," *Business Lawyer,* vol. 20 (1965), pp. 1015, 1036-40; William E. Guthner, Jr., *Prohibited Transactions and Unreasonable Accumulations of Income,* 13 U.C.L.A. Law Review 996, 1006-1007 (1966); Karst, pp. 198-99; Herman T. Reiling, *Income Tax Policy as to Charitable Foundation Misuse,* 10 St. Louis Law Journal 462 (1966); Marcus Schoenfeld, *Initial Impressions of the Treasury Report on Foundations,* 14 Cleveland Marshall Law Review 286, 295 (1965).

33. Patman Report, 21 December 1966, p. 13, 16 October 1963, pp. IV-VII, 20-58.

34. Ibid., 16 October 1963, pp. VII-VIII, 61-74.

35. Ibid., 31 December 1962, pp. 9-13.

36. Ibid., p. 13.

37. I.R. Code, Sec. 502, 511-13.

38. John Walsh, "Foundations: Patman Maintains Pressure for Tighter Regulation of Tax-Exempt Organizations," *Science,* 7 August 1964, pp. 559-61; Frank, pp. 36-41; *Preventing the Operation of Untaxed Business By Tax-Exempt Organizations,* 32 University of Chicago Law Review 581 (1965).

39. Golden, pp. 555, 572; *Wall Street Journal,* 3 April 1967. The procedure employed was as follows: The foundation's business assets were leased to a wholly-owned subsidiary at a rental high enough to

absorb substantially all the income earned by the subsidiary's business operations. Although the subsidiary was subject to the payment of the regular corporate income tax, it in fact paid little or none since the rent it paid to the foundation, if "reasonable," was a deductible expense; and the "rent" received by the foundation was specifically excluded from the definition of "unrelated business" income. I.R. Code, Sec. 512 (b)(3).

40. Daniel J. Baum and Ned B. Stiles, *Power Pools, Private Foundations and Private Corporations,* 13 U.C.L.A. Law Review 938, 952-53, (1966).

41. Treasury Report, pp. 36-37.

42. John G. Simon, "The Patman Report and the Treasury Proposals," New York University Conference on Charitable Foundations, vol. 7 (1965), pp. 141, 158-59; one commentator suggests that the grace period should be 25 years, Folk, pp. 1015, 1023; Ronald E. Gother, *Analysis and Criticism of the Treasury Proposal to Limit Stock Ownership by Private Foundations,* 13 U.C.L.A. Law Review 1017 (1966); Schoenfeld, p. 297.

43. Riecker, pp. 113-15; Lawrence M. Stone, "Background of the Treasury Department Report on Private Foundations," New York University Conference on Charitable Foundations, vol. 7 (1965), p. 181; Reiling, loc. cit.

44. Patman Report, 16 October 1963, p. 2.

45. Patman Report, 21 December 1966, pp. 1-3.

46. Reicker, pp. 135-40; Peril, pp. 69-83; *Business Week,* 25 August 1962, p. 85.

47. Patman Report, 21 December 1966, p. 1.

48. Ibid., pp. 8-9.

49. I.R. Code, Sec. 504 (a)(1).

50. Patman Hearings, 21 July 1964, p. 59.

51. Patman Report, 16 October 1963, pp. 2-3.

52. Thus Frederick T. Gates, the Baptist minister who was the closest adviser in matters of philanthropy to John D. Rockefeller, Sr., who founded the Rockefeller Foundation, is quoted by Patman as having warned the Philanthropist: "Your fortune is rolling up, rolling up like an avalanche! You must keep up with it! You must distribute it faster than it grows! If you do not, it will crush you and your children and your children's children." And Dr. Max Mason, head of the Foundation from 1929 to the 1930s, is said to have told a magazine writer in 1959: "Old man Rockefeller did not set up the foundation, or any of its philanthropic enterprises for that matter, with the idea of ever-lastingness. Not only was the interest to be spent, the principal was too; so the prospect of spending itself out of existence had been before the

Rockefeller Foundation from its beginnings." Patman Report, 21 December 1966, pp. 8-9.

53. Patman Report, 31 December 1962, p. 133.

54. Treasury Report, pp. 26-30.

55. Ibid., pp. 49-54.

56. Golden, pp. 555, 570, 571; Guthner, p. 1016; Reiling, loc. cit.; Schoenfeld, p. 296.

57. William E. Hannam, "Family Foundations," *Trusts and Estates,* vol. 102 (Feb. 1963), p. 108.

58. Treasury Report, pp. 41-45. Some commentators feel that the maximum percentage of a donor-controlled corporation that a foundation should be permitted to own should be 10% or less. Karst, pp. 217-20.

59. Simon, p. 141.

60. Folk, pp. 1015-21.

61. Treasury Report, pp. 56-57.

62. Schoenfeld, pp. 298-99.

63. *Preventing the Operation of Untaxed Business by Tax-Exempt Organizations,* 32 University of Chicago Law Review 581 (1965).

64. Substantially the same proposals were recommended for adoption as part of the Treasury's tax reform package submitted to Congress in February 1969. Treasury Dept. 1969 *Reform Studies,* pp. 25-26, 41, 295-306.

65. Thomas A. Troyer, *The Treasury Department Report on Private Foundations: A Response to Some Critics,* 13 U.C.L.A. Law Review 965 (1966).

4. Special Tax Privileges for Corporate Executives— Stock Options Old and New

1. Proxy statements of Bristol-Myers Company, 11 October 1967, pp. 19-20; of International Telephone and Telegraph Corporation, 1 April 1967, p. 25; of City Investing Company, 28 July 1967, p. 31; and of W. R. Grace and Company, 20 April 1967, p. 7.

2. Commissioner v. Smith, 324 U.S. 177.

3. V. Henry Rothschild, *The New Stock Option,* 17th University of Southern California Tax Institute 117 (1965); Theodore Berger, *Stock Options Under the 1964 Revenue Act,* 46 Chicago Bar Record 430, 433 (1965–66).

4. Livingston, "Business Outlook," *Washington Post and Times Herald,* 4 April 1958.

5. *House Hearings on H.R. 8363,* p. 461.

6. Ibid., pp. 473-78.

7. Ibid., p. 460.

8. Ibid., pp. 478-79. Another study prepared by the Treasury of a sample of 215 executives from 350 U.S. corporations for the 1950–60 period showed that when the unrealized profits from unexercised stock options were included with the gains realized from exercised options, the resulting benefits were even greater. Ibid., p. 472.

9. According to a Treasury study of a sample of 215 top corporate executives for the period 1950–60, less than 40% of those who exercised stock options continued to hold all the stock so acquired at the end of the period, and only 50% retained at least 80% of their stock. Over 25% sold more than half of their optioned stock and 6% disposed of all of it. According to another study for the years 1958–60, of 528 executives who acquired 1.7 million shares through stock options, two-thirds had disposed of at least some of the optioned stock acquired—a total of 490,000 shares. Ibid., pp. 488-90.

10. Five percent if the corporation's net worth is more than $2 million, up to 10% if the net worth is less than $2 million.

11. I.R. Code, Sec. 422. Neither the requirement that stock option plans must be ratified by stockholders, nor the disqualifications of executives owning over 5% of outstanding stock represents a substantial impediment. As to the former, it is common knowledge that management proposals rarely fail to obtain stockholder ratification in view of the management's control of the proxy machinery. Stockholders are like sheep, and will approve virtually anything proposed by management.

As to the 5% limitation, only a handful of executives, even those owning thousands of shares, own even 1% of the outstanding stock of the larger publicly-owned U.S. corporations, so that the percentage limitation would disqualify few if any candidates for stock option privileges. In short, the limitation affects only stockholder officers of small corporations. Robert R. Frei, "Stock Options in the Light of the 1964 Revenue Act," *Taxes,* vol. 42 (1964), pp. 872, 885.

12. Frei, pp. 872, 888; Berger, pp. 430, 436; Frederick D. Lipman, "The Use and Misuse of the Qualified Stock Option," *Journal of Taxation,* vol. 24 (1966), pp. 130, 131.

13. Frei, p. 885.

14. Rothschild, pp. 117, 118-19.

15. Proxy Statement of the Bristol-Myers Company.

16. Proxy Statement of City Investing Company.

17. Proxy Statement of International Telephone and Telegraph Corporation.

18. Proxy Statement of W. R. Grace and Company.

19. Regulation 1.421-6 (d)(2). The Internal Revenue Service has

under consideration amendments to its regulations which might eliminate this loophole. However, even if finally adopted, the new regulations will still have to be tested and may not be upheld in the courts.

20. See Chap. 23.

21. *House Hearings on H.R. 8363,* p. 1099.

5. Waning Days of a Tax Windfall for Multi-Corporate Operations

1. I.R. Code, Sec. 11. Under the 1964 Revenue Act the normal rate on the first $25,000 was reduced from 30% to 22%, and the surtax on the net income over $25,000 from 52% to 48%.

2. William P. McLure, "Revenue Act of 1964—Provisions Dealing With the Treatment of an Affiliated Group of Corporations as a Single Taxpayer," *Taxes,* July 1964, p. 414.

3. *House Hearings on H.R. 8363,* pp. 36, 76. Similarly, under the Administration's proposal affiliated corporate groups were to be restricted to a single $100,000 accumulated earnings credit, and one $100,000 exemption in computing estimated corporate income tax.

4. See note 1.

5. E. Randolph Dale, "Climate Improves for Multiple Corporations Despite Penalty Tax," *Journal of Taxation,* May 1964, p. 264, William F. Hannam, "Planning for Controlled Corporations under Revenue Act of 1964," Tax Institute of University of Southern California, vol. 17 (1965), pp. 85, 113-14; Paul E. Bomze, *Multiple Corporations under 1964 Revenue Act,* 38 Temple Law Quarterly 245, 262 (Spring, 1965); Treasury Dept. 1969 Reform Studies, pp. 242-43.

6. I.R. Code, Sec. 1562.

7. Bedrick F. Schonberger, "Multiple Surtax Exemptions," *Journal of Taxation,* Sept. 1964, p. 136; H. Stewart Dunn, Jr., "Affiliated and Related Corporations," New York University Institute of Federal Taxation, vol. 23 (1965), pp. 255, 263-65; Reinhold Groh, "Privilege of a Controlled Group to Elect Multiple Surtax Exemptions," *Taxes,* July 1965, pp. 425, 426.

8. I.R. Code, Sec. 1561, 1563.

9. I.R. Code, Sec. 1563.

10. William A. Cromartie, "Affiliated Organizations and Multiple Corporations," *Taxes,* vol. 43 (1965), pp. 31, 55; Bomze, pp. 254-55. Even the parent-subsidiary corporate relationship can sometimes be avoided by "spinning off" the stock of a subsidiary to the stockholders of the parent, tax-free under I.R. Code, Sec. 355.

11. See Chap. 23.

12. Under I.R. Code, Sec. 61, 269, 482, or 1551.

13. Richard L. Kessler, "Multiple Corporations Under the Revenue

Act of 1964," *Illinois Continuing Legal Education,* vol. 3, no. 3, pp. 93, 100-101, 106-107, 110-11; Peter Elder, "Operating Problems of Multiple Corporations," New York University Institute of Federal Taxation, vol. 24 (1966), p. 1145; Peter K. Maier, "Use of Multiple Corporations Under 1964 Revenue Act," *Taxes,* vol. 42 (1964), pp. 565-66, 570-81.

14. Maier, p. 575.

6. The Submerged Iceberg—Capital Gains That Escape Taxation

1. See Chap. 23.

2. I.R. Code, Sec. 1.

3. Harold M. Groves, *Taxation of Capital Gains,* 2 Tax Revision Compendium 1194 (1959).

4. Philip J. Hanrahan, *A Proposal for Constructive Realization of Gains and Losses on Transfer of Property by Gift and at Death,* 15 Kansas Law Review 133, 141-43 (1966–67).

5. I.R. Code, Sec. 1014 (a).

6. I.R. Code, Sec. 1201 (b).

7. I.R. Code, Sec. 1014 (a). Actually the "basis" of the assets in the hands of the heirs is either the "stepped-up" fair market value at death, or the fair market value one year after death if an election is made to use the later date; I.R. Code, Sec. 2032 (a).

8. *Senate Hearings on H.R. 8363,* pp. 128-29.

9. Hanrahan, pp. 135-48.

10. Admittedly the taxpayer who sells such assets during his lifetime receives the benefit of the cash receipts which remain after having paid the tax on the gains—proceeds which he may spend during his lifetime, thereby *pro tanto* reducing the ultimate tax on his estate.

11. U.S., Congress, Joint Economic Committee, *The Federal Tax System, Facts and Problems,* 88th Cong., 2nd sess., 1964, p. 164; *House Hearings on H.R. 8363,* pp. 657-60, 685-86.

12. IBM, Polaroid, and Xerox are examples of such companies whose stocks have enjoyed spectacular stock market rises during the past ten years.

13. Philip E. Heckerling, *The Death of the "Stepped-Up" Basis at Death,* 37 Southern California Law Review 247, 252-53, 261-62 (1964); Harold M. Somers, "The Case for a Capital Gains Tax at Death," *American Bar Association Journal,* vol. 52 (1966), p. 346; Hanrahan, p. 136.

14. *Senate Hearings on H.R. 8363,* pp. 307, 1465, 2185; Hanrahan, p. 141.

15. Hanrahan, pp. 142-43. Present Treasury estimates put the value of asset appreciation passing at death at $11½–$15 billion each year, and the annual revenue loss at approximately $2½ billion. *Treasury Dept. 1969 Reform Studies,* pp. 4, 110, 334; *Wall Street Journal,* 20 January 1969.

16. I.R. Code, Sec. 1015 (a).

17. Henry Cabot Simons, *Federal Tax Reform* (Chicago: University of Chicago Press, 1950), pp. 44-46; Groves, pp. 1193-94, 1199; Philip M. Stern, *The Great Treasury Raid* (New York: Random House, 1964), p. 92; Heckerling, p. 273; Hanrahan, p. 144.

A somewhat less drastic approach to taxing capital gains at death, an alternative sometimes referred to as the "carryover basis," has been suggested by others. Under this proposal no capital gains tax would be imposed at death. However, the estate or the heirs would be deemed to receive these assets *not at their fair market value at the time of death, but at the decedent's original cost.* When the assets are sold by the estate or its beneficiaries, a capital gains tax would have to be paid on the entire gain, i.e., the difference between the sales proceeds and the original cost. Thus the major inequity implicit in the present system, which permits the entire gain accrued up to the time of death to escape capital gains tax completely, would be removed.

There are a number of serious objections to this "carryover of basis" alternative. In the first place, the payment on the gain is postponed beyond the death of the original owner, and perhaps postponed indefinitely, since it is not until the estate or its beneficiaries dispose of the assets that liability for the tax is incurred. Thus where stock is owned in a closely held family business, the appreciation in value could accrue for generations without a capital gains tax being paid. And again, taxpayers in the higher income tax brackets will be encouraged to make gifts of appreciated assets to members of their families with smaller incomes, so that when the assets are eventually sold, less taxes will be payable on the appreciation. From every point of view the alternative proposal is inferior to the imposition of a capital gains tax at the time of death.

18. Early in 1969, the Treasury again included in its tax reform suggestions to Congress a proposal that the appreciation in value of property transferred by lifetime gift or on death be subjected to the capital gains tax.

19. *House Hearings on H.R. 8363,* pp. 126-40.

20. Rene A. Wormser, "The Case Against a Capital Gains Tax at Death," *American Bar Association Journal,* Sept. 1965, pp. 851, 855.

21. Heckerling, p. 250; Hanrahan, p. 154.

22. Heckerling, p. 250; Wormser, pp. 853, 854.

23. Hanrahan, p. 157; Abraham Tannenbaum, *Basis of Property Transmitted at Death—Need for Revision,* 3 Tax Law Review 166, 170 (1947).

24. Hanrahan, p. 155; Heckerling, p. 273.

25. *Senate Hearings on H.R. 8363,* p. 2183.

7. Oil and Gas—A Major Leak in the Tax Structure

1. *Senate Hearings on H.R. 8363,* p. 2125.

2. *New York Times,* 29 April 1968.

3. U.S., Congress, House, *Congressional Record,* 90th Cong., 1st sess., 12 October 1967, p. H 13352.

4. "The Tax Gap," *New York Post,* 1 November 1967.

5. Ibid.

6. *Senate Hearings on H.R. 8363,* pp. 1465-68, 2374.

7. U.S., Congress, Joint Economic Committee, *The Federal Tax System, Facts and Problems,* 88th Cong., 2nd sess., p. 113.

8. Income consisted of all receipts, including receipts from oil properties, less the deduction of all ordinary costs, including operating expenses, depreciation costs, depletion, exploration costs, and losses due to abandonment of unproductive wells. It did not include, however, the allowance for percentage depletion in excess of cost depletion, deductions for current development costs, net long-term capital gains exclusions, and certain other exclusions.

9. *Senate Hearings on H.R. 8363,* pp. 287, 2369-74; *House Hearings on H.R. 8363,* pp. 278, 293; U.S., Congress, Senate, *Congressional Record,* 88th Cong., 1st sess., vol. 109, part 18, 12 December 1963, p. 24397.

10. Treasury Dept., 1969 Reform Studies, pp. 101, 414-17.

11. "The Tax Gap," loc. cit.; *The Federal Tax System, Facts and Problems,* p. 115.

12. While there are differences in rates and other distinctions, the special tax allowances permitted oil and gas producers apply as well to many other extractive industries, including the mining of coal, ores, and various metals. But since the great bulk of these allowances accrue to the oil and gas industry, this discussion is largely confined to oil and gas.

13. These are expenditures for wages, fuel, repairs, hauling, and supplies, incident to and necessary for drilling a well and preparing it for production, as contrasted with the cost of physical property having salvage value, such as casing, tubing, pumping equipment, and other tangible items which must be capitalized and recovered through depreciation.

14. I.R. Code, Sec. 263 (c).

15. I.R. Code, Sec. 167.

16. I.R. Code, Sec. 611-14.

17. I.R. Code, Sec. 263 (c), Reg. 1.612-4.

18. In any other industry these expenditures would be considered as capital investments and therefore recoverable only gradually as depreciation over a twenty- or twenty-five year period, at $4,000 or $5,000 each year.

19. *Congressional Record*, 12 October 1967, p. H 13352.

20. Even if the deductions for drilling and development are carried forward in the form of a net operating loss carryover, and are used to reduce future taxable income, that need not be subtracted from net income from the mineral property for the purpose of the percentage depletion limitation. *House Hearings on H.R. 8363*, p. 37.

21. Claude Hogan, *Tax Implications of Oil and Gas Transactions*, 7 Rocky Mountain Mineral Law Institute 613, 657 (1962).

22. *Senate Hearings on H.R. 8363*, p. 275.

23. The Treasury proposed that to the extent that deductions taken with respect to a mineral property exceeded the gross income in any taxable year, the amount of the excess would be carried forward so as to reduce a taxpayer's net income from the property in subsequent years, solely for the purpose of computing the 50% net income limitation on depletion. *House Hearings on H.R. 8363*, pp. 114-15.

24. The Treasury's proposal was that on a sale of an oil property wherein costs which are capital in nature are recaptured or repaid, and which had previously been deducted from ordinary income, such recaptured costs would be added back and taxed at ordinary income tax rates rather than at capital gains rates. Such costs would include, in addition to drilling and development costs previously deducted, the amount of depletion, cost or percentage, which the taxpayer had deducted from his ordinary income with respect to the property, but only to the extent of his basis in the property. Ibid., pp. 57, 142-44.

25. Ibid.

26. Clark W. Breeding, *Tax Considerations in Financing the Drilling of a Well*, 12 Tulane Tax Institute 293, 314 (1963).

27. Statistics on the risk of unsuccessful drillings vary. Many sources indicate that the percentage of productive wells to dry holes is extremely low, varying from 10% to 20%. Charles O. Galvin, *The "Ought" and "Is" of Oil and Gas Taxation*, 73 Harvard Law Review 1441, 1444 (1960); Peter O. Steiner, "The Non-Neutrality of Corporate Income Taxation—With and Without Depletion," *National Tax Journal*, vol. 16 (1963), pp. 238, 247; F. J. Blaise, "What Every Tax Man Should Know About Percentage Depletion," *Taxes*, vol. 36

(1958), pp. 395, 400-402; *Petroleum Facts and Figures,* 1967 Edition, American Petroleum Institute, pp. 11-14, 16-17. But one authority, quoting the *Oil and Gas Journal,* insists that the figures cited indiscriminately by industry spokesmen are unreliable, and that the risk of dry holes, especially among the larger oil companies, is far less. John A. Menge, *The Role of Taxation in Providing For Depletion of Natural Resources,* 2 Tax Revision Compendium 967, 975 (1959). Between 1956 and 1965 the drilling programs of McCulloch Oil Corporation had 23.3% success for exploratory wells and 72.5% success for development wells. *New York Times,* 19 February 1967, Sec. 3.

28. Peter L. Wentz, *Tax Planning for the Investor in Oil and Gas,* 11 University of Illinois Law Forum 602, 611 (1959).

29. Godfrey William Welsch, "Oil and Gas Properties Offer Unique Advantages in Family Tax Planning," *Journal of Taxation,* vol. 22 (1965), p. 120.

30. Such as an overriding royalty, a net profit interest, or a carried working interest.

31. Another way that A can achieve the same result would be to have the various trusts for his children acquire directly a fractional interest in the property before drilling is commenced; then under a "farm out" agreement between himself and the trusts, he would undertake the cost of drilling and development and each of the trusts would retain an overriding royalty or a net profits interest.

32. An "oil payment" or an "oil production payment" is an assignment of the right to receive a specified amount of oil revenue in dollars or a specified number of barrels from an oil property. The purchaser of such a payment is usually assured by geological estimates that there is sufficient oil remaining in the ground to cover the payment.

33. Treasury Dept. 1969 Reform Studies, pp. 256, 258-59.

34. *House Hearings on H.R. 8363,* p. 656.

35. I.R. Code, Sec. 901 et seq.

36. *Senate Hearings on H.R. 8363,* p. 2396.

37. *House Hearings on H.R. 8363,* pp. 118-21.

38. See, for example, *Federal Tax System, Facts and Problems,* p. 114; Blaise, p. 395; Horace M. Gray, *Tax Reform and the Depletion Allowance,* 2 Tax Revision Compendium 979 (1959); Galvin, p. 1441; Menge, p. 967; Maurice E. Pelouet, "Depletion for U.S. Income Tax Purposes," *Oil and Gas Tax Quarterly,* vol. 15 (1966), p. 137.

39. *Senate Hearings on H.R. 8363,* pp. 2495-96.

40. Harry J. Rudick, *Depletion and Exploration and Development Costs,* 2 Tax Revision Compendium 983, 984 (1959); L. J. Randall, *Depletion and Development Costs of the Mining Industry,* 2 Tax Re-

vision Compendium 1033 (1959); Scott C. Lambert, *Percentage Depletion and Exploration and Development Costs*, 2 Tax Revision Compendium 1009 (1959).

41. *The Federal Tax System, Facts and Problems*, pp. 117-18; Blaise, pp. 413-17.

42. U.S. Treasury Department, *Tax Reform Studies and Proposals*, 11 March 1969, part 4, p. 2.2.

43. The vote in the Senate in favor of a sharper reduction of the depletion allowance was 38 yeas and 52 nays, 2 paired, and 8 not voting. Yeas: Aiken, Bayh, Boggs, Brooke, Byrd, W. Va., Case, Cooper, Eagleton, Goodell, Gore, Hart, Hartke, Hatfield, Hughes, Inouye, Jackson, Javits, Kennedy, Magnuson, McCarthy, McGovern, McIntyre, Metcalf, Mondale, Muskie, Nelson, Pastore, Pell, Prouty, Proxmire, Ribicoff, Russell, Smith, Me., Spong, Tydings, Williams, N.J., Williams, Del., Young, Ohio. Nays: Allen, Allott, Bellmon, Bennett, Bible, Burdick, Byrd, Va., Cannon, Church, Cook, Cotton, Cranston, Curtis, Dodd, Dole, Dominick, Eastland, Ellender, Ervin, Fannin, Fong, Gravel, Gurney, Hansen, Harris, Holland, Hruska, Jordan, N.C., Jordan, Idaho, Long, Mansfield, Mathias, McClellan, McGee, Miller, Montoya, Moss, Murphy, Packwood, Pearson, Randolph, Saxbe, Schweiker, Scott, Sparkman, Stennis, Stevens, Talmadge, Thurmond, Tower, Yarborough, Young, N.D. Present and giving live pairs, as previously recorded: Fulbright, against; Griffin, for. Not voting: Anderson, Baker, Goldwater, Hollings, Mundt, Percy, Smith, Ill., Symington.

44. U.S., Congress, Senate, *Congressional Record*, 91st Cong., 1st sess., 1 December 1969, p. S15268.

45. *Senate Hearings on H.R. 13270*, pp. 702, 703.

8. Another Tax Shelter for the Wealthy—State and Local Bond Interest

1. U.S., *Treasury, Annual Report of the Secretary on the State of the Finances*, 1966, p. 777, Table 56. The Treasury currently estimates the annual revenue loss from the exemption at $1.8 billion. *Wall Street Journal*, 20 January 1969.

In 1965, according to a leading underwriter and distributor of such bonds, there were about $97.8 billion of state and local tax-exempt bonds outstanding, and about $11 billion of new issues were being added every year. *Investing for Tax-Exempt Income* (Merrill, Lynch, Pierce, Fenner and Smith, 1966), p. 6.

On the basis of the proportion of tax-exempt bonds known to be held by taxpaying individuals and corporations, a conservative estimate of the annual federal tax revenues due, if the interest were not exempt, would be at least 1% of the principal of the bonds outstanding. Kirby, *State and Local Bond Interest, House Committee on Ways and Means, 86th Congress, 1st session,* 1 Tax Revision Compendium 679-80 (1959). There are additional losses in state income tax revenues due to tax exemption under state laws.

2. Leading Wall Street underwriters and distributors of state and municipal bonds invariably point out in their brochures that this type of investment is almost as safe as U.S. government bonds; that even during the worst depression in our history, during the 1930s, over 98% of all such bonds were never in default; and that of those which were temporarily in default, the vast majority eventually met their obligations in full.

3. McCulloch v. Maryland, 17 U.S. (4 Wheat.) 316 (1819).

4. U.S., Congress, *Congressional Record,* 63rd Cong., 1st sess., 1913, p. 1262 App. vol. 6, Doc. No. 94.

5. George E. Lent, "The Origin and Survival of Tax-Exempt Securities," *National Tax Journal,* Dec. 1959, p. 301.

6. Letter of Secretary of the Treasury, Relative to Tax Exempt Securities, 16 January 1922; Annual Report of the Secretary of the Treasury, 1922, p. 320, quoted by Lent, p. 305.

7. Lent, pp. 306-14; Hart H. Spiegel, *Financing Private Ventures with Tax-Exempt Bonds,* 17 Stanford Law Review 224 (1965).

8. Roswell Magill, "Plugging the Loopholes," *Readers Digest,* Jan. 1962.

9. Lent, p. 315, quoting B. U. Ratchford, "Intergovernmental Tax Immunities in the United States," *National Tax Journal,* vol. VI (1953), p. 327; Jack E. Gelfand, *Tax Exempt Securities and the Doctrine of Reciprocal Immunity,* 32 Temple Law Quarterly 173 (1959); Spiegel, p. 225: *U.S. v. Atlas Life Insurance Company,* 85 S. Ct. 1379.

10. William A. Klein, *Borrowing To Finance Tax-Favored Investments,* 1962 Wisconsin Law Review 608.

11. It is assumed that the securities C sells have not appreciated in value above his cost, so that no capital gains tax is incurred on his sale.

12. Klein, p. 612.

13. Gelfand, p. 179.

14. Alfred E. Abby, *Municipal Industrial Development Bonds,* 19 Vanderbilt Law Review 25 (1965); Spiegel, pp. 225-27; Arthur O. Armstrong, Jr., *Municipal Inducements,* 48 California Law Review 58 (1960); *The "Public Purpose" of Municipal Financing for Industrial Development,* 70 Yale Law Journal 789 (1961).

15. Spiegel, p. 227; *New York Times,* 18 September 1967; *U.S.*

News & World Report, 9 May 1966, p. 104; *New York Times,* 12 November 1967, Section 3; *Wall Street Journal,* 27 June 1968.

16. *Wall Street Journal,* 22 November 1963; *Business Week,* 14 December 1963, p. 45.

17. Abby, pp. 64-66; *New York Times,* 18 September 1967, 12 November 1967, Section 3.

18. Some of the criticism emanating from banking circles seems to have arisen less out of outrage at this particular abuse of tax exemption than out of concern that public criticism of tax-exemption for industrial development bonds may spill over to a re-examination of the whole question of tax-exempt securities, and thereby jeopardize the long-standing tax immunity of conventional state and local bonds. *Business Week,* 3 December 1960, p. 93; *U.S. News & World Report,* 9 May 1966, p. 104.

19. *Wall Street Journal,* 22 November 1963.

20. *San Francisco Chronicle,* 25 March 1964; *Wall Street Journal,* 18 February 1964.

21. Spiegel, p. 225.

22. Address of Stanley S. Surrey, Assistant Secretary of the Treasury, before the Federal Bar Association, 23 February 1967, p. 5.

23. I.R. Code, Sec. 103 (c), enacted by Public Law 90-364. The bill contained a number of restrictions, including a provision that the amount of the issue in excess of $1 million would be tax-free only if the company's total investment in plants in the community in the three years before and after the bond issue in question did not exceed $5 million. *Wall Street Journal,* 27 June 1968, 30 October 1968.

9. The Incorporated Pocketbook Is Not Dead

1. Under Internal Revenue Code, Sec. 243, only 15% of the dividends received by one corporation from another are includible for corporate tax purposes, on the theory that when the money is eventually paid out to the recipient's stockholders in the form of dividends, it will be taxed to them.

2. I.R. Code, Sec. 541.

3. I.R. Code, Sec. 531; Donald C. Lubick, "Personal Holding Companies, Yesterday, Today and Tomorrow," *Taxes,* vol. 42 (1964), p. 855.

4. See Chap. 6.

5. If M judiciously distributed the stock among members of his family, he might succeed in setting up a number of these corporate tax shelters for holding his securities. Each corporation's tax could be kept

at almost the lowest corporate rate by splitting the dividend income among them. See Chap. 5.

6. I.R. Code, Sec. 541, imposes a tax of up to 85% of undistributed income. Under the Revenue Act of 1964 the rate was reduced to 70% of undistributed personal holding company income.

7. A sufficient factual basis always had to be provided in order to justify the retention of the accumulation, so as not to run afoul of the tax on unreasonable accumulations of corporate profits under I.R. Code, Sec. 531.

8. It was necessary to avoid having 50% of the value or voting power owned directly or indirectly by five persons or fewer. I.R. Code, Sec. 542.

9. Former I.R. Code, Sec. 542.

10. I.R. Code, Sec. 541-65.

11. Actually called "adjusted ordinary gross income," I.R. Code, Sec. 542, 543.

12. I.R. Code, Sec. 543.

13. Ibid.

14. *Improper Accumulations of Surplus and Personal Holding Companies,* 24 New York University Institute of Federal Taxation 927, 967-68 (1966); Kenneth H. Liles, *A New Look at Personal Holding Company Problems,* 24 New York University Institute of Federal Taxation 863, 883 (1966). Such a taxpayer will have to demonstrate, of course, the need for retaining such additional investment income in his business to avoid running afoul of I.R. Code, Sec. 531, which imposes an additional tax on businesses with large unnecessary accumulated surpluses.

15. I.R. Code, Sec. 536, allows corporations threatened with Personal Holding Company status up to 2½ months after the end of the year to distribute sufficient dividends to meet the various percentage tests.

16. Since these contracts are a recent development the Internal Revenue Service has not had an opportunity to test them fully in court, one of the problems in attempting to plug tax loopholes. The plug must be big enough to avoid seepage around the sides. In this area many tax practitioners are of the opinion that the plug was a little too small.

17. Such as switching from net leases to leases under which the landlord provides certain services and therefore receives a large rental in return. 24 N.Y.U. Institute (1966) pp. 969-70.

18. Arthur A. Feder, *Relieving the Impact of the Revenue Act of 1964 on New Personal Holding Companies,* 23 New York University Institute of Federal Taxation 723, 741 (1965); Arnold Fisher and

Benedict Kohl, "Personal Holding Company Rules Tightened; More Corporations Vulnerable," *Journal of Taxation*, May 1964, p. 258; N.Y.U. Institute (1966), pp. 961-62, 969-70; Allan B. Aronson, *Real Estate Tax Shelter for Personal Holding Companies and Individuals*, 25 N.Y.U. Institute on Federal Taxation 747, 756-59 (1967); Marvin S. Shapiro, *Personal Holding Companies under the 1964 Revenue Act*, 17 University of Southern California Tax Institute 187, 200-201 (1965); Liles, pp. 884-85.

19. 24 N.Y.U. Institute (1966), pp. 967, 969-70; Liles, p. 883; Feder, p. 741.

20. 24 N.Y.U. Institute (1966), pp. 947, 962; Shapiro, p. 201; Liles, pp. 884-85; Lubick, pp. 855, 869.

21. *Hearings on H.R. 8363,* p. 860.

10. One Good Loophole Deserves Another—The Proliferation of Special Tax Treatment

1. I.R. Code, Sec. 1201-1202. See Chap. 6.

2. Stanley S. Surrey, *Definitional Problems in Capital Gains Taxation,* 2 Tax Revision Compendium 1203, 1232 (1959).

3. In 1961, 36% of the income of taxpayers with adjusted gross incomes of $100,000 or more consisted of capital gains. In 1959, 63% of the income of taxpayers having adjusted gross incomes of $500,000 or more consisted of capital gains, while among those with incomes up to $15,000, capital gains comprised only 4% of their income. U.S., Congress, Joint Economic Committee, *The Federal Tax System, Facts and Problems,* 88th Cong., 2nd sess., 1964, pp. 81, 220. In 1959, thirty-seven individuals with incomes over $5 million reported an average of $6,280,000 in capital gains, half of which was excluded from their adjusted gross incomes, and the balance taxed at the maximum 50% rate. *Senate Hearings on H.R. 8363,* pp. 279, 284.

4. *Senate Hearings on H.R. 8363,* pp. 840-41.

5. See Chap. 21.

6. Surrey, pp. 1210, 1229.

7. Ibid., pp. 1227-28. These arrangements include distributions of preferred stock dividends which are sold by the stockholders and redeemed by the corporation; transfers of part of the assets to a new corporation, the stock of which is "spun off" to the shareholders and later sold by them; redemptions of stock and partial liquidations; and complete liquidations followed by the reincorporation of part of the assets by many of the same stockholders.

8. Reuben Clark, *The Paradox of Capital Gains,* 2 Tax Compendium 1243, 1246 (1959); Richard Katcher, *Capital Gains Problems*

and Proposals, 14 University of Southern California Tax Institute, 769, 775-77 (1962); Leonard L. Silverstein, *The Capital Asset Definition,* 2 Tax Revision Compendium 1285, 1291 (1959); Dan Throop Smith, *Tax Treatment of Capital Gains,* 2 Tax Revision Compendium, 1233, 1235 (1959).

9. I.R. Code, Sec. 402 (a)(2).

10. Smith, p. 1237.

11. I.R. Code, Sec. 1231 (b)(2), 631.

12. I.R. Code, Sec. 1235, 1221 (3).

13. I.R. Code, Sec. 421.

14. I.R. Code, Sec. 1231 (b)(3)(4).

15. I.R. Code, Sec. 1231 (b)(4).

16. U.S., Congress, Senate, *Congressional Record,* vol. 97, 1951, pp. 11, 741.

17. *House Hearings on H.R. 8363,* pp. 148-57. Another capital gains loophole which the administration sought unsuccessfully to eliminate involved the proceeds of the sale by a life tenant of his interest in a life estate which he had acquired by gift or inheritance; the net effect was to deprive the government of tax on a substantial part of the income during the life tenancy. I.R. Code, Sec. 273, 1014 (a); Treasury Regulations (1957), Sec. 1.1014.4(b)5; *House Hearings on H.R. 8363,* pp. 156-57.

18. I.R. Code, Sec. 631 (c).

19. See Chap. 4.

20. *House Hearings on H.R. 8363,* pp. 144-46; 451-58; George Kondelis, *Observations on the Proposed Capital Gains Reforms,* 38 Temple Law Quarterly 289, 310 (1964); C. A. Freeze, "Tax Considerations in Planning for Livestock Operations," *Journal of Taxation,* vol. 9 (1958), p. 51; *Current Capital Gains Problems,* 22 New York University Institute of Federal Taxation 185, 192-93 (1964); Jon K. Mulford, *Tax Planning for Capital Gains in Livestock Operations,* 38 University of Colorado Law Review, 572, 583 (1966).

Of course not every investor in livestock raising and breeding had these favorable tax results since there were substantial risks involved, and competent supervision was needed by absentee investors in order to avoid losses from dishonest or slipshod management. Mulford, p. 578.

21. *House Hearings on H.R. 8363,* pp. 451-52.

22. Ibid., pp. 144-46. The remedy suggested in 1963 by the Treasury was to place a limitation on the amount of deductions on livestock, farming, and similar operations which wealthy investors could utilize to reduce their taxes from other sources and at the same time reap

long-term capital gain tax advantages when the livestock or other property was ultimately sold. In order to be sure that true farmers and ranchers would not be affected by the limitation, an exception was to be made in the case of taxpayers whose non-farming or non-cattle-raising adjusted gross incomes did not exceed $15,000 per year. A substantially similar proposal was included in the tax reform package submitted to Congress by the Treasury in early 1969. See Chap. 23.

23. I.R. Code, Sec. 631, 1231 (b) (2).

24. According to Treasury Department statistics, the overwhelming majority of timber property owners are small farmers whose average ownership is only 49 acres. Though the large lumber, pulp, plywood and paper companies constitute only .5% of all owners of timber, they hold collectively 62 million acres, or 13% of all timber land outside the state and national forests. Two hundred and eighty-three large companies in the forest industry have timber land holdings averaging more than 200,000 acres each, with seven companies owning more than 1 million acres each. *House Hearings on H.R. 8363,* pp. 391-92, 414-16.

25. In 1959 three large timber companies received 42% of the $44 million capital gains tax benefits realized by the timber industry. In the plywood industry four large companies received 95% of all capital gains benefits; and in the paper industry the fifteen largest companies received over 82% of such benefits. At the same time, the capital gains tax benefits of 99% of all owners of timber land were relatively minimal or non-existent. Ibid., p. 407.

Treasury figures for 1965 disclose a similar pattern. Treasury Dept. 1969 Reform Studies, pp. 101-102, 434-35.

26. During the 1962–66 period the large lumber and paper companies were able to minimize their tax liabilities by shifting almost 10% of their income to the capital gains category. It is estimated that the tax preferences granted the timber industry cost the Treasury over $125 million a year in tax revenues. Treasury Dept. 1969 Reform Studies, pp. 101-102, 434, 437-38.

27. *Senate Hearings on H.R. 13270,* p. 703.

28. *House Hearings on H.R. 8363,* pp. 388-419.

29. *Executives Tax Report* (Prentice Hall), vol. 12, 13 August 1962.

30. Under the Treasury proposal sales of timber would have been treated as ordinary income, except that individual timber owners would have been permitted to treat up to $5,000 realized on timber cutting or sales each year as capital gains; this exception, it was claimed, would cover 90% of all timber property owners. At the same time, in order to encourage sound conservation and reforestation practices, *all* timber

owners and operators were to be granted the privilege of deducting all costs of reforestation, conservation, and forest management as current expenses. Such a program, the Treasury explained, would stabilize the present timber ownership of small farmers, encourage reforestation, conservation, and development of the nation's timber resources, curtail indiscriminate and wasteful cutting of large timber tracts because of unwarranted tax benefits, aid the deteriorating economic position of the small sawmill operator and logger, and otherwise create healthier competitive conditions in the timber industry. *House Hearings on H.R. 8363,* pp. 57-58, 151, 392-99.

31. The proposal has met with criticism in some quarters on the grounds that it penalizes the organized pulp and lumber industry and fails to give sufficient acknowledgment to the risks attendant on growing timber over long periods of time or to the fact that the capital gains preference granted the industry is a major incentive for investment and for sound conservation, reforestation, and management practices. Kondelis, pp. 312-13.

32. Maurice E. Pelouet, "Depletion for United States Income Tax Purposes," *Oil and Gas Tax Quarterly,* vol. 15 (1966), pp. 137, 141; F. J. Blaise, "What Every Tax Man Should Know About Percentage Depletion," *Taxes,* vol. 36 (1964), pp. 395, 421.

33. I.R. Code, Sec. 613.

34. *Senate Hearings on H.R. 8363,* p. 1468.

35. Philip M. Stern, *The Great Treasury Raid,* (New York: Random House, 1963), p. 170.

36. I.R. Code, Sec. 613.

37. Sho Sato, "Ground Water Rights and Depletion Deduction," *Natural Resources Journal,* vol. 6 (1966), pp. 236, 239-40.

38. *Wall Street Journal,* 6 August 1969.

39. See Chap. 7.

40. See Chap. 7.

41. Sulfur and uranium were reduced from 23% to 22%; gold, silver, oil shale, copper, and iron ore were unchanged; certain other minerals reduced from 15% to 14%.

11. Keeping Income in the Family and Saving Taxes at the Same Time

1. Large business interests under common control frequently split income by the use of multiple corporations. See Chap. 5.

2. I.R. Code, Sec. 1.

3. In this example and those that follow it is assumed, unless other-

wise stated, that itemized deductions equal 15% of gross income and the personal exemption is $625.

4. Assuming exemptions of $625 each for himself, his wife, and their five children.

5. I.R. Code, Sec. 2503, 2513, 2521.

6. We are assuming that H's salary and rate of return on his investments have not changed, and that he is no longer able to take the dependency deduction for each of his children because of their independent incomes. This return is based on exemptions for Mr. and Mrs. H only without reduction by the Maximum Tax on Earned Income, which does not become fully effective until 1972.

7. Based on deductions amounting to 15% of gross income and $625 personal exemption.

8. However, under the 1969 Act, the accumulated income will be taxed to the child when he receives it as though he received it in the year earned.

9. It will often be worthwhile for a father in a very high tax bracket to make annual family gifts in excess of his and his wife's generous gift tax exemptions, and pay a gift tax on such gifts.

10. There also had to be a separate trust agreement for each trust, and each trust had to be for a separate purpose, e.g., one for the child's education, one for his life insurance needs, one for emergency needs by reason of accident or sickness, etc. Each trust also had to have a different combination of family members who would receive the principal of the trust when it ended. Allen T. Malone, *Income Splitting As a Means of Avoiding Taxes,* 19 Vanderbilt Law Review 1289, 1311 (1966).

11. Such as the right to revoke or amend the trust or to receive income or principal of the trust. I.R. Code, Sec. 671 et seq.

12. I.R. Code, Sec. 665 (b)(1)-(4).

13. U.S., Congress, Joint Committee on Tax Evasion and Avoidance, *Hearings,* 75th Cong., 1st sess., 1937, pp. 264, 278.

14. I.R. Code, Sec. 665.

15. Malone, pp. 1309-11. (See Chap. 23.)

16. I.R. Code, Sec. 671-78. Robert A. Lewis, "Gift and Income Tax Implications of Grantor-Trustee Reversionary Trusts," *Taxes,* vol. 46 (1968), p. 336.

17. It is assumed that the income will be payable or accumulated for the benefit of the child, and not used to discharge the father's obligation of support.

18. Taking into account the dividend exclusion and the right of the

child's trust to use the standard deduction at 13% on its income tax return.

19. Treasury Regulations, Sec. 25.2512-5 (f).

20. I.R. Code, Sec. 704 (e)(2).

21. In order to insure recognition of the propriety of the arrangement, the partnership agreement should set forth the percentage share of earnings of each partner; state that in computing such shares a reasonable compensation for the services to be performed and the capital contributions of each partner was considered; and provide that each partner has the right to participate in management decisions, to take out his distributions of partnership earnings, and to withdraw from the partnership altogether. Malone, p. 1297.

22. I.R. Code, Subchapter S, Sec. 1371-77.

23. A stil further refinement would be a gift–lease-back arrangement, whereby the plant and equipment of a business is transferred by the owner to trusts for numerous grandchildren. The trustee immediately leases the property back to the business at a reasonable rental, providing the latter with a large income tax deduction for rent and the trusts with income taxed at low or nominal rates.

24. See Chap. 17.

12. Generation-Skipping and Other Means of Avoiding Estate Taxes

1. Fortunes of $10 million are not exceptional today. In fact wealth of such size was too picayune to be mentioned in a *Fortune* article referred to in the *New York Times* of 29 April 1968. In 1958 there were 40,000 millionaires, and the number has grown considerably since then. *Time Magazine,* 3 December 1965, p. 88.

2. Gilbert Hine (Vice President and Trust Officer, National Bank of Commerce, San Antonio, Texas), "Vision vs. Revision," *Trusts and Estates,* vol. 103 (1964), p. 162.

3. See Chap. 11 and I.R. Code, Sec. 2503, 2513, 2521.

4. Under I.R. Code, Sec. 2052, estates amounting to less than $60,000 are exempt from federal estate tax.

5. A second gift tax may also be eliminated by the use of a trust. If T, Sr. gives property outright to his son, he may be liable for a gift tax if the gift is large. If sometime thereafter the son decides to donate the property to one of his own children, a second gift tax may be payable. On the other hand, if the father's original gift to his son is in trust, with the son receiving only the income for life and the remainder distributable to the grandchildren, the property passes to the grandchildren without the payment of any additional gift tax.

6. The Rule Against Perpetuities was formulated in the Duke of Norfolk's Case, decided by the English courts in 1685. The rule stated that a trust may continue for any number of lives in being at the creation of the trust but not beyond that point. Thereafter the limitation was extended to cover the time necessary for the birth of a posthumous child, and as a result an arbitrary twenty-one years was permitted to be tacked on to the lives-in-being concept. Had it not been for the sagacity of English justices in the seventeenth century trusts might have been permitted to continue for unlimited generations, including many generations unborn, without the payment of additional estate taxes.

7. Erwin N. Griswold, *Powers of Appointment and the Federal Estate Tax,* 52 Harvard Law Review 929 (1939); W. Barton Leach, *Powers of Appointment and the Federal Estate Tax, A Dissent,* 52 Harvard Law Review 961 (1939).

8. I.R. Code, Sec. 2041.

9. In addition to those already mentioned there are innumerable indirect benefits and emoluments in which the beneficiaries of trusts or members of their families may participate. Among other things, they may receive substantial commissions as trustees or co-trustees; their sons or sons-in-law may serve as attorneys for the estate in return for tidy legal fees; stock market, real estate, and insurance transactions of the estate may be handled by members of the family in Wall Street or in the real estate or insurance brokerage business; and there is nothing to prevent beneficiaries or other family members from receiving lucrative salaries as officers or employees of family corporations whose stock forms part of the estate.

10. W. Barton Leach, "Powers of Appointment," *American Bar Association Journal,* vol. 24 (1938), pp. 807, 809.

11. Griswold, p. 955.

12. The maximum gift tax rate is 57¾%, whereas the maximum estate tax rate is 77%. I.R. Code, Sec. 2502, 2001.

13. I.R. Code, Sec. 2513; see Chap. 11.

14. I.R. Code, Sec. 2523.

15. I.R. Code, Sec. 2513.

16. After exemptions and exclusions.

17. I.R. Code, Sec. 2056.

18. The origin of the marital deduction is briefly as follows: Under the laws of certain states, called "community property states," the wife (or husband) is deemed to own one-half of the property that his or her spouse has accumulated during his or her lifetime. When one of them dies only one-half of the joint property is subject to estate tax;

the other half is not taxed until the other spouse passes away. As a result, prior to 1948, wealthy persons residing in California and other states having community property laws enjoyed a substantial advantage in the payment of estate taxes. The possibility loomed of wealthy persons shifting their residences to the more favored states. The enactment by Congress of the marital deduction provisions in 1948 was designed to make estate tax treatment uniform throughout the country.

19. I.R. Code, Sec. 2042. The insured, however, must be careful to divorce himself from the incidents of ownership of the policy, including the right to designate or change the beneficiaries, to borrow on the policy, or to cancel it.

The Internal Revenue Service has claimed that not only the premiums paid by a taxpayer during the three years prior to death, but also the proportion of the policy proceeds attributable to those premiums, are includible in the estate for estate tax purposes. But the Service has not been uniformly sustained by the courts, and the ultimate determination of the applicable law is questionable.

20. U.S., Congress, House, Committee on Ways and Means, *Minority Report on H.R. 1337,* 83rd Cong., 2nd sess., 1954, p. B14; Charles L. B. Lowndes, *A Practical Program for Reforming the Federal Estate Tax,* 5 Villanova Law Review 1, 29 (1959); J. Nelson Young, *Estate Planning and the Tax Structure,* 15 University of Illinois Law Forum 437, 464 (1963).

21. In February 1969 the Treasury recommended that in addition to a lifetime transfer tax on the interpolated terminal reserve value of the policy, a deathtime transfer tax should be imposed on the portion of the life insurance proceeds equal to the increase in cash value of the policy resulting from the premiums paid during three years before death plus the difference between the face amount of the policy and its cash value at death. Treasury Dept. 1969 Reform Studies, p. 362.

22. I.R. Code, Sec. 2039. In 1962, when the Self-Employed Individual Tax Retirement Act was enacted, a similar tax exemption for death benefits paid under pension plans of professionals and other self-employed persons not covered by corporate pension plans was eliminated.

The Treasury has recently proposed eliminating this loophole. Treasury Dept. 1969 Reform Studies, pp. 363-64.

23. Davis v. U.S., D.C. Utah 1960, 5 Amer. Federal Rep. (2nd) 1902, 60-1 U.S. Tax Cases, Par. 11943; Broderick v. Gore, 224 Fed. 2nd 892, CCA 10 (1955); Angela Fiorita, 33 Tax Ct. 440 (1959), acquiesced in by the Commissioner of Internal Revenue 1960-1 Cumulative Bulletin 4; Estate of Orville B. Littick, 31 Tax Ct. 181

(1958), acquiesced in by the Commissioner of Internal Revenue 1959-2 Cumulative Bulletin 5.

24. As a transfer during his lifetime made in contemplation of death. I.R. Code, Sec. 2035. The result would be the same if the decedent had created a trust, with a life interest reserved to himself until death, and with the remainder payable on his death to his children.

25. Apart from the fact that there may be included in the property left in trust, stock in the family business from which the son, as a chief executive, will draw a generous salary.

26. *Forbes Magazine,* 1 December 1967, p. 41.

27. In 1957 and 1959 virtually every decedent leaving an estate of more than $10 million had made lifetime gifts to members of his family, with the percentage of those making such gifts dropping as the size of the estate decreased. In the case of estates under $300,000, only 10% of the decedents had made lifetime gifts to family members. This trend has continued to the present day.

Similarly, according to the Treasury, the use of generation-skipping trusts is ten times as great among those leaving estates of $1 million or more than it is among those leaving estates of $300,000 or less; and the great preponderance of family trusts created by those leaving $2 million or more are of the generation-skipping variety. Carl F. Shoup, "Federal Estate and Gift Taxes," The Brookings Institution (1966), Appendix; Treasury Dept. 1969 Reform Studies, pp. 31, 338-89.

28. Randolph Paul, *Federal Estate and Gift Taxation* (Boston: Little, Brown & Co., 1942), p. 31; U.S., Congress, Joint Committee on the Economy of the U.S., *Address by Louis Eisenstein,* 84th Cong., 1st sess., 16 December 1955; Stanley Surrey, *An Introduction to Revision of the Federal Estate and Gift Taxes,* 38 California Law Review 1, 4 (1950); Lowndes, pp. 1, 3; Harry J. Rudick, *What Alternative to the Estate and Gift Taxes,* 38 California Law Review 150, 158 (1950).

29. In 1939 estate and gift taxes raised 6.6% of total federal tax receipts. By 1943 the percentage had dropped to about 2%, and since that time has remained between 1% and 2% of federal tax revenues. Shoup, appendix.

30. U.S., Congress, Joint Committee on the Economic Report, *Federal Tax Policy for Economic Growth and Stability,* 84th Cong., 1st sess., 1955, p. 690.

31. Surrey, p. 3; Adrian W. DeWind, *The Approaching Crisis in Federal Estate and Gift Taxation,* 38 California Law Review 79, 81 (1950). The American Law Institute Federal Estate and Gift Tax

Project, with Professor A. James Casner of the Harvard Law School as the Reporter, has for some time been working on proposals for major reforms in the estate and gift tax law. The project, under way since 1963, envisages either major revisions to the present tax system or an entirely new integrated estate and gift tax law. One major recommendation under consideration is the taxation, under a progressive rate schedule, of the aggregate amounts received by the beneficiaries of estates, trust, and gifts from all such sources over their lifetimes.

32. Finance Act of 1894, 57 & 58 Vict. c 30 Sec. 2 (1) (b).

33. Young, p. 462; Lowndes, p. 4; Surrey, p. 10; DeWind, p. 116; Rudick, p. 167-75.

34. Rudick, loc. cit.

35. Under present law, if a man possessing $1 million makes a lifetime gift of $300,000 to a son, he will pay a gift tax at a low rate, i.e., lower than the estate tax rate. On his death, if he leaves half of his remaining estate to his wife and half to his children, the half left to the wife passes free of tax (under the marital deduction provision), while the other half will be subject to an estate tax. Finally, when the widow dies and leaves what she had received from her husband to the children, another estate tax will be payable. The children have thus received the entire amount of their father's estate subject to three different taxes, i.e., a gift tax and two estate taxes.

Under the proposal, there would in effect be only one overall tax instead of three. On the transfer to the son there would be a tax on $300,000. When the father died the $300,000 previously given away would be added to his estate for valuation purposes. Any amount left to his widow, whether half, three-quarters, or all of his estate, would be free of estate tax. But on her death all that she had received from her husband, and all amounts previously transferred by him to his children during his life or by his will (i.e., $1,000,000), would be subject to an estate tax in the $1 million tax bracket, subject to a credit for the gift and estate taxes previously paid.

36. See Chap. 23.

13. Tax Abuses of Corporate Pension Plans and Similar Arrangements

1. I.R. Code, Sec. 401 et seq.

2. Except where contracts with labor unions require the employer to set up such plans.

3. Although the Internal Revenue Service requires certain minimum actuarial standards (or minimum annual contributions up to a specified

maximum to be deducted by the employer), these standards (or minima and maxima) are arrived at by the actuary whose calculations and assumptions are rarely disturbed by the Service. The legislation permitting the setting up of such plans is so vague, indefinite, and flexible, that it is difficult to demonstrate that any particular plan fails to meet the minimum actuarial standards.

4. Under the law the employer has the right to increase or decrease the amount of the annual contribution on the basis of new determinations and assumptions arrived at by the actuary, and to discontinue the plan altogether in the interests of the business.

5. Assuming a federal and state combined tax rate of 55%.

6. I.R. Code, Sec. 501.

7. I.R. Code, Sec. 402.

8. I.R. Code, Sec. 2039.

9. I.R. Code, Sec. 402. On the other hand, the same code section provided that distributions from pension plans in installments, both on retirement and on death, were subject to taxation at ordinary rates.

10. See note 5.

11. I.R. Code, Sec. 79.

12. Revenue Ruling 68-334.

13. Contributions of the employer up to 15% of the compensation of covered employees is a deductible expense for the corporation, and the earnings of the profit-sharing trust are exempt from income tax. I.R. Code, Sec. 404, 501.

14. *House Hearings on H.R. 8363,* pp. 148-50, 499-500. At the same time the Treasury suggested that such payments be subject to certain averaging provisions which would soften the effect of the receipt of the lump sum payment in a single year.

15. The Treasury cited several examples of large lump sum distributions to certain executive employees which received the advantage of being taxed at the preferential capital gains rate. One company was shown to have made two lump sum distributions of more than $500,000 each, one of $400,000, and two of $325,000. Another company made distributions to certain of its top executives of $800,000, $400,000, and $365,000; and one employer paid a lump sum benefit to a single individual amounting to $843,000. Ibid., pp. 499-500.

16. Instances of executives being covered by life insurance policies of $300,000, $400,000, and in one case $900,000, were cited by the Treasury. *Senate Hearings on H.R. 8363,* pp. 142, 306.

17. *House Hearings on H.R. 8363,* pp. 20, 50-51, 108-109. The Treasury was prepared to make an exception for the first $5,000 of such insurance coverage, the cost of which under the Treasury pro-

posal would not be considered taxable income. The $5,000 exception would in effect mean that the great majority of employees with modest insurance coverage would be unaffected.

18. Russell B. Long, "Tax Reform and Economic Growth," speech delivered at the National Conference on Federal Tax Reform, *The Taxpayer's Stake in Tax Reform* (Washington, D.C.: Chamber of Commerce of the United States, 1968).

19. U.S., Congress, House, Committee on Ways and Means, *House Report 2333,* 77th Cong., 2nd sess., 1942, p. 103.

20. U.S., Congress, House, Committee on Ways and Means, *Hearings on Revenue Act of 1942,* 77th Cong., 2nd sess., pp. 1004-1005, 2406-2407.

21. Now I.R. Code, Sec. 401.

22. The Self-Employed Individual Tax Retirement Act of 1962. Public Law, 87-792.

23. Report of the President's Committee on Corporate Pension Funds and other Private Retirement Funds and Welfare Programs, January 1965.

24. Robert Scheff, *Qualified Pension Plans,* 26 New York University Institute on Federal Taxation 1041 (1968).

25. The Treasury estimates that it loses about $3 billion annually in tax revenues as the result of the exclusion from taxation of contributions to pension plans by private employers, and about $1.5 billion a year from the exclusion of employer-paid premiums in connection with group life insurance and medical plans. *Wall Street Journal,* 20 January 1969.

26. The tax reforms submitted recently to Congress contain a proposal to subject all employee death benefits paid to his family under qualified pension plans to the payment of a transfer tax. Treasury Dept. 1969 Reform Studies, pp. 363-64.

14. Loopholes That Are Tailor-Made—The Special Bill

1. Louis Eisenstein, *The Ideologies of Taxation* (New York: Ronald Press, 1961), pp. 3-4, 11.

2. Stanley S. Surrey, *The Congress and the Tax Lobbyists,* 70 Harvard Law Review 1145, 1147 (1957); Philip M. Stern, *The Great Treasury Raid* (New York: Random House, 1964), pp. 44-48; Charles O. Galvin, *The Deduction for Percentage Depletion and Exploitation and Development Costs,* 2 Tax Revision Compendium 933, 941 (1959).

3. I.R. Code of 1939, Sec. 117 (p) added by 65 Statute 504 (1951).

4. U.S., Congress, Senate, *Congressional Record*, 82nd Cong., 1st sess., vol. 97, part 9, 21 September 1951, p. 11814.

5. Surrey, pp. 1147-56, 1176-82; William L. Cary, *Pressure Groups and the Revenue Code*, 68 Harvard Law Review 745, 748-56 (1955).

6. Stern, Chap. 3.

7. Cary, p. 752.

8. *New York Times*, 7 December 1967.

9. "Aluminum and Politics," *Wall Street Journal*, 26 April 1967; "Five Billion Bonanza," *New York Post*, 11 January 1968.

10. Surrey, p. 1156.

11. U.S., Congress, Senate, *Congressional Record*, 91st Cong., 1st sess., 8 December 1969, p. S 16101.

12. *Wall Street Journal*, 27 May 1970.

13. Surrey, pp. 1176-82.

14. Cary, p. 747.

15. Tax Windfalls in Real Estate

1. Treasury Dept. 1969 Reform Studies, pp. 444-45.

2. I.R. Code, Sec. 167.

3. Land has an unlimited life and may not be depreciated.

4. His cash flow was $825,000; that is, $1,015,000 of real income less mortgage amortization payments aggregating $190,000.

5. I.R. Code, Sec. 1245.

6. I.R. Code, Sec. 1231.

7. Burton Crane, *New York Times*, 31 May 1959; Stanley W. Penn, *Wall Street Journal*, 17 July 1961; *Wall Street Journal*, 30 January 1963.

8. *House Hearings on H.R. 8363*, pp. 362-64, 422, 428.

9. Under the Treasury's proposal, if property were sold after having been held for six years or less, all the previous deductions for depreciation recovered in the sales price would have been taxed as ordinary income. But if sold after six years, the amount of this "recapture" by the government would have diminished as the holding period lengthened; after 14½ years none of these extra tax benefits would have been "recaptured." Ibid., pp. 141-42. N's tax-free benefits under such a proposal, though somewhat reduced, would still have been huge. He would have been allowed to deduct only $40,000 for depreciation each year, but he still would have paid a tax at the 25% capital gains rate on about half of the $400,000 of depreciation deductions that he recovered when he sold the property after ten years.

10. U.S., Congress, Senate, Committee on Finance, *Hearings on H.R. 10650, Part I, (Revenue Act of 1962)*, 87th Cong., 2nd sess., 1962,

Exhibit VI, Statement of the Secretary of the Treasury, pp. 88-89, 352-70 (reprinted in *House Hearings on H.R. 8363,* pp. 432-50).

11. Ibid.

12. *House Hearings on H.R. 8363,* p. 447. Syndicates of this type have in recent years fallen into disfavor with investors because of publicity given to their managers' excesses.

13. I.R. Code, Sec. 1250. The Treasury's "recapture" of excess tax benefits was confined to the difference between the deductions on an accelerated depreciation basis and ordinary straight-line depreciation. But even this was curtailed. After a property was held for a mere 20 months, the amount of "recapture" steadily declined, so that if held for ten years and sold at a profit, there was no "recapture" at all of extra tax benefits. *Senate Hearings on H.R. 8363,* p. 145. This is why N was permitted to convert $670,335 of depreciation deductions into capital gain on a sale after ten years.

14. *Wall Street Journal,* 29 October 1968. A Treasury study of the 1966 tax returns of 13 individual real estate investors, each with substantial gross incomes, disclosed that as a result of accelerated depreciation and other deductions, 11 of the 13 paid virtually no income tax or none at all. Treasury Dept. 1969 Reform Studies, pp. 443-44.

15. I.R. Code, Sec. 1245, provides that on the sale of personal property at a price higher than its depreciated basis, the portion of the gain representing depreciation previously taken and deducted by the taxpayer will be taxed, not at the capital gains rate, but at the ordinary rate.

16. Charles S. Franklin, *Real Property Depreciation Recapture— An Ineffectual Reform of the Tax Laws,* 19 Vanderbilt Law Review 1336 (1966); Selwyn A. Horvitz, *The Puddle and the Lake,* 20 Tax Law Review 285 (1965).

16. The Tax Abuses of Philanthropy Curtailed

1. On the other hand, there are some who suggest that private philanthropy is failing today to contribute adequately to the relief of the country's most critical and pressing problems, such as the poverty and unemployment of minorities, shortages in housing and educational facilities, and urban blight, and that only programs financed by governmental agencies can take effective steps to solve these problems. The inference is that it may be necessary to consider some curtailment of the flow of private funds to charitable institutions and their redirection in the form of additional tax revenues to the government, where they may be channeled into areas not reached by private charity.

Andrew Hacker, "When Big Business Makes Gifts," *New York Times,* 12 November 1967, Magazine section, p. 34.

2. I.R. Code, Sec. 170 (b)(c), 503 (b).

3. I.R. Code, Sec. 170 (b).

4. I.R. Code, Sec. 2055, 2522.

5. Treasury Dept. 1969 Reform Studies, pp. 178-205.

6. Harry Yohlin, "The Tax Blessings of Charitable Giving," *Practical Lawyer,* vol. 10 (1964), pp. 43, 49-51.

7. C. Emery Glander and Earl E. Mayer, Jr., *Tax Savings Through Gifts to Education,* 25 Ohio State Law Journal 222, 226-29 (1964).

8. Former I.R. Code, Sec. 170 (b)(1)(C).

9. *House Hearings on H.R. 8363,* pp. 107, 242-45.

10. *Senate Hearings on H.R. 8363,* p. 284.

11. *House Hearings on H.R. 8363,* p. 106.

12. Rene Wormser, "Gifts to Charity Can Put Money in Your Pocket If You Are Rich Enough," *Journal of Taxation,* vol. 4 (1956), pp. 211, 212; *Federal Tax Incentives for Higher Education,* 76 Harvard Law Review 369 (1962); Richard Katcher, *Capital Gains Problems and Proposals,* 14 University of Southern California Tax Institute 769, 791 (1962).

13. *Federal Tax Incentives for Higher Education,* pp. 369, 371. Those who disagree that the escape of the capital gains tax and the allowance of a charitable deduction for the full market value of donated property constitutes a tax loophole, point out that wealthy taxpayers owning securities which have greatly increased in value over the years have other alternatives besides selling the property and paying the capital gains tax. They may, for the time being, hold on to the shares and avoid paying the capital gains tax; and if they retain them until death they will escape payment of a capital gains tax altogether. Furthermore while they continue their ownership, the shares may further increase in value. *Americans Like To Give,* Council for Financial Aid To Education, Inc., April 1962, p. 8.

14. Philip M. Stern, *The Great Treasury Raid* (New York: Random House, 1964), p. 247.

17. Tax Favoritism Based on Marriage, Age, or Family Status

1. I.R. Code, Sec. 1-2.

2. These states were originally settled by the French and Spanish, and their laws in large part were derived from French civil law.

3. I.R. Code, Sec. 2.

4. In each of these examples the tax has been computed after deductions and personal exemptions.

5. Joseph A. Pechman, *Income Splitting,* 2 Tax Revision Compendium 473, 485 (1959).

6. Eugene J. Brenner, *An Inquiry Into the Possibility of Lowering the Tax Rates by Increasing the Tax Rates Through Elimination of Income Splitting,* 2 Tax Revision Compendium 687, 490-92 (1959).

7. Pechman, p. 479.

8. Pechman, p. 477; Martin Atlas, *Personal Exemptions,* 2 Tax Revision Compendium 525, 530 (1959); Everett M. Kassalow, *To Restore Balance and Equity In Family Income Taxation,* 2 Tax Revision Compendium 515, 520-21 (1959); Philip M. Stern, *The Great Treasury Raid* (New York: Random House, 1964), pp. 62-71; Paul J. Strayer, *Treatment of Family Income,* 2 Tax Revision Compendium 537 (1959).

9. Pechman, pp. 479, 481.

10. I.R. Code, Sec. 1.

11. Pechman, pp. 482-83.

12. I.R. Code, Sec. 151 (b)(c).

13. I.R. Code, Sec. 37.

14. *New York Times,* 13 December 1967.

15. Ibid.; *Wall Street Journal,* 20 January 1969.

16. *House Hearings on H.R. 8363,* pp. 87-89, 209-15.

17. Ibid., pp. 87-89, 209-15. Under the 1967 proposal a special additional deduction, $2300 for single persons and $4,000 for married couples, would have replaced the additional personal exemption and retirement income credit for those over 65. This special deduction would have been reduced by income, including Social Security and Railroad Retirement benefits, in excess of $5,600 for single persons, and in excess of $11,200 for married couples; in no event was the deduction to be less than one-third of the Social Security benefits. H.R. 5710, 90th Cong., 1st sess., 1967; Stanley S. Surrey, Assistant Secretary of the Treasury, speech before the Federal Tax Institute of New England, 29 April 1967, pp. 7-10.

Both proposals, particularly the one advanced in 1967, would have the effect of giving virtually all the added tax benefits to elderly people with incomes of $10,000 or less, of reducing the present tax advantages of well-to-do older persons, and of eliminating the unwarranted penalty of additional taxation on modest amounts of wages earned by the elderly.

18. See Chap. 23.

19. I.R. Code, Sec. 151, 152.

20. Of course if the income from property donated by parents to children is used for their support it will be taxable to the parent. But

as long as the income from the property given to the child is deposited in the child's bank account, there is little likelihood of it being considered as available to the parent for the child's support and thereby endanger the allowance of the child as a dependency exemption.

21. C. Lowell Harriss, *Parent and Child—And Taxes—Some Problems in Dependency,* 2 Tax Revision Compendium 531, 532-33, 535 (1959); Kassalow, p. 521.

22. Harriss, loc. cit.

23. Harriss, pp. 533-34.

24. Pechman, pp. 474, 484-86; Kassalow, pp. 520-21; Atlas, p. 530; Strayer, p. 537.

25. Pechman, loc. cit. For example, the present exemption for each dependent could be retained for taxpayers who have incomes up to a given dollar amount yearly, such as $10,000; and the amount of the personal exemption for each dependent increased up to a maximum of, say, $1500 in the case of persons with incomes of $25,000 annually.

18. Tax-Free Benefits That Do Not Meet the Eye—Imputed Income

1. William A. Klein, *Borrowing to Finance Tax Favored Investments,* 1962 Wisconsin Law Review 608, 634; Melvin White and Ann White, "Horizontal Inequity in the Federal Tax Treatment of Home Owners and Tenants," *National Tax Journal,* vol. 18 (1965), p. 225; U.S., Congress, Joint Committee on the Economic Report, *Federal Tax Policy For Economic Growth and Stability,* 84th Cong., 1st sess., 1955, p. 297.

2. White and White, pp. 226-28.

3. Klein, p. 635.

4. Klein, pp. 620-21; Boris I. Bittker, *A "Comprehensive Tax Base" As A Goal of Income Tax Reform,* 80 Harvard Law Review 925, 944 (1967).

5. Klein, p. 632; William L. Cary, *Pressure Groups and the Revenue Code,* 68 Harvard Law Review 745, 764-65 (1955).

6. Cary, p. 764-65.

7. Joseph A. Pechman, *Income Splitting,* 2 Tax Revision Compendium 473, 480 (1959).

8. I.R. Code, Sec. 214.

9. Cary, pp. 771-72.

10. The Treasury has recently estimated that the exemption from taxation of the interest element connected with regular life insurance policies cost it about $900 million a year; and that deductions by home owners for local property taxes and interest on their home mortgages

result in revenue losses of about $1.8 billion and $1.9 billion each year, respectively. *Wall Street Journal,* 20 January 1969.

19. Tax Windfalls for Banking Institutions

1. Treasury Dept. 1969 Reform Studies, Committee Print, pp. 458-61.

2. Ibid., pp. 102-103, 461.

3. Other reasons that probably motivated Congress to grant favored tax treatment to mutual savings banks and savings and loan associations were the great number of people whose modest savings were deposited with them, and the fact that a large proportion of their loans was invested in home mortgages. Ibid., pp. 466-67.

4. Under I.R. Code, Sec. 593, and various administrative rulings of the Treasury Department. The bad debt reserve permitted other businesses is only enough to cover expected and ordinary losses.

5. Treasury Dept. 1969 Reform Studies, p. 465.

6. Ibid., pp. 462-63.

7. I.R. Code, Sec. 582.

8. Treasury Dept. 1969 Reform Studies, p. 468.

9. Ibid.

10. I.R. Code, Sec. 265 (2).

11. Treasury Dept. 1969 Reform Studies, p. 49.

12. Ibid.

13. Ibid., pp. 102-103; U.S., Congress, House, Committee on Ways and Means, *Report to Accompany H.R. 13270,* 91st Cong., 1st sess., 1969, House Report No. 91-413, pp. 122, 129-30.

20. Obstacles to Tax Reform

1. Russell B. Long, "Tax Reforms and Economic Growth," speech before the Conference on Federal Tax Reform, *The Taxpayer's Stake in Tax Reform* (Washington, D.C.: Chamber of Commerce of the United States, 1968), pp. 16-17.

2. U.S., Congress, House, *Congressional Record,* 90th Cong., 1st sess., 12 October 1967, p. H. 13351.

3. Stanley S. Surrey, *The Congress and the Tax Lobbyist,* 70 Harvard Law Review 1145, 1170-75 (1957).

4. Ibid., pp. 1162-66.

5. *House Hearings on H.R. 8363,* pp. 839-40.

6. Philip M. Stern, *The Great Treasury Raid* (New York: Random House, 1964), p. 292.

7. Drew Pearson, "Oily Tax Loophole," *New York Post,* 5 September 1967.

8. Long, p. 20.
9. *Senate Hearings on H.R. 8363*, p. 1469.
10. *House Hearings on H.R. 8363*, p. 534.
11. *Senate Hearings on H.R. 8363*, pp. 1733-38.
12. *House Hearings on H.R. 8363*, pp. 1959-70.
13. Ibid., p. 1979.
14. Surrey, pp. 1175-76.
15. *Senate Hearings on H.R. 8363*, p. 309.

21. Ideologies, Principles, and Dogmas

1. R. A. Musgrave, *In Defense of An Income Concept*, 81 Harvard Law Review 44, 47 (1967); Charles O. Galvin, *More On Boris Bittker And The Comprehensive Tax Base*, 81 Harvard Law Review 1016, 1017 (1968).

2. Louis Eisenstein, *Some Second Thoughts on Tax Ideologies*, 23 New York University Institute on Federal Taxation 1, 5 (1965).

3. Musgrave, p. 46; Horace M. Gray, *Tax Reform and the Depletion Allowance*, 2 Tax Revision Compendium 979-80 (1959).

4. R. A. Musgrave, *The Theory of Public Finance* (New York: McGraw-Hill, 1959), Chap. 4, 5.

5. Gray, p. 980; Musgrave, *In Defense of An Income Concept*, p. 47; "A Discussion of 'The Ideologies of Taxation,'" *Tax Law Review*, vol. 18 (1962-3), pp. 1, 7.

6. Musgrave, *In Defense of An Income Concept*, p. 45.

7. Louis Eisenstein, *Ideologies of Taxation* (New York: Ronald Press, 1961), p. 224.

8. Eisenstein, *Some Second Thoughts on Tax Ideologies*, pp. 1, 2.

9. Ibid., p. 3.

10. According to certain 1959-60 statistics accumulated by the Treasury, capital gains (of which one-half were excluded from adjusted gross income) totaled about $12 billion a year. Over 80% of all income tax returns showing income over $50,000 reported some capital gains. For taxpayers in the $50,000-$100,000 income category, over 55% of their capital gains were derived from the sale of stocks, bonds, or other securities. *House Hearings on H.R. 8363*, pp. 367-68.

11. Dan Throop Smith, *Tax Treatment of Capital Gains*, 2 Tax Revision Compendium 1233, 1234, 1239-40 (1959); Reuben Clark, *The Paradox of Capital Gains*, 2 Tax Revision Compendium 1243, 1247 (1959); *The Troubled Distinction Between Capital Gains and Ordinary Income*, 73 Yale Law Journal 693, 697-99 (1964); Wilbur A. Steger, *Economic Consequences of Substantial Changes in the*

Method of Taxing Capital Gains and Losses, 2 Tax Revision Compendium 1261, 1280-81 (1959). (While the above articles mention these arguments, the authors do not necessarily espouse them.)

12. Richard Katcher, *Capital Gains Problems and Proposals,* 14 University of Southern California Tax Institute 769, 778-79 (1962); Clark, p. 1244.

13. Eisenstein, *Some Second Thoughts on Tax Ideologies,* pp. 1, 7.

14. *House Hearings on H.R. 8363,* pp. 127, 165, 370; Harold M. Groves, *Taxation of Capital Gains,* 2 Tax Revision Compendium 1193, 1195-96 (1959); Stanley S. Surrey, *Definitional Problems in Capital Gains Taxation,* 2 Tax Revision Compendium 1203, 1215 (1959).

15. See Chap. 6.

16. Clark, pp. 1247, 1250; Katcher, p. 784; Merle H. Miller, *Taxation of Capital Gains,* 2 Tax Revision Compendium 1257 (1959); Leonard L. Silverstein, *The Capital Asset Definition,* 2 Tax Revision Compendium 1285, 1295 (1959).

17. Charles Rabb, "Tax Bait in the Ghetto," *The Nation,* 4 November 1968, p. 464.

18. Stanley S. Surrey, *Federal Tax Policy in the 1960's,* 15 Buffalo Law Review 498-99 (1966).

19. Boris I. Bittker, *A "Comprehensive Tax Base" as a Goal of Income Tax Reform,* 80 Harvard Law Review 925, 926 (1967); Mortimer M. Caplin, "Federal Tax Policy," *The Taxpayer's Stake in Tax Reform,* (Washington, D.C.: Chamber of Commerce of the United States, 1968), pp. 5-6; Stanley S. Surrey, Assistant Secretary of the Treasury, "Tax Policy Developments in the Corporate Area," address before the Federal Bar Association, Washington, D.C., 23 February 1967, pp. 6-7.

20. Surrey, *Federal Tax Policy in the 1960's,* pp. 477, 488-89; Lawrence M. Stone, *U.S. Tax Policy,* 18 University of Southern California Tax Institute 1, 8, 14-18 (1966); Caplin, loc. cit.

21. *New York Times,* 5 December 1968.

22. There are now two major tax credits permitted by law: the credit for foreign taxes paid and the retirement income credit. The first reduces taxes by the entire amount paid to various foreign governments for certain income taxes, and the second reduces the taxes of those over 65 by a percentage of their income from sources other than wages.

23. If instead of a full tax credit, a 50% credit were permitted, A and B would each be permitted to deduct $50 from their tax bills.

24. C. Harry Kahn, *Personal Deductions in the Federal Income Tax, A Study by the National Bureau of Economic Research* (Princeton: Princeton University Press, 1960), pp. 89-90.

25. Kahn, p. 88.

26. Wilbur Mills, Address before the National Association of Manufacturers, 4 December 1968.

27. "A Discussion of 'The Ideologies of Taxation'," *Tax Law Review,* vol. 18 (1962–63), pp. 1, 21.

28. I.R. Code, Sec. 1.

29. An analysis of the estate tax rate scale shows an even greater distortion of the theoretically progressive rate concept.

30. During the period 1957–66, the capital gains of persons reporting adjusted gross incomes of $50,000 or more per year soared from a total of about $1⅓ billion to almost $4⅓ billion, with most of the gains accruing to those with adjusted gross incomes of $100,000 a year or more. U.S. Treasury Department, Internal Revenue Service, *Statistics of Income 1966—Individual Income Tax Returns,* Table 69, p. 235.

31. *Senate Hearings on H.R. 8363,* pp. 237, 281-82, Tables 3, 5.

The average effective tax rate of those with amended gross incomes (which was arrived at by taking into account, among other things, all capital gains) of $500,000 or more in 1959 was:

Amended Gross Income	Average Tax Rate
$250,000 to $499,999	32.4%
$500,000 to $749,999	53 %
$750,000 to $999,999	28.6%
$1,000,000 to $1,999,999	23.8%
$2,000,000 to $4,999,999	24.6%
$5,000,000 and Over	23.7%

Moreover, over 61% of all taxpayers who reported adjusted gross incomes of over $500,000 in 1959 paid at an effective rate of less than 20%; and one taxpayer with an annual gross income of $1.3 million paid less than 1% of that income in taxes.

32. Ibid., pp. 307-308.

33. Treasury Dept. 1969 Reform Studies, pp. 80-84, 89-97.

34. *Senate Hearings on H.R. 8363,* p. 237.

35. Eisenstein, *Some Second Thoughts on Tax Ideologies,* p. 21-25.

36. Stone, p. 6.

37. Eisenstein, *Some Second Thoughts on Tax Ideologies,* p. 19; I.R. Code, Sec. 1.

The following table illustrates how families with two children, in the various income brackets, have fared in this respect since 1954:

If the Family Net Income Was:	The After-Tax Income Increase Was:
$ 3,000	2 %
5,000	1.6%
10,000	2.3%
25,000	3.8%
50,000	6.2%
100,000	8.3%
200,000	16 %

38. Henry H. Fowler, Secretary of the Treasury, "The Uses of Tax Policy," address before the Kentucky Chamber of Commerce, Louisville, Ky., 10 April 1967, p. 16; Caplin, p. 8; Senator Russell B. Long, "Tax Reforms and Economic Growth," *The Taxpayer's Stake in Tax Reform* (Washington, D.C.: Chamber of Commerce of the United States, 1968), p. 16.

39. Eisenstein, *Some Second Thoughts on Tax Ideologies,* p. 25-28.

22. Is an Ideal Income Tax Possible?

1. Joseph A. Pechman, *What Would a Comprehensive Individual Income Tax Yield?,* 1 Tax Revision Compendium 251 (1959); Boris I. Bittker, *A "Comprehensive Tax Base" as a Goal of Income Tax Reform,* 80 Harvard Law Review 925 (1967); R. A. Musgrave, *In Defense of an Income Concept,* 81 Harvard Law Review 44 (1967); Charles O. Galvin, *More on Boris Bittker and the Comprehensive Tax Base,* 81 Harvard Law Review 1016 (1968); Joseph A. Pechman, *Comprehensive Income Taxation,* 81 Harvard Law Review 63 (1967); Boris I. Bittker, *Comprehensive Income Taxation,* 81 Harvard Law Review 1032 (1968); Philip M. Stern, *The Great Treasury Raid* (New York: Random House, 1964), pp. 304-309; Charles O. Galvin, *Progress in Substantive Tax Reform,* 17 University of Southern California Tax Institute 1 (1965); Walter J. Blum, "Federal Income Tax Reform —Twenty Questions," *Taxes,* vol. 41 (1963), p. 672; William A. Klein, "Federal Income Tax Reform, A Reaction to Professor Blum's Twenty Questions," *Taxes,* vol. 42 (1964), p. 175; Walter J. Blum, "More on Twenty Questions," *Taxes,* vol. 42 (1964), p. 180; Report of the Royal Commission on Taxation (Canada, 1966).

2. Bittker, 80 Harvard Law Review, 935-78; Musgrave, pp. 49-60; Galvin, *More on Boris Bittker,* 1017-18, Pechman, *Comprehensive Income Taxation,* p. 66.

3. Musgrave, p. 56; see also Bittker, 80 Harvard Law Review 951.

4. Musgrave, pp. 56-57.

5. Ibid., pp. 55, 60-61.

6. Bittker, 80 Harvard Law Review 977-80.

7. Musgrave, pp. 61-62.

8. Bittker, 80 Harvard Law Review 962-96.

9. Musgrave, p. 58-59.

10. Musgrave, p. 62; Pechman, *Comprehensive Income Taxation,* pp. 65-66.

11. Bittker, 80 Harvard Law Review 928-33, 982, 81 Harvard Law Review, 1034.

12. Musgrave, loc. cit., Galvin, loc. cit., Pechman, *Comprehensive Income Taxation,* p. 63.

13. Caplin, p. 7; *Senate Hearings on H.R. 8363,* p. 904; Stern, pp. 10, 305.

23. Proposals for Reform

1. Charles O. Galvin, *Progress in Substantive Tax Reform,* 17 University of Southern California Tax Institute 1, 10 (1965).

2. See Chap. 1, note 3.

3. Russell B. Long, "Tax Reforms and Economic Growth," *The Taxpayer's Stake in Tax Reform* (Washington, D.C.: Chamber of Commerce of the United States, 1968), p. 15, 18-19.

4. Boris I. Bittker, "An Optional Simplified Income Tax," *Tax Law Review,* vol. 21 (1966), pp. 1, 13-17; Paul M. Dodyk, *The Long Amendment and the Mills Proposal,* 25 New York University Institute of Federal Taxation 1443, 1469-71 (1967).

5. U.S. Treasury Department, *Tax Reform Studies and Proposals,* 91st Cong., 1st sess., 5 February 1969, Committee Print Parts 1-3.

6. Ibid., pp. 13-14, 35, 94-95, 132-42.

7. Ibid., pp. 19-21, 37-38, 178-205.

8. Ibid., pp. 15-16, 36, 152-63.

9. Ibid., pp. 23-24, 40, 241-56.

10. Ibid., pp. 16-17, 36, 164-71.

11. Ibid., pp. 25-26, 41, 295-306.

12. Ibid., pp. 26-27, 42, 315-27.

13. Ibid., pp. 28-30, 42-44, 331-51.

14. Ibid., pp. 28, 29, 30-32, 43-44, 351-401.

15. P.L. 91-172, 91st Cong., 1st sess., 1969.

16. See Chap. 15.

17. See Chap. 16.

18. See Chap. 6.

19. See Chap. 13.

20. See Chap. 11.

21. See Chap. 7.

22. See Chap. 5.

23. See Chap. 4.

24. See Chap. 10.

25. See Chap. 19.

26. See Chap. 3.

27. See Chap. 2.

28. Philip M. Stern, *The Great Treasury Raid* (New York: Random House, 1964), pp. 10-16.

29. *Wall Street Journal,* 20 January 1969. Treasury Secretary Barr's estimates of tax revenue lost each year included the following: exclusion from tax of private employers' pension contributions—$3 billion, multiple corporate surtax exemptions—$1.8 billion, excess depreciation allowed in respect to real estate—$.5 billion, percentage depletion in excess of cost allowed to the oil, gas, and mining industries—$1.3 billion, avoidance of capital gains tax on property passing at death—$2.5 billion, exemption from taxation of municipal and local bonds—$1.8 billion, exclusion from tax of employer-paid premiums on group life and medical insurance and payments for medical care—$1.5 billion, and the exclusion of the interest on the savings of regular life insurance policies—$.9 billion.

30. U.S., Congress, Staff of the Joint Committee on Internal Revenue Taxation and the Committee on Finance, *Summary of H.R. 13270 (Tax Reform Act of 1969),* 91st Cong., 1st sess., 1969, p. 112.

31. Long, p. 18.

Index